R. M. OGILVIE

ROMAN LITERATURE
AND
SOCIETY

PENGUIN BOOKS

Penguin Books Ltd, Harmondsworth, Middlesex, England
Penguin Books, 625 Madison Avenue, New York, New York 10022,
U.S.A.
Penguin Books Australia Ltd, Ringwood, Victoria, Australia
Penguin Books Canada Ltd, 2801 John Street, Markham, Ontario,
Canada L3R 1B4
Penguin Books (N.Z.) Ltd, 182–190 Wairau Road,
Auckland 10, New Zealand

First published 1980

Copyright © R. M. Ogilvie, 1980
All rights reserved

The Acknowledgements section, which begins on p. 293, constitutes
an extension of this copyright page

Made and printed in Great Britain by
Richard Clay (The Chaucer Press) Ltd, Bungay, Suffolk
Set in Monotype Bembo

PELICAN BOOKS

ROMAN LITERATURE AND SOCIETY

Robert Ogilvie was born in 1932 and educated at Rugby
and Balliol College, Oxford. He was a Fellow of Clare
College, Cambridge, from 1955 to 1957 and of Balliol from
1957 to 1970. He was headmaster of Tonbridge School
from 1970 to 1975 and is now Professor of Humanity at the
University of St Andrews.

His publications include commentaries on the Roman
authors Livy and Tacitus, and books on Roman religion,
the history of early Rome and Lactantius. He is a Fellow of
the British Academy and the Royal Society of Edinburgh.

CONTENTS

PREFACE

With many excellent and accessible translations of the Latin classics
now on the market and with a renewed interest at large in all aspects
of the Roman world, it seemed worthwhile to attempt to write a
brief survey of Latin literature which would serve as an introduction,
for students and others, to the major Latin writers. I have tried, in
particular, to relate their works to the evolving social conditions of
the times. Inevitably such a study must be derivative, but I have
reread every author and tried to form a fresh and independent
opinion about him. In the two appendixes I have given brief biblio-
graphies which may be of use.

Acknowledgements for quotations are printed at the end of the
book. I am responsible for translations where no translator is named.

I have two particular debts that I should like to acknowledge:
first, to Dr Adrian Gratwick, who put his voluminous knowledge of
early Latin literature at my disposal, and, secondly, to Mrs May Dick
for her skilful and patient typing.

June 1978   R. M. Ogilvie, Errachd

I

ROMAN SOCIETY AND
LITERATURE

LITERATURE reflects the interests and prejudices of society. To appreciate Roman literature you have to understand the sort of audiences for which it was written and to know something of the historical background. Not that Virgil or Horace cannot be read today, in translation or in the original, as poets in their right. There have after all been many people like Thomas Burnet, who wrote in 1716: 'I am now at my leisure hours reading Horace with some diligence and find that the world was just the same then that it continues to be now', or Mgr Ronald Knox, who traced his religious life as a 'Spiritual Aeneid'. But this is to read ourselves into ancient literature. The best of classical writers have more to say, if you can make the imaginative leap into the conditions and circumstances of their own time.

Roman authors wrote for a wide variety of audiences, and Latin literature ranges over nearly six centuries, from the plays of Plautus at the beginning of the second century B.C. to the poems of Claudian and the history of Ammianus Marcellinus at the end of the fourth century A.D. Plautus wrote for a single public performance in the theatre; his plays were bought by a magistrate or an agent, and staged as a popular attraction at the games. They survive for us because his popularity ensured that they were repeated, and acting copies, often with considerable alterations, were handed down. Cicero wrote the majority of his speeches to persuade an immediate audience, either in a court of law or in the Senate. They would have perished for ever, as so much Roman oratory has, if he had not been vain enough to issue them in book form for the enjoyment of his friends. Caesar wrote his *Gallic Wars* as a piece of political propaganda to enhance his position with the Roman nobility and with the electorate. But most writers, poets like Catullus or Horace or Virgil, and historians, like Sallust or Livy, wrote with a small sophisticated audience in mind – an audience drawn from the tightly-knit group of families who comprised the governing class at Rome. They were men who had had a predominantly literary education themselves and who, above all, were imbued with the culture of Greece. They were rich and able to indulge the leisure which the political system afforded them. Although periodically called upon to hold demanding magistracies at home and in the provinces, senators were not allowed to engage directly in trade.

There were three chief ways in which an author would bring his work to the attention of his audience. The commonest was by giving a public recitation. Roman literature, it should be remembered, was almost always intended to be read aloud and we miss much of its impact by silent, visual reading. Indeed it was a matter of surprise that Caesar and St Ambrose could read silently to themselves. An aspiring author hired a hall and invited his friends to a reading. Livy, we are told, drew only small audiences to his readings but those who came came because of his eloquence and the beauty of his personality. Tacitus relates that audiences in his day have become so discriminating that they expect to carry away some memorable and witty quotation from any such performance. Claques were hired to fill the benches. 'The reciter', says Seneca, 'brings an enormous historical work, written very small, tightly rolled up: after he has read a considerable part of it, he says "I will stop now, if you like." Immediately there is a shout of "More, more!" from his hearers who would really like to see him struck dumb on the spot.' When the Younger Pliny realized that he read poetry badly, he employed one of his freedmen but was worried how he should react: should he behave as a disinterested spectator or should he enter into the spirit of the performance? In the satirical poet Persius we have a lurid account of an affected reciter draped in a billowing snow-white toga, with curled hair and a huge diamond ring on his finger, lolling back in his high chair as he began to declaim in melting tones. Roman authors hoped that as a result of public recitations the word would be spread around about their newest work and that they would receive constructive criticism to improve it.

Works were also launched at private parties, especially dinner-parties. Virgil left the *Aeneid* incomplete at his death in 19 B.C. but he had recited parts of it, especially the end of Book 6, to Augustus before he died. An older contemporary of Virgil, Varro (see p. 101), says that the host at a dinner-party should choose passages to be read which were both uplifting and amusing. But guests were not always so lucky. The poet Martial, at the end of the first century A.D., writes: 'There is one reason, and one reason only, why you give a dinner-party, Ligurius. You want the chance to recite your terrible poems. I have taken off my slippers. The fish and lettuce are served. Here comes Book 1. The main course is delayed so that we can hear Book 2. Then, before dessert, Book 3, Book 4, Book 5. If you serve roast pig like this, course after course, it is revolting. Give those horrible poems to the fishmonger to wrap fish and chips in. Otherwise no one will ever come and dine with you.' The habit lasted long. At the beginning of the third century A.D. the emperor Severus Alexander was still giving literary dinner-parties. When he dined with his friends, he invited Ulpian or other learned men who, he said, refreshed and fed him. When he dined privately, he had a book at table, usually Greek, but he liked reading Latin poets.

Thirdly, there was the book trade. Considering how cumbersome it was to produce books in the Roman world, it is remarkable how widely they did circulate. For most of the classical period, books were made out of the fibres of the papyrus plant, which grows mainly beside the Nile. The fibres were flattened, laid at right angles over each other, and glued or pressed together to make sheets, which were rolled up. To read a book required both hands, gradually unwinding a roll (*volumen*). This made it awkward to handle, especially if you wanted to go back and verify a reference; in addition the material was fragile and easily damaged. The book as we know it was not invented until the first century A.D., when craftsmen at Pergamum (hence 'parchment') cured sheepskins to provide more durable pages, and it was not generally adopted until the very end of the Roman Empire.

To provide a large number of copies of a book required substantial capital, both in money and in trained slave-copyists. This does not seem to have existed before the first century B.C. Earlier works were copied either because they were needed for schools (e.g. the poet Ennius) or because they were in demand for repeat performances (e.g. Plautus). It was Cicero's friend and correspondent Atticus who for the first time moved into the big business of book production. He had a large staff of slaves whom he employed in copying the works of Cicero and his other friends. Cicero's letters are full of fascinating details about book production as he tries to get last-minute corrections into the text of works, such as his treatise on oratory, the *Orator*. Atticus proved that the copying of books was a commercial undertaking, and after him there was a succession of publishers who catered for the Roman market. That market was undoubtedly a big one. The library of the Epicurean consul L. Piso (58 B.C.) has been found at Herculaneum, and its range and variety are impressive. Lucullus (consul in 74 B.C.) had amassed a huge collection of books, mainly looted from Greece, which he allowed his friends to consult. Cicero is for ever requesting his correspondents to try to acquire this or that volume for him.

Books were not expensive (the first book of Martial's poems, some 700 lines, cost only five *denarii*; the Good Samaritan gave two *denarii* to have the wounded man looked after), but they were scarce. The circulation of works would never have been widespread had not leading Romans been inspired by the Greek example to found public libraries. The first was established in Rome by C. Asinius Pollio in 39 B.C., although Caesar had had ambitious plans for one, for which he had enlisted the help of Varro but which was frustrated by his death in 44 B.C. Augustus built two, the more important in 28 B.C. in the Temple of Apollo. By the fourth century there were no fewer than twenty-nine libraries in Rome alone. Readers could not only consult works but also borrow them. The emperor Marcus Aurelius wrote to his old tutor: 'I have been reading two of the Elder Cato's speeches. It is no good sending your slave to the Temple of Apollo for them, because I have taken them out and have them with me in the country.' Most provincial cities would have had a sizeable library: there is even evidence for one at St Albans. Ephesus had a particularly splendid one.

But it was not only the cultivated upper classes that authors wrote for. Roman education may have been narrow in scope – no science, no philosophy, no history – but it was remarkably pervasive. The conduct of ordinary day-to-day business presupposed that the citizen was literate. The walls of Pompeii were covered with graffiti, urging the voter to vote for X or Y, announcing the attractions at the forthcoming games, quoting Virgil or merely promoting the latest best buy at the local supermarket. Veterans from the army were issued with a written discharge. Just as in early times the calendar of public events was published on a whitened board, so in the last century of the Empire Diocletian tried to control inflation by publishing a list of fixed prices. All over the Roman world you come across pathetic magical curses, often written in a semi-literate script on lead tablets: 'Here drowns a lock of hair: the river waits for its owner' or, from Arezzo, 'I vow, pray, sacrifice that you, Hot Springs or Nymphs or whatever you like to be called, should kill and put to death Q. Letinius Lupus, alias Caudadio, the son of Sallustia Veneria or Veneriosa, within the year'. Recently discovered debris at Vindolanda on Hadrian's Wall contains numerous letters, accounts, diaries and so on written on wooden tablets. Soldiers have left their messages in quarries, on fresh-baked tiles or scrawled on the sides of jars and pots. And the rubbish-pit of an insignificant village in Egypt, Oxyrhynchus, has, because of the freak nature of the climate, preserved fragments of a host of Greek and Roman authors that were otherwise lost. To such an outpost of the Empire do we owe Aristotle's *Constitution of Athens*, the poems of Bacchylides, an epitome of Livy and parts of Sallust's history.

All our evidence suggests that basic literacy, even among the lower classes, was the rule rather than the exception at Rome. It was acquired slowly and painfully. In the Empire, teachers were supported by the state, but education still had to be paid for by parents. The primary stage, from seven to eleven years of age, was simple and so cheap enough. The aim was unambitious, no more than to teach children to read and write and do simple arithmetic. The technique was repetitive: the pupils copied letters which had been incised on their wax tablets until they were word-perfect. With the secondary stage (eleven to fifteen), children were introduced by the schoolmaster (*grammaticus*) to literature. In early times the prescribed books were the poets Terence, Ennius and Naevius;

but for the greater part of the life of the Empire it was Virgil and Terence of the poets and Cicero and Sallust of the prose writers who monopolized the curriculum. Ovid and Horace were sometimes read but not commonly. It is interesting to see how in the fourth century Lactantius and St Augustine were still brought up on the same syllabus. A statuette from Gaul (fourth century A.D.) shows a schoolmaster reading out the opening sentence of Cicero's *First Catilinarian Speech*. The study of these authors was not very subtle; you learned long passages by heart, analysed the grammar in painstaking detail and memorized the content ('Who was Anchemolus's stepmother in the *Aeneid* and how many jars of Sicilian wine did Acestes give to the Phrygians?'). Nevertheless, despite its inadequacies, such an education did introduce the finest of Roman literature to a wide audience. Horace's father, a poor man, made large sacrifices to give his son the best possible education. The great governor of Britain, Agricola (A.D. 78–84), set up special schools to teach the sons of British chieftains. If the majority of Romans did not go on to the third stage of education (the rhetorician's school) or study Greek literature and philosophy at Athens or Rhodes, they were nonetheless firmly grounded in Latin letters. And much Roman literature was written specifically for such an audience – the Elder Cato's work on agriculture, Vitruvius's *Architecture*, or Vegetius's handbook on military science, to name but three that happen to survive of the hundreds of technical books that are known to have been written over the span of six hundred years.

The aim of the following chapters is to trace the fluctuating relationship between the Roman author and his public.

2

THE EARLY REPUBLIC

FROM very early times Rome had been washed by the tides of Greek culture. She first became a city when Etruscans settled in Rome and brought with them their sophisticated ideas of architecture, organization, religion, trade and town-planning, which they themselves had developed as a result of their close commercial contacts with the Greek world. Rome soon acquired many of the characteristics of a Greek city, as one Greek historian of the fourth century, Heraclides Ponticus, noted: temples of Greek design, civic institutions devised on Greek models, foundation-legends and other traditions based on Greek originals. The founder of the Roman race, Aeneas, was a hero from the Greek epic of the Trojan War. At first many of Rome's contacts were not directly with Greece itself but either with the Etruscans or with the Greek colonists of Italy and Sicily. There are well authenticated accounts of dealings with Aristodemus of Cumae and with the rulers of Sicilian cities in the fifth century B.C. Rome derived a number of cults such as Ceres, Libera and Liber, and Apollo from Greek sources during the first hundred years of the Republic. But such contacts were limited. It is questionable how far there is any Greek influence in the Twelve Tables, the great code of law produced in 450 B.C., and scholars have very diverse views about the stories which say that Romans consulted or made offerings to the oracle of Apollo at Delphi during this period. Nevertheless, right from its establishment, Rome showed herself receptive to Greek ideas.

The turning-point was when Rome first came directly into contact with mainland Greece, as Pyrrhus, King of Epirus, crossed over to help the city of Tarentum against the Romans in 280 B.C. From then on the Romans had continuous and close relations with Greece. Their merchants began to travel widely in the Aegean, exploiting the slave trade on the island of Delos, doing business in corn at Rhodes or trafficking farther afield among the kingdoms of Asia Minor. Perhaps one of the most significant documents for the whole period is an inscription recently unearthed on the Greek island of Chios which contains one of the earliest references to the legend of Romulus and Remus, and which can be dated to the early third century. Romans were setting out their claims to be true cousins of the Greeks, and the Greeks, for their part, responded by taking an interest in Rome and her history. Aristotle had informed himself about the Gallic Sack of Rome; the Alexandrian poet Lycophron or an editor (about 280 B.C.) thought it valuable to include some lines on early Rome in his tragic poem *Alexandra*; and Timaeus, the great historian from Tauromenium in Sicily (*c.* 355–260 B.C.), treated Roman affairs in some detail.

The First Carthaginian (or 'Punic', since Carthage was a colony of Phoenicia) War (264–241 B.C.) brought Rome even closer in touch with Greece. Rome had, indeed, from now on to try to win the support of the Greeks in her immediate struggles with Carthage. The dangers became all the more acute in the Second Carthaginian War when Hannibal persuaded Philip V, King of Macedon, to open a second front against the Romans. Roman armies were forced to take the field in Greece itself, until, under T. Quinctius Flamininus, they won a decisive victory over Philip at Cynoscephalae in 197 B.C. But that was not the end. Another great Hellenistic king, Antiochus III of Syria, befriended the exiled Hannibal and intervened in mainland Greece. This emergency again required Roman action. The Romans crossed into Asia Minor and, under Scipio Africanus, inflicted a crushing defeat on Antiochus at Magnesia in 190 B.C. Both wars entailed intensive propaganda to secure the good-will of the Greek peoples and to promote the image of the Romans not as barbaric foreigners but as true Greeks. And after both wars, although Rome proudly claimed to have restored Greek independence and to have withdrawn all her military forces, nevertheless the Romans maintained from now on a continuous and dominant presence in the Greek East. One small sign of this is the spate of dedications by Romans at such sanctuaries as Delphi and Delos.

There was, however, no native tradition of literature at Rome, or, for that matter, in Etruria (Etruscan writings, except on religious matters, are a shadowy and insubstantial phantom). If Rome was to make her case known, she had to create Latin forms of self-expression. She did this by borrowing heavily from contemporary fashions in Greek historiography, oratory and poetry, and recasting them in Latin. It is important to realize that at this period the Romans did not go back for inspiration to the great classical models of Sappho or Alcaeus, Herodotus or Thucydides, Aeschylus or Sophocles. Their needs were much more urgent and immediate. Contemporary Greek was the language and literature of communication and it was that which the Romans made their own, so much so that they also found it acceptable and congenial to naturalize other forms of Greek literature, such as New Comedy, which were widely popular in the Greek world but which did not obviously serve Rome's purpose of cultural respectability. In short, the civilized world was a Greek world. It is no accident that during the second century B.C. Hellenistic styles of art and architecture – in temple-building, funerary monuments, domestic houses and the like – became widely diffused throughout Roman Italy.

To stake her claim Rome had to adopt Greek literary vehicles and in so doing became herself imbued with Greek tastes and interests.

EPIC

Poetry precedes prose as a literary form: the Homeric poems were written down two hundred and fifty years before the first works of Greek prose were composed. The *Iliad* and the *Odyssey* were national poems to the Greeks, one thing that united all the different city-states as heirs of a common heritage. At Rome the earliest attempt to produce a national epic – as opposed to a translation of a Greek epic – that would make the Roman case resound throughout the civilized world was *The Punic War* by Cn. Naevius (*c.* 270–201 B.C.), who dealt with the history of the First Carthaginian War. Naevius's poem suffered from two fatal drawbacks. In the first place he adopted a native Latin metre (Saturnian) which is too jerky to provide the basis of a fluent and extended narrative poem. The Saturnian was used for popular chanting – triumph songs and the like – and its rhythm can be captured in the translation of a line shouted about Julius Caesar:

All the Gauls did Caesar vanquish, Nicomedes vanquished him.

Secondly, the Latin language at this date was still a rude and limited tool which had not yet developed an appropriate vocabulary for heroic poetry. The few fragments of Naevius's epic which survive have force but little elegance.

Yet Naevius's work was epoch-making – for the first time a Roman was aware of the destiny of his country – and it inspired Q. Ennius (239–169 B.C.) from Calabria in S. Italy, who was brought up in the three cultures of Greek, Latin and Oscan, to attempt a more ambitious project, no less than the epic story of the whole of Rome's history.

Ennius had the good fortune to attract the attention of leading Romans such as the Elder Cato, Scipio Africanus and M. Fulvius Nobilior, who gave him encouragement and patronage as a writer. Fulvius in particular was wedded to the ideals of Hellenic culture. He had fought a successful campaign in Ambracia in 164 B.C., and on his return he had founded a 'Temple of Hercules and the Muses' at Rome which consciously recalled the great Museum of Alexandria. It was to be a centre of learning and scholarship, and in it were deposited historical and chronological records as well as works of poetry and philosophy. It is against this background that Ennius must be judged. As he himself claimed, he was not a bard, like Naevius (*vates:* a rough, inspired, instinctive writer), but a poet aiming to create delicate and finely wrought masterpieces. Indeed he had tried his hand successfully at tragedies and comedies; but it was his epic, the *Annales*, covering the history of Rome from Aeneas's flight after the fall of Troy (1184 B.C. traditionally) to his own day (184 B.C.), in fifteen books, which secured his reputation until it was supplanted by Virgil's *Aeneid*. Some 550 lines survive and they suffice to show him as a poet re-creating Hellenistic ideals of metre and diction in Latin. He introduced the hexameter rhythm into Latin, which at once became the standard metre for serious poetry. Its introduction involved considerable discipline and sacrifice, since many words in Latin (e.g. *cīvĭtās*) cannot be used in hexameters. Partly to compensate for this, Ennius experimented with the formation of new Latin words, especially compound adjectives modelled on the common Homeric compound epithets. By these means he built up a poetic diction which was to be the basis of the Latin used by poets such as Catullus, Lucretius, and Virgil. One fragment, dealing with the state of society in time of war, may convey something of the serious and profound tone of the poem:

When news of battles is proclaimed, Wisdom is thrust out of sight, action is done with violence; the spokesman of good counsel is scorned and the tough warrior is applauded. Men do not any longer dispute with learned speeches but stir up bitter feeling with recriminations. They seek their own not through the law but by the sword; they seek total mastery and press ahead with massive might.

Underlying all of this activity was the self-confidence that Latin could naturalize Greek and, more importantly, the desire to present the Roman achievement as something which would stand comparison with the noblest of Greek achievements. Rome had woken to the realization that, within a mere three generations, she had become the dominant power of the Mediterranean and she was actively determined to be worthy of that role.

COMEDY

A Roman visitor to any Hellenistic city would have noticed that the most prominent structure, surpassing the temples and the Senate House, was the semi-circular theatre. Drama, both light and serious, played a unique part in the citizen's life. By the third century acting was highly professional. There were guilds of actors who toured the cities from S. Italy and Sicily to Asia Minor. After the death of Menander (292 B.C.), the master of the New Comedy of plot and character, the plays performed were mainly revivals of famous classics, but the very fact that the audience knew them already, and may even have studied them at school, meant that the standards of performance were that much higher.

The theatre was such a Greek institution that it was inevitable that, as Rome began to take over the mantle of Alexander the Great, she should have shown an interest in it. Unfortunately, although we are lucky enough to possess twenty-seven comic masterpieces by Plautus and Terence, we know very little of the origin of drama at Rome, and are almost totally ignorant of the nature of serious or tragic Roman drama until the time of Seneca (p. 210). Just as Cato and Ennius were anxious to establish the respectable background of the foundation of Rome, so later scholars were at pains to point to native elements – Italian slap-stick, farce and repartee – as the origin of Roman comedy. These may indeed have influenced the comedian's treatment and the audience's reaction but the plays which have survived show all too clearly that it was a conscious decision to take over Greek comedy and make it Roman rather than a gradual cross-fertilization which led to the spectacular successes of Plautus. According to the scholar Varro – and there is no reason to doubt him – Andronicus, who also 'translated' the *Odyssey*, in 240 B.C. produced the first play at Rome. The date is significant, for it was precisely the First Carthaginian War that made Rome a permanent force in the Greek world. We know nothing about the play, but from the start Roman drama differed in major ways from the Greek. The plays were an integral part of public life. They were performed at the five major games or festivals which, lasting fourteen days in all, were given by magistrates, called aediles, who were concerned to use the opportunity of their office to win popularity in the hope that this would further their electoral chances for the higher magistracies of the praetorship and consulship. There was, therefore, no professional organization, there was no guild of artists, indeed there was no permanent theatre at Rome until 55 B.C. Ambitious entrepreneurs, having signed up an author and actors and assembled the necessary staging, approached the aediles and bargained for the right to put on a performance. It was a typically Roman way of doing things, like the tax-collectors who negotiated with the censors a contract for the collection of taxes in a province. At all times the Romans displayed a healthy regard for private enterprise.

Instead of inventing a new genre or new themes, the playwrights, as so many other Latin writers were to do, adopted and adapted Greek originals. In the case of comedy, these were the plays, chiefly, of Philemon, Diphilus and Menander, a number of whose works have recently come to light. They kept the same metrical pattern, a six-footed iambic line for spoken dialogue (akin to blank verse), a longer line for more impassioned chanting and a variety of lyric rhythms for singing. They kept the Greek costume and the Greek masks. Above all they kept the basic types of character. New Comedy, in particular Menander, operated with a conventional set of characters – the young man in love, the clever slave, the pimp, the parasite, the dirty old man and so on. Little attempt was made to particularize different examples of the same type; the same names (e.g. Daos for a slave) and the same masks were used from play to play. Like P. G. Wodehouse, Menander was interested in the economy and consistency of the plot, usually centred on love, and his plays were closely tied to specific situations and places.

Open a play of Plautus and you will instantly feel the difference. Plautus's original name is uncertain. He was born at Sarsina, in Umbria, about 254 B.C. and came to Rome where he worked as a stage-hand and then as an actor. Hence his full name, Titus Maccius ('buffoon') Plautus ('flat-footed'). After an abortive career in business, he returned to the stage and wrote a large number of plays which were so popular that they gained him the reward of Roman citizenship. Superficially he appears to be doing no more than translating ('turning') Greek texts, but his originality is evident at every level. Instead of stock names, his characters are called such splendidly fantastic things as Pyrgopolynices or Ballio (perhaps intended to take off Scipio), and instead of performing an intricate minuet, the characters are involved in one long, complex razzimontade. Plautus deserts his original in order to insert episodes for no other reason than a taste for imbroglio and mayhem. Above all he loves tricks and deceptions – a girl who acts as her own identical twin (in the *Miles Gloriosus*) or the excruciating device in the *Poenulus* whereby the father of two free-born Carthaginian girls temporarily held by the pimp Lycus is made to pretend that he really is their father in order to threaten Lycus with an action for illegal detention of free-born girls. The consequence of this is that Plautus adds scenes, usually inspired by other Greek plays, with a total disregard for the loose ends and inconsistencies that result. A good example is the *Miles Gloriosus* ('The Swaggering Soldier'). It is an open question what source or sources lay behind it. The play that we have falls into two quite separate sections. The first is an elaborate story about a girl who escapes from her keeper, a self-important general, through a secret passage into the house next door, where she is seen by her keeper's slave making love to a young man. The pretence of the identical twins, with all the appropriate stage business, is made up to bamboozle the slave. The second is an equally farcical plot to cut the boastful general down to size. The two plots do not really marry up, but the play as a whole carries one along by its sheer gusto. Why? The secret lies in its verbal dexterity. Plautus loved words. He loved them for their sound and their associations; he loved alliteration and assonance, bombast and braggadocio. The *Miles* opens with a splendid scene between the pompous general, Pyrgopolynices, and his parasitical toady, Artotrogus.

PYRGOPOLYNICES: My shield, there – have it burnished brighter than the bright splendour of the sun on any summer's day. Next time I have occasion to use it in the press of battle, it must flash defiance into the eyes of the opposing foe. My sword, too, I see, is pining for attention; poor chap, he's quite disheartened and cast down, hanging idly at my side so long; he's simply itching to get at an enemy and carve him into little pieces . . . Where's Artotrogus?

ARTOTROGUS: Here, at his master's heels, close to his hero, his brave, his blessed, his royal, his doughty warrior – whose valour Mars himself could hardly challenge or outshine.

PYRGOPOLYNICES [reminiscent]: Ay – what of the man whose life I saved on the Curculionean field, where the enemy was led by Bumbomachides Clytomestoridysarchides, a grandson of Neptune?

ARTOTROGUS: I remember it well. I remember his golden armour, and how you scattered his legions with a puff of breath, like a wind sweeping up leaves or lifting the thatch from a roof.

PYRGOPOLYNICES [modestly]: It was nothing much, after all.

ARTOTROGUS: Oh, to be sure, nothing to the many more famous deeds you did – [aside] or never did. [He comes down, leaving the Captain attending to his men.] If anyone ever saw a bigger liar or more conceited braggart than this one, he can have me for keeps . . . The only thing to be said for him is, his cook makes a marvellous olive salad . . .

PYRGOPOLYNICES [missing him]: Where have you got to, Artotrogus?

ARTOTROGUS [obsequiously]: Here I am, sir. I was thinking about that elephant in India, and how you broke his ulna with a single blow of your fist.

PYRGOPOLYNICES: His ulna, was it?

ARTOTROGUS: His femur, I should have said.

PYRGOPOLYNICES: It was only a light blow, too.

ARTOTROGUS: By Jove, yes, if you had really hit him, your arm would have smashed through the animal's hide, bones, and guts.

PYRGOPOLYNICES [modestly]: I'd rather not talk about it, really.

(tr. E. F. Watling)

Another example of how Plautus lets his verbal exuberance run away with him, thereby ruining the story-line but immensely improving the humour, comes from the *Pseudolus*, produced probably in 191 B.C. and regarded as one of his best comedies. The plot is simple. Calidorus loves Phoenicium, who has been sold to a pimp, Ballio. Calidorus's faithful slave achieves a happy ending by a series of ingenious ruses. But what sticks in the mind is the talk of Ballio. Early in the play he lines up his team.

Now then, my pretties, all *you* have to do is to enjoy your little selves in comfort, ease and luxury, and make yourselves the most desirable companions for the highest gentry in the town. I'm going to put you to the test today. I'm going to find out which of you is only interested in her own freedom, or her stomach, or in lining her own purse, or just going to sleep. I shall have to decide which I'll choose to make a free woman of, and which to put back on the market. I want to see your lovers bringing me a whole pile of presents today. I want supplies for a year brought to this house this day, or else tomorrow you'll be out on the streets. As you are aware, today is my birthday. So where are they? Where are the lads for whom you are supposed to supply the light of love, the joy of life, the sweet sips of honeysuckle lips, the pressed caress . . .? Where are they? I want to see them in massed battalions outside this door, with their hands full of presents for me. Why do you suppose I provide you with clothes and ornaments and everything you could possibly need? And what return have you shown me for it so far? Nothing but dead loss. Drink is the only thing you miserable creatures are interested in; your stomachs are filled to bursting, while I go dry.

(tr. E. F. Watling)

Yet there is a further difference between Plautus and his models which in some ways is the most intriguing. Throughout Rome's history Latin ideas were to be dressed in Greek clothes. Virgil's *Eclogues* and *Georgics* at first sight look like no more than Theocritus and Hesiod transplanted to Rome; Horace's *Odes* disclaim any other intention than to be imitations of Alcaeus and Sappho. Yet those appearances are very deceptive. Modern critics have claimed indeed that when Virgil or Horace are 'being Greek' they are being unrealistic and purely literary. But there is more to it than that. The

Romans assimilated the Greek world to such an extent that one simply cannot distinguish the Greek elements from the Latin: they all coalesce to form part of a civilized, cosmopolitan, Roman scene. This will become clear later when Horace, Propertius and Virgil are considered in detail; for Plautus, it meant that his scenes are not confined to Athens but take place in a universal city which comprises the Roman, Greek and Carthaginian worlds equally. A play nominally set in Athens will turn on the interpretation of a fine point of Roman law; free-born Carthaginian girls will be treated as possessing the same legal rights to freedom as Athenian or Roman girls. Who was the employer of Pyrgopolynices? Athens? King Seleucus? Rome? In all Plautus's plays the time is 'now' and the scene is 'here', and it is that dramatic illusion which is all-important.

Plautus, unlike his successor Terence, was popular and greatly admired. By reshaping New Comedy so that it was no longer specifically Attic but *Romanograecopunica* he did as much as anyone to establish the place of Rome as a civilized power. And his plays are very funny.

Plautus wrote for the masses, as did his successor Caecilius Statius, whose popularity was such that his plays were still being revived in Cicero's day and had won the accolade of being included in school curricula. We can only form a very inadequate impression from a handful of casual quotations. It is quite different with Terence. Born in Carthage in 185 B.C., he came to Rome as the slave of a senator Terentius Lucanus, who freed him and gave him his name, P. Terentius Afer ('the African'). Terence died at the age of twenty-five, when he had written only six plays, but his achievement was such that these six plays, although seldom popular in their own time, proved to be the most influential single force in European drama. Terence operated within the same conventions as Plautus and Caecilius. He based his plays on the same shallow repertoire of New Comedy. The distinctive feature about his dramatic technique is his artistry, artistry in plot and in language. Gone are the noisy, implausible, prolix characters who dominated the stage at the expense of the story-line. Terence's characters talk in an economical, conversational Latin (his opponents called it 'thin'; he himself defended 'the natural purity of spoken words'), and, when he departs from the plots of Menander or other New Comedy authors, his aim is to achieve not greater flamboyance but greater realism. Both *The Mother-in-Law* (*Hecyra*) and *The Self-Tormentor* (*Heauton Timoroumenos*) are masterpieces of subtle psychological analysis that need no pimps or parasites to sustain the interest. The peculiar flavour of Terence can be captured simply by reading the opening lines of his very first play, *The Woman from Andros* (*Andria*).

> [*Simo, a gentleman in late middle age, and his elderly freed slave Sosia come on right with servants carrying food and drink for a party.*]

SIMO: Take those things in, you boys; hurry up. Sosia, wait a minute, I want a word with you.

> [*The servants go into his house.*]

SOSIA: No need to say it, sir. I expect you want me to take charge of all that.

SIMO: No, it's something else.

SOSIA: But what better use can you make of my skill?

SIMO: I don't need your skill for what I'm planning at the moment; this demands the qualities I have always observed in you – loyalty and secrecy.

SOSIA: I'm at your service, sir.

SIMO: You know that ever since I bought you for my slave as a boy you have found me a just and considerate master. I gave you your freedom because you served me in a free spirit, and that was the highest reward at my disposal.

SOSIA: I don't forget it, sir.

SIMO: And I don't regret it.

SOSIA: I'm only too glad if anything I've done or do pleases you, sir, and I'm grateful for your gracious approval. But I'm a bit worried about the way you're reminding me about the circumstances – it looks like a reproach for ingratitude. Please tell me briefly what you want of me.

SIMO: I will. Let me start by saying that you're wrong about these preparations. There isn't going to be a real wedding.

SOSIA: Then why pretend there is?

SIMO: I'll tell you the whole story, then you'll know all about my son's conduct, my own plans and the part I want you to play in the matter. As soon as Pamphilus was grown up and free to live his own life – for no one could have known the truth or guessed his disposition as long as he was restrained by youth, timidity and his tutor –

SOSIA: That's true.

SIMO: The usual things young men do, their crazes for keeping horses or hounds or dabbling in philosophy, all took up his time to a certain extent, but he hadn't any special enthusiasms. I was pleased.

SOSIA: And rightly, sir. 'Nothing too much' is the best rule in life, I think.

SIMO: Let me tell you the sort of life he lived: he was patient and tolerant with all his friends, fell in with the wishes of any of them and joined in all their pursuits, never contradicting nor putting himself first. That's the best way to steer clear of jealousy, win a reputation and make friends.

SOSIA: A well-planned life! Agree with everything nowadays, if you want friends; truthfulness only makes you unpopular.

SIMO: Meanwhile a woman came here from Andros three years ago and settled down in the neighbourhood, the victim of poverty and the indifference of her relatives: a beautiful girl, in the flower of her youth.

SOSIA: Oh dear; I suspect she brings trouble with her.

SIMO: At first she led a modest life, thrifty and hard-working, trying to make a living out of spinning and weaving. Then lovers began to come offering payment, first one and then another; human nature takes to pleasure all too easily after a spell of hardship, and so she accepted their offers and soon afterwards set up as a professional. One day her current lovers happened to take my son there to dinner. 'Now he's caught,' I said to myself at once; 'she's got him.' I used to watch his friends' servant-boys coming and going every morning and call to them: 'You there! Can you tell me who was in favour with Chrysis yesterday?' (That was the woman's name.)

SOSIA: I see.

SIMO: They said it was Phaedrus or Clinias or Niceratus, for these three shared her at the time. 'What about Pamphilus?' 'Oh, he only stayed to dinner and paid his share.' I was delighted. I made the same inquiry another day, and found nothing at all to implicate Pamphilus. Naturally I concluded that he was a model of continence, tried and tested, for if a man's will has come up against characters like theirs and remained unmoved, you may feel sure of his self-control in his own way of life. To add to my satisfaction, everyone spoke well of him with one voice and congratulated me on my good fortune in having a son blessed with such character. Well, to cut a long story short, my neighbour Chremes was persuaded by what he'd heard to approach me of his own accord and offer his only daughter with a substantial dowry to my son in marriage. I approved and accepted the match, and today is the day fixed for the wedding.

SOSIA: What's stopping it then?

SIMO: You'll hear. A few days after we made the agreement our neighbour Chrysis died.

SOSIA: Good, I'm glad to hear it. Dear me, she made me nervous for Pamphilus.

SIMO: At the time my son was always at the house with the lovers of Chrysis, helping them with the funeral. He was often depressed and sometimes wept bitterly. I was quite pleased at the time, for if he took this woman's death so much to heart, I thought, when they were only slightly acquainted, what would he feel if he had been really in love? And how will he take it when death comes to me, his father? I assumed that everything was prompted by his sensitive nature and sympathetic disposition. In short, I went to the funeral myself to please him, still with no suspicion that anything was wrong.

SOSIA: What are you getting at, sir?

SIMO: I'll tell you. The body was brought out and we followed. Presently among the women who were there I caught sight of a girl whose beauty was –

SOSIA: Not bad, perhaps.

SIMO: And her expression, Sosia, was so modest and lovely – nothing could be more so. Her grief seemed to me to exceed that of the other women, just as she outshone them all in the grace and refinement of her bearing, so I went up to the attendants and asked them who she was. They told me she was the sister of Chrysis. Then the truth came home to me. Why, that was it – the reason for his tears and tender-heartedness.

SOSIA: I dread to think what's coming next!

SIMO: Meanwhile the procession moved off, we joined it and came to the cemetery. The body was laid on the pyre. Everyone wept. Then the sister I spoke of, careless of what she did, went dangerously near the flames. Thereupon Pamphilus, in his terror, let out the secret of his well-hidden love. He ran up and caught her round the waist. 'Glycerium, my darling,' he cried, 'what are you doing? You'll kill yourself.' Then you could easily see that they had long been lovers; she fell back into his arms and wept, so confidingly . . .

SOSIA: Did she indeed!

SIMO: I returned home angry and disappointed in him, but I had no real grounds for reproving him. I could imagine his answer: 'What have I done, father? What's wrong? A girl tried to throw herself on the fire, and I held her back and saved her life. What harm have I done?' Proper enough.

SOSIA: You're right, sir. If you start blaming folk for saving lives, what will you do with those who do real harm or damage?

(tr. Betty Radice)

There is a rare freshness about this scene, and also considerable irony and sophistication. Simo's motives and feelings too are a great deal more complicated than he himself would allow.

But it is a quiet and unspectacular opening. Terence's plays are indeed to be appreciated not by the crowds but by the connoisseurs, as the prologue to the *Hecyra*, spoken by the distinguished actor L. Ambivius Turpio, ruefully admits.

Now for my sake give a fair hearing to my plea. Once more I am presenting *The Mother-in-Law*, a play for which I have never been able to gain a hearing uninterrupted, so much has misfortune dogged its progress. You can remedy this by your understanding, if you will support our efforts. At the first production, much talk of some boxers, as well as the rumour that a tight-rope walker would appear, the mob of their supporters, shouting and women's screaming forced me off the stage before the end. I then decided to follow my old practice with this new play and try it out. I put it on a second time. The first part was doing well when news arrived that there was to be a gladiators' show. In surged the people, pushing, shouting, jostling for a place, leaving me powerless to hold my own.

(tr. Betty Radice)

In his own prologues Terence does not conceal the fact that he was most at home with Roman aristocracy.

The author ... takes it as a high compliment if he can win the approval of men who themselves find favour with you all and with the general public, men whose services in war, in peace, and in your private affairs, are given at the right moment, without ostentation, to be available for each one of you.

(Prologue to *The Brothers*; tr. Betty Radice)

And it is significant that at this period a changed attitude to Greek culture was making itself felt among Roman nobles, an attitude which can best be defined as one of scholarly appreciation. The Hellenic arts were no longer novelties to be enthusiastically naturalized: they were to be enjoyed with deeper awareness. After the Battle of Pydna (168 B.C.) Rome was completely mistress of the Greek East, and a flood of statues, paintings and other works of art began to pour back to the capital, accompanied by Greek artists and writers anxious for recognition and employment. In this climate cultivated Romans became more discriminating. Chief among them was P. Cornelius Scipio Aemilianus (185-129), the son of L. Aemilius Paulus and adopted son of the great Scipio Africanus. He had a profound and genuine interest in the arts. He had been brought up on the Greek pattern, surrounded, as Plutarch tells us, not only by Greek teachers, scholars and rhetoricians but also by Greek sculptors, painters, overseers of horses and hounds, and instructors in hunting. He befriended the Greek historian Polybius, who movingly described his relationship as one of teacher and friend, and the Stoic philosopher, Panaetius (p. 79). He also numbered among his intimate friends the writer C. Laelius and the satirist C. Lucilius (p. 142). His library was enriched by books acquired from the Macedonian royal library. Yet it would be wrong to think of a philhellenic coterie. Other Romans, no friends of Scipio, shared the same taste, such as A. Postumius (consul in 151 B.C.) or P. Licinius Crassus, who could speak five Greek dialects. Now for the first time Roman oratory, as Cicero observed, begins to be influenced by the principles of Greek rhetoric, and it is only appropriate that it was in 155 B.C. that the great philosopher Carneades created a sensation by delivering some lectures in Rome on 'Justice' in which he claimed that Rome's empire was based upon injustice. Whether these were the circles which Terence claimed approved of his plays is immaterial. What is relevant is that Rome was growing up, and her educated citizens were becoming more mature and less raw.

HISTORY

The writing of history is a curious phenomenon. We may take it for granted, but in fact it is rare in other cultures.

The Jews wrote no history: they wrote about the dealings of Jehovah with his people. The Persians wrote no history; their kings wrote about themselves. Neither the Carthaginians nor the Etruscans wrote any history. It requires a certain temperament and outlook, which the Greeks happened to have, the curiosity to look at events and ask what happens, how it happens and why it happens.

Just such questions must have faced many Romans at the end of the third century B.C. when they dealt with the Greeks, on business or political or even military affairs. It is like the oldest question in Homer asked of strangers: 'Who are you? Where do you come from? What are you doing?' It is characteristic of the Romans that they saw that such questions needed answering and responded to them in the one way possible – a Greek way. The first Roman historian was a member of a famous family – Q. Fabius Pictor – who had himself achieved a reasonably distinguished level in public life. Indeed, after the defeat of the Romans by Hannibal at Cannae he was sent on a mission to Delphi to seek advice about the future (216 B.C.). His history does not survive, so that we are driven back on guesses and inferences, but it was the primary source for all later Roman historians. As a recent discovery has startlingly proved, Fabius's *Annals* were widely disseminated; a second-century B.C. library catalogue from Tauromenium in Sicily includes him with a short summary of the contents of his work. Nor can we be sure when it was actually composed: possibly during the Second Carthaginian War to drum up support against Philip of Macedon; more probably after the Peace Treaty of 202 B.C. But significantly it was written in Greek, not Latin, partly because Latin was still evolving as a literary language, partly because it was directed towards an international audience, that is an audience whose common language would have been Greek.

Fabius, as the fragments show, dealt in great detail with the foundation and early history of Rome and with more recent events leading up to the Carthaginian War; the period from 500 to 300 B.C. was evidently more thinly covered. His approach was not that of Herodotus or Thucydides, but of contemporary Hellenistic historians such as Duris or Timaeus. He had a taste for anecdotes and biographical (even if imaginary) stories. He may have worked up many legends of ancestors of famous families like the Claudii, Fabii or Valerii which were still prominent in his own day. But his achievement was to give, however spuriously, a substantial and credible background to Rome, which made her a city whose history could stand comparison with that of any in the Hellenic world. Romantic and fictitious it may have been, but it was also original and persuasive.

The decisive emancipation, however, was due to M. Porcius Cato (234–149 B.C.; consul in 195 B.C., censor in 184 B.C.). Cato is a fascinating study in contradictions. He publicly committed himself against the evils of Greek influences of every kind: 'Their race is quite worthless,' he wrote, 'and unteachable, and I speak as a prophet that when it gives us its literature it will ruin everything.' Yet both his historical and oratorical works owe their success precisely to Greek inspiration. With equal force, as censor, he attacked all forms of luxury and extravagance; yet his surviving handbook on agriculture (p. 102) is mainly concerned to help a landlord maximize his profits from his estates. We do not know what inspired him to write his historical work, *Origines*; what we do know is that it was the first major work of history to be composed in Latin. It was written over a period of years. The first three books, dealing with the foundation of Rome and the other Italian cities, were perhaps completed in the 180s; Books 4 and 5 dealt with the Carthaginian Wars and brought the story down to 167 B.C.; the last two books treated events up to within a few months of Cato's own death. The pattern is notable. Like Fabius, Cato concentrated on early times and on contemporary history, and was content to leave the intervening period, for which records and research were deficient, to be briefly summarized. Unlike Fabius, however, he felt no compulsion to justify Rome as if it were a Greek city. He does indeed link Rome and Greece (the Aborigines are held to have come from Achaea and Roman austerity to have been inspired by the Lycurgan constitution at Sparta), but he is writing for a Roman audience and not, defensively, for a Greek one. History has a practical purpose, to aid the statesman to understand Rome's place in the world. The *Origines*, it was said, was written for the education of Cato's son. But Greek supplied the model. The very title is a translation of a familiar Hellenistic form of literary history – 'Foundations' or *Ktiseis* – and from the fragments we can see how Cato tried to develop an appropriate prose style in Latin.

Most of the fragments are quoted by later grammarians and antiquarians for the sake of curious details, but one of the most extensive is a passage from a speech on behalf of the Rhodians delivered by Cato himself in 167 B.C., which he incorporated in the *Origines* and which illustrates another development. We know little about the history of Roman oratory. Metellus, who died in 221 B.C., was said to have been 'the best orator' of his day, and Cicero calls M. Cornelius Cethegus (consul in 204 B.C.) the first truly eloquent Roman; but nothing survived to enable later generations to know how they, or Scipio or Fabius or any other great figure, actually spoke. But what is significant is that the first memorable speech delivered by a Roman was that given by T. Quinctius Flamininus *in Greek*, when he promised Greece its independence in 196 B.C. at the Isthmian Games. There was a history of Greek rhetoric, but not of Roman. Cato, for all his supposed anti-Hellenism, seems to have been the first to transplant Greek rhetorical techniques and ideals and adapt them to Latin: he is described as having acquired 'the whole armoury taught by rhetoricians'. A short passage shows typically Greek devices – the careful antitheses, the subtle distinction between action and volition, the imaginary prosecutor and so on:

... He who speaks against them most strongly says 'They wished to become our enemies.' Is there any one of you, I want to know, who, in a matter in which he himself is involved, thinks it right to be punished because he is accused of having *wished* to do wrong? No one, I think; for I would not in a matter which related to me ... What more? Is there, I want to know, any law so severe, which says, 'If anyone *wishes* to do such and such a thing, let the fine be a thousand sesterces provided that is less than half his estate; if any one *wishes* to have more than five hundred acres, let the penalty be so much; if any one *wishes* to have a greater number of sheep, let him be fined so much?' Yet we all *wish* to have more of all of these, and we go unpunished for it ... But if it is not right for honour to be given because someone says that he *wanted* to do right but did not, will it be prejudicial to the Rhodians because they did not do harm, but because they say that they wished to do harm?   (tr. G. Kennedy)

Cato, therefore, whether consciously or not, was very much a child of his time. As Ennius naturalized epic and as Plautus naturalized comedy, so he was the first to recognize that the Latin language had the capacity to produce works of history and oratory which, however much they might owe to Greek, were original works in their own right. Cato's example was to set the pattern for the whole subsequent history of Latin literature.

3

THE LATER REPUBLIC

ROME and her vast Empire were governed by a tiny group of families. If you look at the annual lists of consuls, the chief magistrates, you find the same names recurring year after year – Claudii, Caecilii, Domitii, Licinii, Julii, Cornelii, Antonii, Calpurnii and so on. They maintained this hold on power by their network of dependants. Roman society was hierarchical. A leading politician, in addition to a long history of family tradition, enjoyed a special social position. He acted as patron to a large number of clients, both in Rome and in the provinces with which his family had close connections. The relationship was a finely wrought one. The patron had a duty to look after the interests of his clients – to defend them when necessary in a court of law, to give them hospitality, to offer them advice and help in times of need. In return he expected their backing at the polls or on public occasions when a display of his supporters would add to his prestige and popularity. From very early times it was accepted that it was the duty of a Roman to take an active part in the running of the state. Thereby he acquired the 'dignity' that was the prerogative of his family and his class. As Cicero was to write, 'we may perhaps excuse men for not going into politics if they are exceptionally clever and have devoted themselves to scholarship, or if bad health or some more serious reason had led them to withdraw from public life ... but, so far from regarding it as praiseworthy, we should, I think, consider it discreditable if, without any such excuse, they simply profess to despise a career in politics, which most people admire'.

The crowning glory was the office of consul, but to reach that a man had to be elected to a succession of minor offices: the quaestorship, which dealt largely with financial administration, the aedileship, which supervised the running of the games and public festivals, the tribunate of the people, which secured him a voice in the Senate, and the praetorship, which ran most of the legal business of Rome. In addition he would be expected to serve for a year or so on the staff of a provincial governor and also to take his own turn as a governor – an opportunity welcomed by most because it afforded a chance to recoup the heavy expenses involved in political life. All these offices were elective and often strenuously contested and, although Rome was theoretically a democracy, in practice its electoral bodies were so composed that a man with money, connections and clients stood the best chance. There were two assemblies. The centuriate, which elected the consuls and handled certain pieces of major legislation, consisted of some 196 units or 'centuries', drawn from five classes based on wealth. The voting system was so organized that a majority could be secured simply by the vote of the richest class. The tribal assembly was made up of the thirty-five tribes, in which all Roman citizens were registered, acting as voting units. It put a premium on those living in or near to the city itself who could actually turn up and vote; there was no postal ballot.

The nobles had a stranglehold on office, and they maintained it by a complicated method of alliances between families. Dynastic marriages were normal practice, facilitated by the almost complete power which the male head of a family enjoyed over the affairs of other members of it. When Caesar wanted to cement his political coalition with Pompey in 59 B.C. he decided to break his daughter's engagement to Q. Servilius Caepio and marry her instead to Pompey.

(Despite a difference of thirty years in their ages, the marriage proved surprisingly happy and successful.) Less dynastic but equally formal was the custom of publicly asserting your 'friendship' (*amicitia*) with another statesman, which was a method of proclaiming your political alignment. Such 'friendships' could be just as publicly renounced or broken as made.

In such a highly competitive world, there was not enough room at the top. Time and again in the last century of the Republic, ambitious men reached an eminence which they could only maintain by destroying the fabric of democracy and assuming autocratic power but which in turn drove their opponents to have recourse to equally violent and autocratic measures. First Marius and then, in a counter-coup backed by the nobles, L. Cornelius Sulla became to all intents and purposes sole ruler of Rome. Twenty years later Pompey had gained a prestige and military backing after his victorious campaign in the East that made him seem a threat to other men's aspirations and to the Republic. Julius Caesar, at least, had no intentions of allowing his aspirations to be cut down by Pompey or anyone else. By an astute pact in 59 B.C. with Pompey and Crassus he bought himself first five and then ten years' grace to win fame and fortune and, above all, a veteran army at his back. His decisive defeat of Pompey at Pharsalus in 48 B.C. spelled the breakdown of the old constitution. Had not assassination intervened, Caesar, already perpetual dictator, might have become king and god. His death allowed the old dynastic feuds to continue for another generation as Antony and Octavian, Caesar's adopted son, tried to divide and rule. But the tensions and passions were too strong. The Battle of Actium (31 B.C.) sealed the fate of the Republic. Thereafter, whatever the name ('princeps' or emperor), whatever the outward trappings, Rome was under the rule of one man – a situation which Cicero and other thinkers had foreseen and realized was the only possible salvation of the state. Augustus, as Octavian now called himself, was fortunate to live long enough (he died in A.D. 14) to preside with tact and sensibility over this constitutional transition.

It was extremely difficult for an outsider to break into such a charmed circle. Membership of the Senate depended on elected office, and elected office depended on birth and connections. Until the Empire it was rare for a 'new man' to win through to the top. He had to have some outstanding talent which would win him the patronage of a noble family. C. Marius, one of Rome's greatest military geniuses, attracted the attention of the noble family of Metelli, who started him on the first rung of the ladder. Cicero had only his gift of eloquence to help him; he owed his first break to Marius himself, now an elder statesman, who happened to come from the same small Italian town as Cicero, Arpinum. For all his gifts and successes, Cicero was never really accepted by the Roman establishment, and the story of his life is one of pathetic frustration.

Words were all-important in public life. Business was decided by public debate either in the Senate (with some 300–500 members) or before the assemblies, so that the man who could sway the vast Roman electorate or persuade his critical colleagues was the man who would get on. And politics spilled over to the courts. Most of the major trials held in the period from 80 to 50 B.C. had a strong political undertone, whether they were actual prosecutions of rival politicians for corruption, bribery, extortion etc. or whether they were for such nominal crimes as murder or violence. A successful prosecution or defence had major political consequences. Indeed it was customary for a young and aspiring noble to seek to make his mark by some particularly spectacular case. Cicero's success was assured by his flamboyant attack on C. Verres, governor of Sicily, in 70 B.C.

This is why the third stage of Roman education (between the ages of fifteen and eighteen) was almost exclusively taken up with training in public speaking. The Romans had inherited the precise science of rhetoric from the Greeks (p. 38) and adapted it to their own needs and conditions. The education was designed to produce fluency and ingenuity. A boy started with a series of preliminary exercises – retelling a story in his own words or building up a short passage to illustrate a particular moral or maxim. He would study the structure of a speech and the style appropriate to different types of oratory. He would learn conventional arguments, derived from character, situation, occasion, probability, necessity and so on. He would read and reread specimen examples, such as speeches of the Elder Cato and (later) of Cicero himself. He would stock his mind with telling precedents from past history. Finally he would try his hand at composing imaginary speeches, either on a set subject (e.g. 'Hannibal after Cannae debates whether to march on Rome') or for or against a particular case (e.g. 'The law states that no foreigner is allowed to mount the city-wall, on pain of death. The city is besieged and a foreigner repels a party of enemy who were scaling the walls. Should he be put to death?'). Many of these rhetorical exercises, as we shall see (p. 170), survive from the early Empire.

There were authors who tried to formalize the principles of public speaking. The earliest surviving handbook, addressed to one C. Herennius, was probably written by Q. Cornificius in the 80s. Cicero himself devoted at least five books to the subject – *Brutus, Orator, On the Orator, On Invention* and *On the Best Style of Speaking* – but it is as a practitioner of the art rather than a theorist that Cicero lives.

CICERO'S CRIMINAL CASES

Criminal cases at Rome were heard before a permanent court usually consisting of seventy-five members of the equestrian class (the predominantly business class, which was second only to the senatorial class), presided over by a praetor. The hearings were in public and attracted great crowds. There was no Public or State Prosecutor, so that all charges had to be brought by individuals. To win a case the advocate relied less on modern techniques, such as establishing an alibi or discrediting the evidence, than on building up the character of his client; his action was to show that his client was not the sort of person who could have committed the crime of which he was accused. The idea that people do the kind of things they do because they are the kind of people that they are is an old one, going back at least to Aristotle's *Poetics* and *Rhetoric*, and is of crucial importance for the understanding not only of oratory but of Roman historical writing as well. We must therefore not be surprised that Cicero dismisses with apparent levity the actual facts in the case and concentrates instead on painting pen-portraits of the chief characters. His tools are a devastating wit – no one knew better than he how to pour scorn and ridicule on an opponent – a passionate indignation and a rare gift of plausible obfuscation. His speeches, which he carefully revised for publication, make lively and amusing reading.

One of the earliest is his defence of Sextus Roscius of Ameria, who was accused in 80 B.C. of murdering his father on his way home from a dinner-party. Cicero does not attempt to establish his innocence but tries instead to pin the crime on two other men, Magnus and Capito, acting for Chrysogonus, a freedman of the all-powerful Sulla who was anxious to lay his hands on Roscius's property. What at first

ROMAN LITERATURE AND SOCIETY

sight seems to be a small-town murder turns, as so often, into a political *cause célèbre*. Cicero was at the very start of his career and his patron Marius, the life-long enemy of Sulla, had recently died; but the speech was a triumphant success and secured Roscius's acquittal. Cicero played on the feelings of the audience in a justly famous passage of high emotion which paints the heinous nature of murder as a crime and the grisly penalty attached to it.

... And so they ordained that anyone found guilty of this crime should be sewn alive into a sack and then thrown into a river.

It was a remarkably wise decision, gentlemen. What they did, in effect, was to cut the culprit off and shut him out of the entire sphere of nature. By depriving him, at one single blow, of sky and sun and water and earth, they created a situation in which the murderer of the very person to whom he owed his own life should in turn be deprived of all the elements which have given life to the world. To throw the condemned man to wild beasts did not seem to them the right solution, in case this contact with such a monstrosity should make the beasts even more savage towards us than they had been before. And the idea of dropping the guilty man naked into a river they likewise rejected, for fear that when his body had been carried down to the sea it would defile that very element which is itself believed to purify every defilement that exists. In a word, they left the criminal wholly bereft of all the things that are most abundantly available to the rest of the world. Breath to the living, earth to the dead, the sea to those who float upon its surface, the shore to those the sea casts up – these are the most universally available things in the world. Yet men condemned for this crime live, as long as they are allowed to go on living, without being able to breathe the air from the sky. They die without the earth coming into contact with their bones. They are tossed about by the sea without its cleansing waters ever reaching them. And, at the end, when they are cast up on the shore, even the rocks do not support their dead bodies to give them rest.

That is the enormous crime you are imputing to Sextus Roscius and that is its horrifying punishment.

(*In Defence of Sextus Roscius* 70–72; tr. Michael Grant)

But it is the characteristic wit of his mature years which makes Cicero such a delight to read. Perhaps the best example of it comes in his speech in defence of M. Caelius Rufus on five charges: organizing riots at Naples, beating up some Alexandrian ambassadors, the seizure of Pallas's goods, the murder of Dion, and, finally – and this was the nub of the case – the attempted poisoning of Clodia Metelli. Caelius is one of the most engaging personalities of the late Republic. Rich, handsome, well-connected, he was a protégé of Cicero, to whom he wrote some brilliantly offhand letters when Cicero was languishing in 51 B.C. as a very reluctant governor of Cilicia. He finally became a praetor and disappeared in the cataclysm of the Civil Wars in 48 B.C. The case in question, however, dates to 57 B.C. Cicero had achieved the consulship in 63 B.C., which he distinguished by the suppression of a conspiracy planned by a thwarted aristocrat, Catiline. In so doing he had earned many enemies, not least P. Clodius, a member of the ancient house of the Claudii. It was his sister Clodia who was at the centre of Caelius's trial. We are no longer dealing with petty crime in small Italian towns but with high Roman society. Clodia was a woman of rare talents. She is, beyond doubt, the Lesbia of Catullus's bitter and passionate poems (see p. 73), and she had also ensnared young Caelius, but there were deep political motives as well behind the prosecution. Caelius was certainly an impetuous young man, and was probably guilty on the first four charges. Cicero casually glosses over them and devotes his scathing wit to the fifth, which had been included only to blacken Caelius's character on the familiar ground that it was character not facts which counted. Caelius was fully acquitted.

Like most great advocates, Cicero preferred to defend rather than prosecute, but on occasion he could be a formidable prosecutor. He had made his reputation with his attack on Verres, the corrupt governor of Sicily, but, of his surviving prosecutions, perhaps the most notable is his biting assault on L. Calpurnius Piso, the consul of 58 B.C. whose daughter had married Julius Caesar. Cicero prosecuted him for his conduct while governor of the province of Macedonia, but once again the case really turned on the depiction of character. For Piso was an Epicurean (it was a time when Epicureanism enjoyed a brief vogue at Rome: see p. 81). Indeed his villa with its rich library including works of a noted Greek Epicurean, Philodemus, has been unearthed at Herculaneum. Cicero calls up all the popular bogies about Epicureanism – 'eat, drink and be merry for tomorrow you die' – to paint a cruel picture of the sham, insincere philosopher who in public appeared in all his bearded austerity but in private indulged in nameless vices and luxuries.

A Greek lives with him. I have always found him well-mannered, at least in Piso's company or by himself. He had readily responded to the young Piso's friendly approaches, although even then he affected a disdainful expression, as if disapproving of the gods themselves. The two men became intimate, indeed inseparable. Now I know that I am addressing not an illiterate audience but one of the most educated and cultivated in the world. So you have no doubt heard it said that Epicurean philosophers measure everything that a man ought to desire by pleasure. It does not matter whether this happens to be true or not, or, if it does, it is certainly irrelevant to the present case. But still it is a tempting sort of argument for a young man and one always dangerous to a person of limited intelligence. And so, the moment Piso heard that pleasure was so exceedingly praised by a philosopher, he inquired no further: that was quite enough for someone of his natural dissipation.

CICERO'S PUBLIC SPEECHES

If most of his forensic speeches had political undertones, Cicero also used his talents directly in the sphere of public affairs, whether in the Senate or before the people. He was at a disadvantage in that he had no social power-base from which to counsel any positive policy of his own. He had always tried to maintain his independence and his tongue was sharp enough to make great men anxious to have him on their side, but in fact he was throughout his life beholden to more powerful figures than himself. In the 60s he had dreams of forming a coalition with Pompey, who for much of the decade was winning glory and wealth in the East. In the 50s, particularly after his exile and recall in 58 B.C., Cicero was careful to advocate the policies of Caesar and Pompey. When the Civil War came, he eventually, after much hesitation, sided with Pompey but managed to miss the decisive Battle of Pharsalus. Reconciled to Caesar he made few public contributions, devoting himself instead to philosophy, but the speeches he did write display a craven subservience to the policies of the dictator. In the end his ineffective temporizing led him to be caught in the vindictive reprisals of Octavian and Antony. In so far as he had a programme, it was centred on the 'Concord of the Orders', a touching hope that senators and *equites* would all unite in a common cause for the welfare of the state. But ambition and dignity are divisive and centrifugal forces.

Cicero's political speeches, therefore, reflect the tensions and circumstances of the moment. As one would expect, they are persuasive and skilful. His *On the Law of Manilius* (66 B.C.) helped Pompey to get the command against Mithridates; his *On the Consular Provinces* gave a spurious respectability to the compact between Caesar, Pompey and Crassus in 55 B.C.

which enabled Caesar to retain the provinces of Gaul for a further five years. But it is only when he escapes from the oppressive shadows of the great nobles, when he sets out to speak for himself and himself alone, that he rises to the highest flights of eloquence.

There were two occasions in his life when for a brief instant he felt himself to be his own master and in command of the political scene. The first was in 63 B.C. when he was consul. One of his defeated candidates, Catiline (L. Sergius Catilina), a colourful if impoverished aristocrat, soured by his disappointment, began to plot a military *coup d'état* with the help of disaffected veteran soldiers throughout Italy and slaves from the big country estates. In four brilliant speeches Cicero awakened the people to the danger. His success in scotching the conspiracy was the highlight of his life which he never failed to recall. He wrote a poem on his consulship and tried to persuade a literary friend, Lucceius, to compose a history.

Nothing is finer than the celebrated opening of the *First Catilinarian Speech*, delivered to the Senate on 7 November 63 B.C.:

How long will you abuse our patience, Catiline? How long will you mock us in your madness? When can we expect an end to your present reckless abandon? Do you not see that your number is up? Are you not impressed by the strong guards on the Palatine Hill, by the sentries throughout the city, by the popular alarm and the solidarity of the responsible citizens, by this session of the Senate held under conditions of unprecedented security, by the looks and reactions of the Honourable Members assembled here? Can you not see that your conspiracy has already been frustrated, rendered impotent by widespread disclosure?

The second occasion came almost exactly twenty years later, after the assassination of Caesar. M. Antony, a devoted lieutenant of Caesar's, hoped to succeed to his power, but there was also the young Octavian, whom Caesar had adopted as his heir. In the stirring months that followed Caesar's death, Cicero emerged from his political semi-retirement to launch a series of vitriolic attacks on Antony. In all he wrote fourteen *Philippics* (named after the speeches made by the Athenian orator Demosthenes against Philip, King of Macedon, in the fourth century B.C.). Some were speeches, some were rather political pamphlets. All were sensational, none more so than the end of the second *Philippic*:

The name of peace is beautiful – and peace itself is a blessing. Yet peace and slavery are very different things. Peace is freedom tranquilly enjoyed, slavery is the worst of all evils, to be repelled, if need be, at the cost of war and even of death. Even if those liberators of ours have withdrawn from our sight, they have left behind them the example of their deeds. They achieved what no one had ever achieved before. Lucius Junius Brutus made war against Tarquin, who was king at a time when kingship was lawful at Rome. Spurius Cassius Vecellinus, Spurius Maelius, and Marcus Manlius Capitolinus were killed because of the suspicion that they aimed at autocratic monarchy. But here, for the first time, are men raising their swords to kill one who was not merely aiming at monarchy, but actually reigning as monarch. Their action was superhumanly noble in itself, and it is set before us for our imitation: all the more conspicuously, because heaven itself is scarcely immense enough to hold the glory which this deed has made theirs. The consciousness of a noble achievement was reward enough; yet no one, I believe, should spurn that further reward which they have also won – immortality.

The day you ought to remember, Antony, is that day on which you abolished the dictatorship for ever. Let your memory dwell on the rejoicing of the Senate and people of Rome on that occasion. Contrast it with the haggling with which you and your friends busy yourselves now. Then you will realize that gain is a different thing from glory. Just as there are diseases, or dullnesses of the senses, which prevent certain people from being able to taste food: so, by the same token, debauchees, misers, and criminals are unattracted by glory.

However, if the hope of being praised cannot entice you to behave decently, is fear equally incapable of scaring you out of your repulsive behaviour? I know the lawcourts cause you no alarm. If that is due to innocence, you are to be commended. But if the reason is your reliance upon force, do you not understand this: that the man whose imperviousness to judicial processes is due to such a cause has pressing reason to feel terrors of quite another kind? For if you are not afraid of brave men and good Romans – seeing that armed satellites keep them away from your person – believe me, your own supporters will not stand you for very much longer. To be afraid of danger from one's own people night and day is no sort of a life; and you can hardly have men who owe you more, in terms of benefactions, than some of Caesar's killers owed to him.

However, you and he are not in any way comparable! His character was an amalgamation of genius, method, memory, culture, thoroughness, intellect, and industry. His achievements in war, though disastrous for our country, were none the less mighty. After working for many years to become king and autocrat, he surmounted tremendous efforts and perils and achieved his purpose. By entertainments, public works, food-distributions, and banquets, he seduced the ignorant populace; his friends he bound to his allegiance by rewarding them, his enemies by what looked like mercy. By a mixture of intimidation and indulgence he inculcated in a free community the habit of servitude.

Your ambition to reign, Antony, certainly deserves to be compared with Caesar's. But in not a single other respect are you entitled to the same comparison. For the many evils which Caesar inflicted upon our country have at least yielded certain benefits. To take a single example, the people of Rome have now discovered what degrees of confidence they can repose in this or that person. They have discovered who are fit to be entrusted with their fortunes, and who, on the other hand, need to be shunned. Do these facts never occur to you? Do you never understand the significance of this: that brave men have now learnt to appreciate the noble achievement, the wonderful benefaction, the glorious renown, of killing a tyrant? When men could not endure Caesar, will they endure you? Mark my words, this time there will be crowds competing to do the deed.

They will not wait for a suitable opportunity – they will be too impatient.

Antony: some time, at long last, think of your country. Think of the people from whom you come – not the people with whom you associate. Let your relationship with myself be as you please: but your country I pray you to make your friend once again. However, your behaviour is a matter for yourself to decide. As for mine, I will declare how I shall conduct myself. When I was a young man I defended our state: in my old age I shall not abandon it. Having scorned the swords of Catiline, I shall not be intimidated by yours. On the contrary, I would gladly offer my own body, if my death could redeem the freedom of our nation – if it could cause the long-suffering people of Rome to find final relief from its labours. For if, nearly twenty years ago, I declared in this very temple that death could not come prematurely to a man who had been consul, how much greater will be my reason to say this again now that I am old. After the honours that I have been awarded, Senators, after the deeds that I have done, death actually seems to me desirable. Two things only I pray for. One, that in dying I may leave the Roman people free – the immortal gods could grant me no greater gift. My other prayer is this: that no man's fortunes may fail to correspond with his services to our country! (tr. Michael Grant)

Yet once again Cicero had misjudged the situation. He had overlooked Octavian, then only twenty years of age. Octavian entered into an alliance with Antony and a third noble, M. Aemilius Lepidus, to form a triumvirate that would effectively run Rome. Cicero's death was the price of that pact, which lasted until the final demise of the Republic in 31 B.C.

CICERO'S CONTEMPORARIES

Because Cicero's speeches survive, it is easy to think that he held a unique position as an orator during the last century of the Roman Republic; but in fact he was surrounded by able competitors, and he was by no means always successful in the causes that he espoused. Interestingly enough he himself gives us pen-pictures of a number of his rivals, particularly in the *Brutus*, a comparative study of Roman oratory dedicated in 46 B.C. to young M. Junius Brutus, the son-in-law of Cato; and although his judgements are framed in the categories of contemporary criticism, they afford us a fascinating glimpse of the political scene. Of the earlier generation of speakers, Cicero singles out C. Aurelius Cotta (consul in 75 B.C.) and P. Sulpicius Rufus (tribune in 88 B.C.). Sulpicius, he wrote, was 'of all orators whom I have ever heard the most spectacular and the most theatrical'. Cotta, by contrast, who did not possess such a strong voice, relied on pure easy diction and skilful manipulation of his audience. The greatest of Cicero's own contemporaries was Q. Hortensius Hortalus (consul in 69 B.C.), whom he characterizes as follows: 'in his choice of words he was brilliant and at the same time fastidious, felicitous in their combination and resourceful in his command of them. He owed his skill partly to his own great talent and partly to his unremitting practice in rhetorical exercises. He always knew his case by heart and divided it sharply into its parts; he seldom overlooked anything that was relevant to the confirmation or refutation of the case; his voice was sonorous and agreeable; his delivery and gesture perhaps even a little too studied for an orator.' Of his younger contemporaries, Caesar and M. Claudius Marcellus (consul in 51 B.C.) were outstanding. Of Marcellus Brutus says: 'his oratory pleases me very much and with good reason. His dedicated study of the art shows in his use of carefully chosen words and in the wealth and variety of his ideas. What he says too receives an external charm and brilliancy from a fine voice and dignified action.' Caesar is 'of all our orators the purest user of the Latin language. He is master of an eloquence which is brilliant and with no suggestion of routine, and which, in respect of voice, gesture and the speaker's whole physique, possesses a certain noble and high-bred quality.'

But there is a crowd of lesser orators depicted in the *Brutus*. Not one of the prominent figures of the political and social world did not have his own gift. C. Memmius, the associate of Catullus and Lucretius, whose imposing monument still stands at Ephesus, was 'a speaker of the subtle, ingenious type with a pleasing diction, but averse to the labour not only of speaking but even of thinking'. C. Licinius Macer, the historian (tribune in 73 B.C.), was exceptional for his invention and arrangement of matter. Crassus succeeded by hard work: 'his oratory was characterized by a pure Latinity, a vocabulary not vulgar or commonplace, by a careful arrangement of matter, devoid of any flower or lustre of ornament; much liveliness of thought, but little of voice or delivery.' C. Licinius Calvus, son of Macer and friend of Catullus, spoilt his style by an excess of theory: 'he handled style with a scholar's knowledge and discrimination, yet from excessive self-examination and perfectionism he lost true vitality. So his language, through over-scrupulousness, seemed attenuated and while scholars and careful listeners recognized its quality, the crowds in court and forum for whom eloquence exists missed its fine flavour and swallowed it down whole.'

Cicero's rhetorical works, therefore, not only give his detailed views on the theory of successful speaking but also enable us to see the contrasting styles and personalities of the speakers who sought to influence the Roman scene. In all this we must always remember that for Cicero oratory was more than just skill in speaking. He identified the orator with the statesman and he held, as we have seen, that to be a statesman, to be actively involved in public affairs, is the highest function that a man can discharge. A good orator must, first of all, be a good man.

SWAYING PUBLIC OPINION

There were other ways of influencing opinion. The Empire was now a large and complex institution and required an efficient and elaborate administration. Communication had to be maintained between Rome and the provinces; friends wanted news on business, personal affairs, family matters. The Romans met this need by a rapid and reliable postal service. Letters were written on waxed tablets which could be re-used over and over again. Most important households had their own corps of postmen who would travel the length and breadth of the empire, and they would also make use of their friends' postmen who happened to be travelling in the right directions. In addition commercial firms, provincial governments and army groups all had their own couriers. With roads so good and so well-served by hostelries, and with the country-side policed, it is no surprise that letters were fast and frequent. It is a fortunate accident that a vast collection of letters written by and to Cicero has been preserved; it seems that his secretary, Tiro, kept copies of letters that he had written as well as some of the originals sent to him, which he published after his death. They fall into two main classes: intimate letters written to his friend and adviser T. Pomponius Atticus, and letters to other friends (including their letters to him). They are a unique source of information not only about Cicero's life but about the politics and social scene of the late Republic. The letters to Atticus are more informal in style and content (they contain a considerable amount of Greek) than the letters to friends, one complete book of which is taken up with formal letters of introduction and recommendation. But the Romans recognized that the letter was a promising art-form, which could be used for many purposes.

On 16 April 49 B.C. Caesar, who had by now openly invaded Italy, wrote to Cicero in a vain attempt to secure at the least his neutrality in the Civil War. The letter is interesting not least for the light it casts on social relationships (note especially the concept of 'friendship').

Although I was convinced that you would take no rash or ill-judged action, nevertheless my anxiety about what people are saying has impelled me to write to you and urge, in the name of our friendship, that you should not make any move, now that things have gone my way, which you did not see fit to make while matters were undecided. For, everything having manifestly turned out to our advantage and the disadvantage of the other side, you will have seriously damaged the good relations between our two selves – as well as acting against your own interests – if you display resistance to the trend of events. It would then be evident that your action resulted not from support of a cause, since the cause is the same as it was when you decided to hold aloof, but from your objection to something that I have done. And that would be the severest blow you could inflict on me.

Our friendship entitles me to ask you not to do it. Besides, what could be more appropriate for a man of peace and integrity, and a good citizen, than to keep out of civil disturbance? There were many who felt that to be so, but were prevented from acting as they wished because of the dangers that would have been involved. Weigh up the evidence provided by my career and by our own assessment of our friendly relations, and you will find abstention from the quarrel the safest and most honourable course.   (*To Atticus* 10.8; tr. M. Grant)

When Cicero was repining in Cilicia in 51 B.C. he relied on his young friend Caelius to keep him up-to-date with the latest gossip. Several of these racy, perceptive letters survive. Caelius gives his views on current politics.

O CICERO, FROM MARCUS CAELIUS

ROME, LATE IN MAY 51 B.C.

With regard to the promise I gave you when we parted, that I would write most diligently about everything that happens in the capital, I have been at pains to secure the services of a man who would go minutely into every detail – so minutely that I'm afraid you may find his efforts too long-winded. However, I know how meticulous you are, and how everyone abroad loves to be told about the slightest thing that happens at home. But I must beg you not to think that in delegating this job to someone else I have been off-hand in fulfilling my undertaking. It is not that I should not enjoy every minute devoted to thinking of you, busy though I am and, as you know, a very bad correspondent; but I am sure you will agree that the very size of the roll I am sending herewith is ample excuse. Heaven knows how much leisure one would need even to write out all this, let alone take note of it: you will find there every single Decree of the Senate, *bon mot*, story or rumour. In case this sample is not to your liking, please let me know, to save me from spending money only to bore you. If anything special happens in public affairs which is beyond the scope of such clerks, I will myself write you a careful account of what happened, what people's reactions were, and what the result is expected to be. As things are, there is nothing much in the air. Those rumours about elections north of the Po only kept warm as far as Cumae; when I got to Rome, I did not hear so much as a whisper about them. And Marcellus, by holding up his proposal about the succession to the governorship of Gaul and postponing it (as he told me himself) until 1 June, has naturally compelled people to express the same opinion of him as they did when we were at Rome together.

If you ran into Pompey, as you were hoping, let me know what you thought about him, what he told you, and which way he seemed to be inclining (he often says one thing and thinks another, and has not the wit to be able to conceal his true aims). As for Caesar, rumours about him are frequent and not very nice, but only whisperers bring them. One says he has lost his horse – a horse? no doubt he has; another, that the Seventh Legion has taken a beating, and that he himself is cut off from the rest of the army and surrounded near Beauvais. No certain news has arrived yet; nor are even these vague rumours in general circulation, only an open secret in circles known to you; Domitius repeats them with his hands to his mouth.

You died on 24 May – according to reports spread by loafers outside the courts (I should like to see them dead); the rumour was all over the Forum and the City that you had been murdered on the road by Quintus Pompeius. As I happened to know that Quintus Pompeius was at that moment taking a slimming course at Bauli and was so hungry that I was quite sorry for the man, I took it calmly, and only hoped that this canard would clear the air for us of any danger that might be hanging over you.

Your friend Plancus is at Ravenna, and in spite of a large bounty from Caesar is not prosperous or even comfortably off.

Your volumes of *The Republic* are universally popular.

(*To his Friends* 8.1; tr. L. P. Wilkinson)

On a more personal and literary note, Servius Sulpicius Rufus wrote to Cicero in 47 B.C. to console him on the death of his daughter Tullia. The letter artistically uses the themes and common-places of a 'consolation', a particular rhetorical genre, of which the Younger Seneca wrote three surviving examples and from which Tacitus was to borrow at the close of his moving biography of his father-in-law Agricola.

There is one thought I should like to put to you which has been a great consolation to me, in case it may also be able to bring you some comfort. On my return journey from Asia Minor, as I was sailing from Aegina towards Megara, I began to look at the lands round about. Behind me was Aegina, before me Megara, to the right the Piraeus, to the left Corinth. There was a time when these were most flourishing cities: now they lie there in dust and ruins. I began to think to myself, 'Why, fancy us insignificant humans taking it hard when one of us dies or is killed, whose life must in any case be short, seeing that in one place "the relics of so many cities lie exposed". Come, control yourself, Servius, and remember you were born a mortal.' I assure you, I felt considerably better for that thought. Do try, if you will, to fix your attention on the same idea. Lately, at one and the same time, many outstanding men perished, the Roman people suffered a crippling loss, and all our overseas possessions were shaken: are you then so distressed for the loss of the little life of one poor woman? If she had not died now, she would have had to die a few years later since she was born mortal.

Then take your mind too off these things, and turn to thoughts worthy of your role: that she lived while life had anything to give her; that she lived as long as we were still a free people; that she saw you, her father, hold office as praetor, consul and augur; that she was married to young men of the foremost rank; that she experienced almost every happiness; and that when the Republic was falling, she departed this life. What possible quarrel could you or she have with fortune on that score?

Finally, do not forget that you are Cicero, the man who used to give others advice and counsel, and do not be like those bad doctors who, when others are ill, profess to be skilled practitioners, but who cannot cure themselves. Take to heart the advice you always give to others and keep a firm hold on it. There is no sorrow that the passage of time does not diminish and soften. It is unworthy of you to wait for this to happen, and not use your wisdom to anticipate it. If there is any consciousness even after death, you may be sure that she, with her love for you and her devotion to all her family, does not want you to do as you are doing. Think of your lost one; think of your other friends and acquaintances, who are saddened by your sorrow; think of your country, and give it the benefit of your help and counsel wherever it is needed.

(*To his Friends* 4.5; tr. L. P. Wilkinson)

To balance those three very different pieces, it is worth reading two letters by Cicero himself. The first is his reply to a somewhat chilly letter of congratulation from Cato; the second is a frightened and confused screed asking for advice from Atticus.

TO CATO, AT ROME   RHODES, AUGUST 50 B.C.

'Glad I am to have the praises of a man so praised as thou', as Hector says, I think, in Naevius; and pleasant indeed is praise that comes from men who have themselves enjoyed it all their lives. I can assure you that with the congratulations you sent me and the declaration you made when voting in the Senate I have attained the summit of my ambitions. And this was to me both the most complimentary and the most gratifying feature, that you willingly conceded to friendship what you could conscientiously concede to truth. Even if our State were composed largely or entirely of Catos (though indeed the emergence of one is a miracle), what laurels, or what triumphal car, could I compare with praise from you? For to my feeling, and in consideration of the well-known integrity and fineness of your judgement, there could be no higher eulogy than that speech of yours, a full copy of which was sent me by my friends.

But the reason for my aspiration (I will not call it desire) I have explained to you in a previous letter; and although it has seemed inadequate to you, it has this much justification, that while such an honour should not be too much coveted, yet it should by no means be despised if the Senate sees fit to confer it; and I trust that that body, in view of the services I have undertaken for the State, will not think me unworthy of such an honour, especially as its conferment would be according to precedent. If it turns out so, I shall only remind you of your own very kind words and ask you, while you have paid me what you consider the highest possible compliment by the opinion you expressed, to rejoice nevertheless if what I have preferred has been done.

It is in this light that I see your actions, your feelings and your words; and your pleasure at the honour done me by the vote of a Thanksgiving Service is attested by your presence at the drafting; for I am well aware that such decrees are usually drafted by the closest friends of the man to whom the honour is being paid.

I shall, I hope, be seeing you before long. May I find the State in a better condition than I fear I shall!

(*To his Friends* 15.6; tr. L. P. Wilkinson)

Though I do not relax nowadays except while I am writing to you or reading your letters, still I feel the lack of subject-matter for a letter and I believe you feel the same. The easy, intimate exchanges we are accustomed to are out of the question in these critical times; and every topic relating to the crisis we have already exhausted. However, so as not to succumb completely to morbid reflections, I have put down certain questions of principle – relating to political behaviour – which apply to the present crisis. As well as distracting me from my miserable thoughts, this has given me practice in judging the problems at issue. Here is the sort of thing:

Should one stay in one's country even if it is under totalitarian rule?

Is it justifiable to use any means to get rid of such rule, even if they endanger the whole fabric of the state? Secondly, do precautions have to be taken to prevent the liberator from becoming an autocrat himself?

If one's country is being tyrannized, what are the arguments in favour of helping it by verbal means and when occasion arises, rather than by war?

Is it statesmanlike, when one's country is under a tyranny, to retire to some other place and remain inactive there, or ought one to brave any danger in order to liberate it?

If one's country is under a tyranny, is it right to proceed to its invasion and blockade?

Ought one, even if not approving of war as a means of abolishing tyranny, to join up with the right-minded party in the struggle against it?

Ought one in matters of patriotic concern to share the dangers of one's benefactors and friends, even if their general policy seems to be unwise?

If one has done great services to one's country, and because of them has received shameful and jealous treatment, should one nevertheless voluntarily endanger oneself for one's country's sake, or is it legitimate, eventually, to take some thought for oneself and one's family, and to refrain from fighting against the people in power?

Occupying myself with such questions, and marshalling the argument on either side in Greek and Latin, I take my mind off my troubles for a little; though the problems I am here posing are far from irrelevant to them. But I am afraid I am being a trouble to you: for if the man carrying this letter makes good speed he will bring it to you on the day when you are due for your fever.

(*To Atticus* 9.4; tr. Michael Grant)

CAESAR

Out of the letter grew the political pamphlet, written for immediate consumption. Most of these ephemeral publications have disappeared, except for some of the verse lampoons written by Catullus (see p. 72), but we know that they were a frequent element in political warfare, and they were still read by later historians like Suetonius and Tacitus. Probably the most famous were composed on the subject of Cato, who had committed suicide in 46 B.C. and whose memory had become the centre of intense propaganda. His son-in-law, Brutus, had commissioned Cicero to write a short account of him. Cicero extolled him as the embodiment of true Roman virtue, the hero of ancient republicanism who had preferred death to the intolerable autocracy of Caesar. Cato, he wrote, was one of the few people who were greater than their reputation. This was too much for Caesar, who sought to counteract the damage that it might do to his programme of political reform by writing a refutation himself and persuading his colleague, A. Hirtius (who was also responsible for writing the final book of Caesar's *Gallic Wars*), to do the same. Both were failures. Cicero asked Atticus in a letter to promote Hirtius's volume so that Cato's reputation might shine out all the brighter. And Caesar's was so intemperate that it lacked all credibility. He set out to denigrate Cato's morals – a perfectly acceptable tradition of Roman oratory, which Cicero had used against Clodia, Piso and Antony – but Cato's character was too renowned for even the most accomplished writer to be able to distort it into that of an eccentric drunkard and miser. Brutus himself, who was holding office under Caesar, also published a work of piety to immortalize the memory of his father-in-law. This war of paper is typical of the age. Two examples do survive in the form of open letters addressed to Caesar, nominally by the historian Sallust (see p. 90). One, written, it appears, in 50 B.C., urges Caesar to intervene directly at Rome, to break up the clique of nobles and to institute a far-ranging policy of reform. The second, dating from 46 B.C., advocated draconian legislation to curb extravagance and luxury at Rome which threatened to destroy the moral fibre of the people. We do not know what effect, if any, these pamphlets had.

In the face of innuendo and calumny, the only defence a politician had was to give as wide circulation as possible to his own version of the facts. Autobiography was a Greek art, perhaps the most celebrated example of it being Xenophon's account of the March of the 10,000 (the *Anabasis*), but it was quickly transplanted to Rome. Sulla defended and justified his career in twenty-two volumes; Cicero, as we have seen, hoped that a literary acquaintance of his, Lucceius, would write up his part in the events of the year 63 B.C.; Augustus was later to set up in various cities of the Empire a long inscription cataloguing the record of his achievements. But the most notable and the most remarkable is Caesar's own story of his governorship of Gaul from 58 to 51 B.C. He called the seven books that he completed 'Commentaries', which meant that they were the raw material of history, the bare facts, not the written-up, final product with all the reflections, speeches, digressions and character-sketches which were regarded as being appropriate to a historical masterpiece. There may have been some deliberate disingenuousness in this, but equally Caesar had very little leisure for sophisticated writing. The books were probably written separately year by year at the end of each campaigning season and published in 51 B.C., because Caesar, who had been out of Rome for so long, feared that his opponents would take advantage of his absence to sabotage his future. His presentation is deceptive. He always refers to himself, as Xenophon had done, in the third person and he gives a very matter-of-fact account of what he had done. Scholars have assumed that he must have been guilty of distortion and suppression of the truth. Yet very few of such charges can be made to stick. He may have been unfair to Labienus, he may have omitted the fact that he brought an elephant to Britain, he may have minimized some of his mistakes; but, considering the sheer difficulty of verifying the facts in the confusion of a mobile war, he presents his case with a cold and fair clarity that was to characterize his later actions as dictator.

Above all, Caesar was a great stylist. Indeed he had written a work on language (*On Analogy*). He was particularly concerned with purity and simplicity of vocabulary. It is significant, for instance, that whereas Latin has at least three words for 'river', Caesar uses one and one only. Except in a very few passages of heightened emotion (e.g. the capture of Alesia) he avoids elevated or poetic vocabulary, and he keeps rhetorical devices such as the use of anaphora or chiasmus to an absolute minimum. The *Gallic Wars* is a masterpiece of studied plainness.

One of the finest examples of Caesar's descriptive writing is his account of his victory over a powerful Belgic tribe near the River Sambre – 'That day he overcame the Nervii'. The Roman legions were disorganized and the battle was going badly.

After addressing the 10th legion Caesar had gone to the right wing, where he found the troops in difficulties. The cohorts of the 12th legion were packed together so closely that the men were in one another's way and could not fight properly. All the centurions of the 4th cohort, as well as a standard-bearer, were killed, and the standard was lost; nearly all the centurions of the other cohorts were either killed or wounded, including the chief centurion Publius Sextius Baculus, a man of very great courage, who was so disabled by a number of severe wounds that he could no longer stand. The men's movements were slow, and some in the rear, feeling themselves abandoned, were retiring from the fight and trying to get out of range. Meanwhile the enemy maintained unceasing pressure up the hill in front, and were also closing in on both flanks. As the situation was critical and no reserves were available, Caesar snatched a shield from a soldier in the rear (he had not his own shield with him), made his way into the front line, addressed each centurion by name, and shouted encouragement to the rest of the troops, ordering them to push forward and open out their ranks, so that they could use their swords more easily. His coming gave them fresh heart and hope; each man wanted to do his best under the eyes of his commander-in-chief, however desperate the peril, and the enemy's assault was slowed down a little.

Noticing that the 7th legion, which stood close by, was likewise hard put to it, Caesar told the military tribunes to join the two legions gradually together and adopt a square formation, so that they could advance against the enemy in any direction. By this manoeuvre the soldiers were enabled to support one another, and were no longer afraid of being surrounded from behind, which encouraged them to put up a bolder resistance. Meanwhile the two legions which had acted as a guard to the baggage at the rear of the column, having received news of the battle, had quickened their pace, and now appeared on the hill-top, where the enemy could see them; and Labienus, who had captured the enemy's camp, and from the high ground on which it stood could see what was going on in ours, sent the 10th legion to the rescue. The men of the 10th, who could tell from the flight of the cavalry and the non-combatants how serious things were, and what peril threatened the camp, the legions, and their commander-in-chief, strained every nerve to make the utmost speed.

Their arrival so completely changed the situation that even some of the Roman soldiers who had lain down, exhausted by wounds, got up and began to fight again, leaning on their shields. The non-combatants, observing the enemy's alarm, stood up to their attack, unarmed as they were; and the cavalry, anxious to wipe out the disgrace of their flight, scoured the whole battlefield and tried to outdo the legionaries in gallantry. But the enemy, even in their desperate plight, showed such bravery that when their front ranks had fallen those immediately behind stood on their prostrate bodies to fight; and when these too fell and the corpses were piled high, the survivors still kept hurling javelins as though from the top of a mound, and flung the spears intercepted by their shields. Such courage accounted for the extraordinary feats they had performed already. Only heroes could have made light of crossing a wide river, clambering up the steep banks, and launching themselves on such a difficult position.   (2.25-7; tr. S. A. Handford)

Caesar employed the same technique later when he published three books of *Commentaries* on the Civil Wars, but except for a magnificent section on the disaster that overtook his young friend Curio, who was killed in a desperate battle in N. Africa, they are less satisfying. The material was too intractable and Caesar's own role too controversial. However, the popularity of the genre can be judged from the fact that two of his officers wrote commentaries on the civil wars in Spain and Egypt, which are of interest precisely because they were written by less educated and less artistic men.

In conclusion, it can be seen that much of the finest prose writing of the late Republic was inspired by the special political and social circumstances of the time, above all by the need felt by leading politicians to maintain and to enhance their position.

4

THE INFLUENCE OF GREECE

'GREEK, everything must be Greek.' From the time that Rome was first brought into contact with the Greek world, from the wars of Pyrrhus and above all the Carthaginian Wars, she began to drink deeply from the springs of Hellenic culture. The first Roman literature – plays, epics, histories and oratory – was directly inspired by Greek models. As time went on, this familiarity with Greek civilization became more and more profound. Greek was the language and culture not only of Greece but of the whole of the Eastern Mediterranean. As Rome was forced to govern increasingly large areas of the East, so her ruling class and her traders increasingly adapted themselves to the Greek way of life. In the late Republic there were at least ten Roman provinces in the East, each of which required a staff of probably ten Roman citizens of the senatorial order to administer it. The poet Catullus, for instance, served under C. Memmius, governor of Bithynia in 57–6 B.C. and the patron of Lucretius; young M. Brutus accompanied his uncle Cato to Cyprus in 58 B.C. In addition Roman merchants established prosperous colonies at strategic places like Delos, Rhodes, Ephesus and Alexandria.

The effect of this contact can be seen in many fields. First of all, educated Romans were fluent in Greek. The Elder Gracchus in the mid-second century could deliver speeches in Greek in Greece, while his contemporary, P. Licinius Crassus (consul 132 B.C.), conducted trials in Asia in no fewer than five Greek dialects. In the first century bilingualism was the norm. A man like Livy (see p. 156) is remarkable in that, although he did read Greek (he made considerable use of the Greek historian Polybius), we can tell that his command of the language was far from perfect. The Romans acquired this linguistic skill at school or from private tutors. There is, for instance, a touching epitaph of a boy of six from Rome who had been sent to school to learn Greek. It was the convention for a young man to complete his education by studying for a while in Greece itself. Athens and Rhodes had particularly famous universities. You can catch glimpses of these groups of 'overseas students' at Athens. When Cicero studied here in 79 B.C. at the relatively advanced age of twenty-seven, with him were his brother and his cousin, his life-long friend T. Pomponius Atticus and an aristocrat, M. Pupius Piso. In 45 B.C. you would have found Horace and Cicero's son, a grandson of Cato and two other young nobles, Valerius Messalla Corvinus and Manlius Torquatus. Caesar travelled to Rhodes in 75 B.C. to study rhetoric under a famous professor, Apollonius Molon, but his studies were interrupted by pirates and other adventures. Such examples could be multiplied.

It was not only study and business that familiarized the Romans with things Greek. As they became wealthier and more leisured, they developed a taste for tourism for its own sake. Opportunities for travels had never been better. Roads were good, sailings regular and fast (ships could cover as much as 120 miles in a day). Visitors went to Athens and the great religious centres of Epidaurus, Olympia and Delphi. Then as now the Greek islands, especially Rhodes, were popular for holidays. As Horace writes:

Others can praise in their verse Mytilene, Rhodes and its glories,
  Great Ephesus, high-walled, twin-harboured Corinth,
Bacchus's home town Thebes, or Delphi, haunt of Apollo,
  Or Tempe up in Thessaly . . .   (*Odes* 1.7; tr. James Michie)

And the well-read traveller would penetrate to Troy and see 'the little mound where great Hector lies'. Egypt had an exotic fascination, with its pyramids, sphinx and singing statue of Memnon, but it was a restricted zone which was difficult for a Roman to obtain permission to visit, because the emperor retained it as his private domain.

In return hundreds of Greeks found employment at Rome, which had always lacked a professional class. Doctors, philosophers, architects, rhetors and other technical experts attached themselves to prominent Romans. Pompey gave his confidence to a historian, Theophanes of Mytilene, just as Sulla trusted his Greek freedman, Epicadus, who completed his autobiography. The chief librarian from Pergamum joined Cato's household; Antiochus of Ascalon, a noted philosopher, and the poet Archias were patronized by Lucullus, as the Epicurean Philodemus was by Piso or the writer Empylus of Rhodes by Brutus. A recent count, based on surviving inscriptions, has established that there were not fewer than 111 Greeks employed in various capacities in the imperial household under Augustus and Tiberius. This tendency continued for most of the first century A.D.

What were the effects of this intercourse? At the visible level, Rome derived a great number of architectural ideas from the Greeks. The designs of aqueducts, baths, villas and public halls are all Greek in origin. So too the Romans surrounded themselves with Greek works of art or copies of them. Successive Roman generals had helped themselves to the treasures of the East. L. Mummius pillaged Corinth for its artistic masterpieces in 146 B.C.; both Sulla and Lucullus brought back a wealth of looted valuables from the Eastern provinces; Verres, according to Cicero, could scarcely see or hear of a decent statue in Sicily without wanting to appropriate it. The same taste can be seen in the houses of Pompeii, not one of which is without its original or imitation *objets d'art*.

Painting, sculpture, mosaics – all enjoyed a vogue just because of their Greekness.

We cannot re-create ancient music, but we can see how steeped in Greek literature cultured Romans were. No longer were they content with the late Hellenistic writers: they went back to the great classical authors – Thucydides, Sappho and Alcaeus, Aristophanes and the tragedians, Aristotle and Plato, and, before all, Homer. Reading was both for education and relaxation.

CATULLUS

C. Valerius Catullus came from Verona, the son of a prosperous local dignitary. In this he was characteristic of almost all the great writers of the first century, few of whom came from Rome itself and who might therefore be presumed to view it with detached and curious eyes. Virgil came from Mantua, Horace from S. Italy, Lucretius, probably, from Naples, Propertius from Assisi, Livy from Padua, Cicero from Arpinum, Ovid from Sulmo. Catullus's exact dates are uncertain, perhaps 87–54 B.C., but he emigrated early to Rome and came under the influence of Parthenius, a Greek poet from Nicaea, who had originally been brought to Rome as a prisoner of war.

The result was explosive. A generation of highly educated and articulate poets grew up who were able to use newly discovered Greek forms as a means of expressing their own immediate feelings on a host of topics – politics, personalities, love, the social scene. They were communicating ideas and feelings to their friends through poetry, in the way that Cicero and others did through letters or pamphlets. Most of these poets are mere names to us, but the works of one, Catullus, have been preserved. His survival, one cannot help feeling, was not a matter of chance. His originality and versatility always secured him a hearing in ancient times as today. As far as we know, nobody had ever written quite like him before.

The collection of poems which survives contains a bewildering medley of different types, ranging from brief squibs and lampoons to love elegies, translations of Sappho (51) and Callimachus (66) and longer poems which stand obviously and consciously in the Greek tradition. But all the poems do have a common background – the use of Greek models as a means of release and self-expression.

The short poems, some 110 in all, are the most easy to appreciate. Many of them deal with contemporary political figures – Caesar, Cicero, Mamurra, Hortensius, L. Gellius, C. Memmius, L. Piso, M. Caelius Rufus and others. They are often spontaneous and pungent comments on what is going on in Rome and, as such, are an invaluable source of social criticism, very much in the tradition of Archilochus or some of the writers of Greek epigrams. Catullus attacks, for example, Caesar and Mamurra, his chief engineer during the Gallic and British wars, for their extravagance and immorality (57):

> They make a pretty pair of debauchees,
> Sex-sick Mamurra and his bedroom brother
> Caesar. No wonder; they've the same disease
> (One caught it in the City and the other
> In his own Formiae) and no medicines
> Can purge their natures of the ingrown muck.
> Pretentious littérateurs, degenerate twins,
> Companions of one sofa-bed, they fuck
> The girls in friendly rivalry and share
> The same unholy itch. A pretty pair!

> (tr. James Michie)

These poems, written in compact and colloquial Latin, are often obscene and often ironical, but they are perfect examples of the detached wit and urbanity in which the New Poets of Catullus's generation revelled. He also wrote short poems of a less personal and more generally social kind – on dental hygiene (57) –

> Egnatius, because his teeth are white,
> Is always smiling. Go and watch a trial –
> At the moment when the lawyer's pleas excite
> Tears on behalf of the accused, he'll smile.
> Attend the funeral of an only son –
> Next to the grief-bowed mother there's that face
> Smiling again. At every turn, whatever
> He does, regardless of the time or place,
> He smiles. It's a disease with him, and one
> I don't consider elegant or clever –   (tr. James Michie)

or pronunciation (84):

> When he wanted to say 'advantage' Arrius said
> 'Hadvantage', likewise 'hambushes' instead
> Of 'ambushes', pronounced with hurricane force
> And huge self-satisfaction. (Well, of course,
> His mother, his uncle with the ex-slave's name
> And both his mother's parents had the same
> Habit.) When Arrius was sent away
> To the East, all ears enjoyed a holiday;
> None of us dreaded aitches; vowels were spoken
> Harmoniously. Since then grim news has broken:
> Now Arrius has crossed the sea, the late
> Ionian's rougher by an aspirate!   (tr. James Michie)

In a different vein he wrote moving verses on the death of his brother or on the ship that brought him home from Bithynia.

But Catullus is remembered chiefly for his poems about his mistress, Lesbia. This sequence of poems, together with a shorter set about his boy-friend Juventius (no less intense, for the cultured world of the late Roman Republic was by no means exclusively heterosexual; see p. 118), was something quite new and paved the way for the impassioned writing of Propertius and Tibullus. There seems no reason to doubt that Lesbia was a pseudonym of Clodia Metelli, a beautiful, aristocratic and wayward lady, sister of P. Clodius, mercilessly ridiculed by Cicero in his defence of Caelius (see p. 47). The poems are not an ordered chronicle of a love-affair but disjointed fragments of articulated experience, articulated because Greek predecessors from Mimnernus to Meleager (140–70 B.C.) had given Catullus the means to express himself. His experience covered every emotion from bliss to despair, from self-pity to outrage and mockery.

Catullus was regarded among the ancients as a 'learned' (*doctus*) poet, whereas we, perhaps, regard him as pre-eminently a spontaneous, almost intuitive, poet; but 'learning' (*doctrina*) meant facility at handling Greek forms and Catullus was always experimenting, adapting Greek metres (elegiac, iambic, lyric, dactylic) and exploring Greek forms in order to convey his ideas and feelings. His inventiveness in this respect has no parallel among Roman writers. His exuberance is always finding an outlet. So it is not surprising that side-by-side with very immediate and topical poems we find in the collection which he made of his works others which are more recognizably literary, such as the wedding song for Manlius Torquatus (61), Greek in spirit and conceit but firmly grounded in Roman practice. Two of these poems were to prove very influential with later writers. The first is an exciting narrative poem in an unusual metre about Attis, who castrated himself in a fit of frenzy inspired by the cult of Cybele (63). It opens:

> Having sailed the sea-deeps in a swift vessel,
> Attis arrived, ardently he entered
> The Phrygian forest, set feverish foot
> In the dark, dense-leaved demesne of the Goddess.
>
> (tr. James Michie)

The driving power of the rhythm and the language make the poem memorable in itself, but every reader must sense behind it both an acute perception of the tensions of adolescent sex and also the realities of the ecstatic religions of the ancient world. One must understand Attis in an intellectual climate that could not only appreciate Euripides' *Bacchae* but also sympathize with the Christian martyr, Origen. At first sight poem 64 is more purely literary: it is a highly contrived Hellenistic short epic. It tells of the marriage of Peleus and Thetis but includes a plot within the plot – a tableau of Ariadne's bitter desertion by Theseus, which was much admired by Virgil who imitated it in his account of Aeneas's desertion of Dido. Yet the poem is not just a literary *tour de force*. It ends on a sombre note of foreboding, as Catullus makes us aware of how he sees the historical process of his own times:

> Such was the happiness the Fates, divinely
> Prompted, foretold for Peleus long ago;
> For then, before religion was despised,
> The Sky-dwellers in person used to visit
> The stainless homes of heroes and be seen
> At mortal gatherings. Then, regularly,
> The father of the gods from his bright shrine,
> When the year brought his feast-days round, would watch
> A hundred bullocks crumple to the ground;
> But when the earth grew deep ingrained with sin
> And covetous Man turned justice out of doors,
> Brothers plunged hands in the blood of brothers, children
> Ceased mourning for their parents, fathers hankered
> For a son's death, more freely to enjoy
> Some fresh young blossom as a second wife,
> And vicious mothers seduced innocent boys
> In blasphemous outrage of the household gods,
> Till, right and wrong, virtue and vice, all weltering
> In mad perversity, were so estranged

And horrified the minds of the good gods
That they no longer condescend to join
Men's feasts and festivals or care to endure
The touch of our too glaring light of day.

(tr. James Michie)

Some of Catullus's poems would have circulated by word of mouth and created an immediate impact by their shocking wit; but others would have been intended for the more leisured appreciation of a like-minded audience. He himself gives us a charming vignette of the circle for which he was writing in a poem (50) to his friend and fellow-poet C. Licinius Calvus (see p. 55):

Yesterday, to while time away,
Licinius, we agreed to play
A naughty game of epigrams, using
My tablets. Scribbling verses, choosing
Any old metre, each one taking
Turns, we had fun, drinking and making
Jokes. And I left so laughter-lit
By your incendiary wit
That food gave me no appetite
And, open-eyed, I spent all night
Bed-wandering in delirium
And longing for the light to come
To talk and be with you. Half-dead
At last, dog-weary on my bed,
I wrote this so that you could read,
Sweet friend, how desperate is my need.
Now, apple of my eye, don't tease me,
By playing proud. Humour me, please me,
Otherwise Nemesis will inflict
Punishment; she's a very strict
Goddess, not to be lightly tricked.

(tr. James Michie)

PHILOSOPHY

Catullus is the first surviving Roman poet whose self-expression reflects his curiosity about himself and his world.

Probably no single factor contributed as much to this questing spirit of the Romans during the last century of the Republic as the advent of Greek philosophy. The Romans had, of course, been exposed to it from early times, indeed from the very first contacts between Rome and Greece, but it was only in the second century that Greek philosophers came to Rome to lecture and Romans went to Athens, Rhodes and other centres to study.

There were three main schools of thought, although inevitably there was some overlapping and common ground between them. The tradition of Plato was carried on in the Academy. Plato, maintaining a dichotomy between the senses and reason, had argued that what we perceive with the senses (*phenomena*) is unreal and deceptive, whereas reality can only be apprehended by reason. From this basis he formulated his Theory of Ideas, both to account for the underlying reality and to explain the phenomenal world. The theory was applied to ethics and politics as well: there is an absolute good and an absolute justice which can be attained through reason. Platonic philosophy was subjected to criticism and revision by Aristotle and others, but it was revived during the second century, in particular by Carneades (214–129 B.C.), although in a very different form. For Carneades, as for Plato, the phenomenal world was illusory. For practical purposes we accept what appears true and what is probable, but we must not confuse this with absolute truth. Similarly in the political sphere when we talk about justice, we are not talking about some ultimate, self-evident reality but only about a convention which happens to be accepted for practical reasons by a particular society. The later Academy laid more weight on a sceptical response to the senses than it did on the rational search for absolute truth. In the first century two great leaders of the Academy, Philo and Antiochus, both of whom taught Cicero in his youth, devoted much of their ingenuity to destructive arguments against rival schools of philosophy – above all the Stoics and Epicureans.

The Stoics, who took their name from the Stoa, or colonnade, where they met and discussed in Athens, were founded by Zeno of Citium, a town in Cyprus (336–263 B.C.). The fundamental innovation which he made was to stress the primacy of sense-perception; all knowledge comes through the sense-organs: objects make impressions on the soul 'like that of a seal on wax', as a later Stoic, Cleanthes, wrote. Reality and hallucination can be distinguished because a true perception is 'an image impressed from an existing thing and in conformity with it and of the sort that would not come from a non-existent thing'. The ability to group or classify impressions under general heads (e.g. to tell that all impressions of a certain kind are impressions not of tables but of chairs) is an innate one: we are born with a mental faculty which can differentiate between impressions. From such a starting-point Zeno argued that everything in the universe is material, because it makes impressions on us and we cannot conceive of anything that does not make an impression on us, but matter is of two kinds. The first is passive, finite and indestructible; the second is active and dynamic, transfused through passive matter, as Cleanthes said, 'like a drop of water in wine'. This latter type of matter is a fiery, intelligent breath (*pneuma*) which gives life and form to individual things and which is God or Divine Providence. Every living thing is permeated by it, and, therefore, human beings, and even animals, are in a real sense fragments of the Divine. It follows that at death we rejoin the great pool of Divine Fire and that during our life our proper end or purpose is to live in accordance with reason (or, what is the same, nature). It also follows that because the Divine Fire is rational, beneficent and providential everything in life is predetermined for the best. Zeno went on to hold that there was a periodical conflagration which consumed the universe, so that the whole historical process started all over again on the same pattern. The appeal of his teaching lay especially in the justification which it gave for morality. The old city-state which had acted as a focus for values (what was good was what was good for Athens) had disintegrated, and a new morality had to be built on a more universal footing.

Stoicism was brought to Rome by Panaetius (c. 180–110 B.C.), who was one of a number of Greeks, like the historian Polybius, patronized by Scipio Aemilianus from 144 B.C. onwards. Panaetius, whose works do not survive, although reflected in many of Cicero's writings, but whose influence it is difficult to overestimate, made certain substantial modifications to Zeno's teaching. He reflected the belief in a periodic conflagration and he particularly endeavoured to adapt the philosophy to Roman social and political ideals. He recognized that it was impracticable for ordinary men to live, in the truest sense, 'according to reason' and developed a middle stage for ordinary men which was concerned with what was appropriate or fitting – obligations. Since we are all part of a single Divine Fire, we are all brothers and our political and moral relationships are determined by that fact. This exactly squared with traditional Roman practice, which recognized the bond between patron and client, head of the family and members of the family, master and slave or freedman, and so on. But Panaetius went further and saw in the Roman constitution with its magistrates, senate and people an actual blend of the types of government (monarchy, aristocracy, democracy) suitable for running a state or 'conglomeration of men united by a common consent to the law and by a community of interest'.

Further concessions to Roman thought were made by Panaetius's successor Posidonius of Rhodes (135–50 B.C.), who became a friend of both Cicero and Pompey. Posidonius, who wrote widely on a range of topics from ethics to ethnography, rejected the simple doctrine that the soul was a unity, a piece of Divine Fire, and reverted to the Platonic view that the soul had three parts and that the emotional part of the soul had to be controlled by the rational part. This was much more in line with the unsophisticated beliefs of the Romans themselves.

Epicurus, an Athenian citizen who was more or less contemporary with Zeno (340–271 B.C.), bought a house and garden outside Athens in 306 B.C. which he made the centre for a small philosophical group. Like Zeno, he started from the assumptions that sensation is the only criterion of truth ('we must keep all our investigations in accord with our sensations') and that we have a mental faculty for categorizing our sensations, but he drew very different conclusions from this basis. The universe consists purely and simply of atoms and void; sensation is caused by films of atoms striking our sense-organs ('it is when something enters us from external objects that we not only see but think of their shapes'). The consequences of such a scientific theory were radical. There could be no divine providence; death was simply atomic dissolution; the soul was material. So it followed that the only criteria for good and evil lay in the sensations themselves, namely pleasure and pain. 'These two states of feeling arise in every animate body . . . the one is favourable and the other hostile to that being, and by their means choice and avoidance are determined.' Epicurus was not, of course, a hedonist in our sense. He saw that static pleasures were preferable to dynamic pleasures, which might bring pain in their train, and that if pleasure is the fulfilment of desire, not all desires are pleasurable and there is a limit to pleasure. Nevertheless his philosophy had its attractions at a time when people were, for quite other reasons, tempted to opt out of the political scene.

His teaching also had reached Rome in the second century. The Epicureans were expelled from the city in 173 B.C. and some time in the second half of the century C. Amafinius wrote a number of works in Latin on Epicureanism which have not survived. But it was Philodemus of Gadara (c. 110–c. 35 B.C.) who, under the patronage of L. Piso, did most to popularize it. Philodemus's epigrams, mainly on the subject of love, have come down from antiquity, but his philosophical works were almost unknown until a number of fragmentary rolls were discovered in Piso's villa at Herculaneum. Given how un-Roman Epicureanism was, reducing the gods to impotence, denying providence, discouraging social and political involvement, it is remarkable what a spectacular, if brief, vogue it enjoyed between 60 and 40 B.C. Not only were men such as Atticus, C. Memmius and Piso confirmed Epicureans, but so were many others – Caesar himself and his general Pansa, Horace and the young Virgil. Part of the reason for this lies in the modifications Philodemus introduced which allowed or even encouraged political activity for the higher (i.e. more pleasurable) good of freedom of speech and freedom from tyranny. One of Philodemus's most famous works was 'On the good king according to Homer', and it was a much quoted saying of the sect that 'tyrants for all their violence could not destroy the internal happiness of the wise man'. Epicureans were actively engaged on both sides when Caesar embarked upon his final autocratic career. Among his friends were the jurist C. Trebatius Testa, who had become an Epicurean in 53 B.C., and C. Matius. Among his enemies were C. Cassius, one of the assassins on the Ides of March, converted to Epicureanism in 46 B.C., L. Manlius Torquatus, who was killed on the Pompeian side in 46 B.C., M. Fadius Gallus, who wrote one of the pamphlets in defence of Cato (see p. 63), and L. Lucceius, the historian.

The sudden interest in philosophy, which made so many men turn to Stoicism or Epicureanism at this juncture to help them decide upon their course of action, may have another reason, or perhaps another consequence. Up till now, the teachings of the Academics, Stoics and Epicureans had been widely available only in Greek. True, educated Romans read and spoke Greek, as we have seen; indeed as early as 155 B.C. Carneades had created a furore by his lectures at Rome (see p. 35). But inevitably the audience that the philosophers reached through the medium of Greek was small. All this was dramatically changed in the 50s.

LUCRETIUS

There are virtually no details about Lucretius's life. His full name, T. Lucretius Carus, tells us nothing of his family, origin or background. He was probably born in 94 B.C. and died in 55 B.C. leaving his great poem *On the Nature of the Universe*, dedicated to C. Memmius, incomplete. Legend holds that Cicero, who refers to the work in a letter of 54 B.C., was responsible for publishing it.

In deciding to set out Epicurus's philosophy in poetry, Lucretius was following an old Greek tradition. Didactic poetry goes back to Hesiod; Empedocles and Parmenides had both composed scientific poems, and in the Hellenistic age the works of Aratus, the *Phaemonena* and *Prognostica*, enjoyed much popularity. Cicero himself as a young man had devoted his talents to a verse translation of the *Aratea*. Lucretius's task was, however, formidable. Epicurus's philosophy was technical and complicated, and the Latin language was not well equipped with corresponding terms, let alone terms which would fit easily into the hexameter metre. And it was not only the scientific or philosophical language which raised problems: Lucretius had to devise a suitable poetic diction to match the tone of his subject. He did this by drawing heavily on Ennius and by elaborating his own vocabulary. The result is a style which, although the lines are usually self-contained and therefore do not often produce long, flowing passages, is capable of great emotional power. Lucretius had a feel for sounds and words, which inspired the admiration and imitation of Virgil.

The chief impression on reading the poem is of the poet's own personality. This emerges partly from his imagery: even when Lucretius uses a traditional image, he invests it with an unusual degree of immediacy and vividness. Thus, describing a reflection in water, he writes (4.414–19):

A puddle no deeper than a finger's breadth, formed in a hollow between the cobble-stones of the highway, offers to the eye a downward view, below the ground, of as wide a scope as the towering immensity of sky that yawns above. You would fancy you saw clouds far down below you and a sky and heavenly bodies deep-buried in a miraculous heaven beneath the earth.

Or, of the movement of atoms in the void (2.112–20):

This process ... is illustrated by an image of it that is continually taking place before our very eyes. Observe what happens when sunbeams are admitted into a building and shed light on its shadowy places. You will see a multitude of tiny particles mingling in a multitude of ways in the empty space within the light of the beam, as though contending in everlasting conflict, rushing into battle rank upon rank with never a moment's pause in a rapid sequence of unions and disunions.

Or again, describing the separation of particles during the formation of the world (5.460–66):

> We may compare a sight we often see when the sun's golden rays glow with the first flush of dawn among the dew-spangled herbage: the lakes and perennial watercourses exhale a vapour, while at times we see the earth itself steaming. It is these vapours, when they all coalesce and combine their substance in the upper air, that weave a cloudy curtain under the sky. (tr. R. E. Latham)

But partly it is due to the sheer intensity of his feelings. It is true that the work is incomplete, but there is a strange lack of proportion about the long disquisition in Book 6 on epidemics, including a free rendering of Thucydides' account of the Plague at Athens, or the vitriolic diatribe against sex (admittedly *not* a static pleasure) in Book 4. The same personal prejudices came out in other places. Were Romans really as subject to *accidie* as 'the owner of some stately mansion, bored stiff by staying at home, [who] takes his departure, only to return as speedily when he feels himself no better off out of doors. Off he goes to his country seat, driving his carriage and pair hot-foot, as though in haste to save a house on fire. No sooner has he crossed its doorstep than he starts yawning or retires moodily to sleep and courts oblivion, or else rushes back to revisit the city' (3.1060–67)? There is the same note of obsessive morbidity in the accounts of fainting from fear (3.151–60: 'when the mind is upset by some more overwhelming fear, we see all the spirit in every limb upset in sympathy. Sweat and pallor break out all over the body. Speech grows inarticulate; the voice fails; the eyes swim; the ears buzz; the limbs totter. Often we see men actually drop down because of the terror that has gripped their minds') or injury (3.170–75: 'When the nerve-racking impact of a spear gashes bones and sinews, even if it does not penetrate to the seat of life, there ensues faintness and a tempting in-

THE INFLUENCE OF GREECE

clination earthwards and on the ground a turmoil in the mind and an intermittent faltering impulse to stand up again'). In a particularly macabre passage Lucretius pictures the effect of scythed chariots in the heat and indiscriminate carnage of battle which lop off limbs

so suddenly that the fallen member hewn from the body is seen to writhe on the ground. Yet the mind and consciousness of the man cannot yet feel the pain: so abrupt is the hurt, and so intent the mind upon the business of battle. With what is left of his body he presses on with battle and bloodshed unaware, it may be, that his left arm together with its shield has been lost, whirled away among the chargers by the chariot wheels with their predatory blades. Another does not notice that his right arm has gone, while he scrambles and struggles. Another, who has lost a leg, does his best to stand up, while on the ground at his side the dying foot twitches its toes. A head hewn from the still warm and living trunk retains on the ground its lively features and open eyes till it has yielded up the last shred of spirit.   (3.640–56; tr. R. E. Latham)

Lucretius does indeed provide a faithful account of Epicurus's whole teaching but he gives it a Roman slant, which made it especially relevant to his contemporaries. In Book 5 he describes the evolution of man and, at lines 1135 ff., the political development which eliminated kings: 'So the conduct of affairs sank back into the turbid depths of mob-rule, with each man struggling to win dominance and supremacy for himself. Then some men showed how to form a constitution, based on fixed rights and recognized laws. Mankind, worn out by a life of violence and enfeebled by feuds, was the more ready to submit of its own free will to the bondage of laws and institutions.' There was a message that would have appealed to the 50s. But it is arguable that the main switch of emphasis was not inspired by a desire to make Epicureanism more Roman but, again, by Lucretius's personal obsessions. Throughout the work two themes recur: the gods have no effect on us and death is of no consequence to us. It is very doubtful whether the Romans were greatly troubled by fear either of the gods or of death, at least at this epoch. The writings of Caesar and Cicero and their contemporaries, as the letter of Servius Sulpicius Rufus quoted above (p. 59) shows, are not heavy with superstitition, and the thousands of funeral inscriptions betray little terror of what may lie beyond the grave. It is only from the time of Augustus that religious guilt and the quest for personal salvation became prominent themes. Roman religion was concerned with acts not beliefs. But for Lucretius these fears are very real and evoke some of his finest poetry, as at 3.870 ff.:

[When a man imagines his body being torn apart by wild animals after his death] he does not banish himself from the scene nor distinguish sharply enough between himself and that abandoned carcass ... He does not see that in real death there will be no other self to mourn his own decease ... For if it is really a bad thing after death to be mauled and crunched by ravening jaws, I cannot see why it should not be disagreeable to roast in the scorching flames of a funeral pyre, or to lie embalmed in honey, stifled and stiff with cold, on the surface of a chilly slab, or to be squashed under a crushing weight of earth.

'Now it is all over. Now the happy home and the best of wives will welcome you no more, nor winsome children rush to snatch the first kiss at your coming and touch your heart with speechless joy. No chance now to further your fortune or safeguard your family. Unhappy man,' they cry, 'unhappily cheated by one treacherous day out of all the uncounted blessings of life!' But they do not go on to say: 'And now no repining for these lost joys will oppress you any more.' If they perceived this clearly with their minds and acted according to the words, they would free their breasts from a great load of grief and dread.   (tr. R. E. Latham)

CICERO

It is difficult to assess the impact which Lucretius made, because so little explicit reference is made to the poem. Cicero and his brother read it and it obviously had a profound influence on the young Virgil, who praises Lucretius directly in the *Georgics*; and it is hard to doubt that the popularity which Epicureanism suddenly acquired was due in some measure to the publication of *On the Nature of the Universe*. But the man principally responsible for naturalizing Greek philosophy and thereby enabling the Romans to develop their own outlook on life was Cicero himself.

Cicero had ranged widely in his studies. He had studied under the Epicurean Phaedrus and was acquainted with Philodemus; he had studied with Philo and Antiochus of the Academy; and he was a friend of Posidonius and even extended years of hospitality to another Stoic, Diodotus, who named him in his will as his heir (*c.* 60 B.C.). But it was a set of accidental circumstances that led Cicero to write the philosophical works which were to be his major legacy to the western world. In the period between 55 and 52 B.C. the political situation at Rome allowed Cicero very little independent freedom of action. There were speeches to be made and court cases, like the defence of Milo, to be undertaken, but they were duties laid on him by his political masters, not undertaken voluntarily. Part of his time, therefore, he devoted to theoretical writing such as *On the Orator, On the Republic* (a politico-historical work which will be considered in the next section) and the now largely lost *On the Laws*. After a flurry of political activity which resulted in the triumph of Caesar, Cicero was once again condemned to frustration, heightened by worrying problems of debt and by domestic troubles, such as the divorce of his wife and the death, early in 45 B.C., of his daughter. He retired to the country and in the space of barely two years composed no fewer than sixteen works on philosophical subjects, most of which survive. Some of these, such as the *On Divination* and *On the Nature of the Gods*, are of a more antiquarian nature, but others, such as *On Ends* (i.e. on the Chief Good and Evil), *On Duties, Discussions at my Tusculan Villa, On Friendship* and *On Old Age*, have a strictly philosophical purpose. In them Cicero aimed to put forward in Latin dialogues the views of the principal philosophical schools and to define his own standpoint.

His objective is most clearly stated by himself in the preface to the second book of *On Divination*.

What greater or better service can I render to the state than to instruct and train the youth – especially in view of the fact that our young men have gone so far astray because of the present moral laxity that the utmost effort will be needed to hold them in check and direct them in the right way? Of course, I have no assurance – it could not even be expected – that they will all turn to these studies. Would that a few may! Though few, their activity may yet have a wide influence in the state. In fact, I am receiving some reward for my labour even from men advanced in years; for they are finding comfort in my books, and by their ardour in reading are raising my eagerness for writing to a higher pitch every day. Their number, too, I learn, is far greater than I had expected. Furthermore, it would redound to the fame and glory of the Roman people to be made independent of Greek writers in the study of philosophy, and this result I shall certainly bring about if my present plans are accomplished.

The cause of my becoming an expounder of philosophy sprang from the grave condition of the State during the period of the Civil War, when, being unable to protect the Republic, as had been my custom, and finding it impossible to remain inactive, I could find nothing else that I preferred to do that was worthy of me.

(tr. W. A. Falconer)

Cicero sometimes simplified and sometimes misinterpreted but he brought philosophy to a wide audience, and his works became standard reading for later generations down to St Jerome and St Augustine.

HISTORY

There was, of course, by now a long tradition of historical writing at Rome going back to Cato and Fabius Pictor (p. 37), but it is important to realize that the earlier generations of historians were interested in something rather different from philosophical history. Fabius, writing in Greek, had set out to show that Rome was as respectable as any Greek city, that it had its foundation legends and eponymous heroes, and that recent events, notably the Carthaginian Wars, revealed Rome as the heir of Hellenic greatness. This political, almost chauvinistic, bias is curiously echoed by Cato, except that for him what matters is the *Latinness* of Rome from its origins to present-day times. The scope for writing the history of Rome was substantially widened in the second century by the use of archival material – pontifical records, inscriptions, family documents and legends, and so on. Although none of the historians of this period survives, they seem to have approached their task in one of two ways: either they simply compiled a chronicle, listing what happened year by year, or they interpreted the past in terms of the present. C. Licinius Macer, for instance, a historian much used by Livy, wrote up early history as a foreshadowing of the policies and deeds of Marius. Valerius Antias did the same, only in his case it was the regime of Sulla which was mirrored and justified. History was an arm of party politics.

The turning-point was the sudden wave of popularity for Thucydides in the later 50s and 40s. Thucydides was (and is) a difficult author; for long he was little read at Rome. Yet in the 50s Lucretius had read him and been impressed by him (he translates the account of the Plague in Book 6). Cicero first mentions him in letters of 50 and 49 B.C.; by the time of the *Orator* and *Brutus* (46 B.C.) he can speak of devotees of Thucydides who try to imitate his abrupt and jagged style. There is therefore good evidence of a vogue for Thucydides, who was distinguished not only for his style and his rigorous weighing of the evidence but also for his profound views on the philosophy of history. Human nature like the human body can be observed. Just as by studying the symptoms of the plague you will be more able to recognize it if it occurs again, so by studying history analytically you will be able to appreciate clearly what happens to you if the same or similar circumstances recur. For human nature remains the same.

The first man to attempt to write history in the true Thucydidean vein was not, as one would expect, Cicero (although his *Republic* contains long passages of historical analysis) but a much more unlikely figure, C. Sallustius Crispus. Sallust was born in 86 B.C. and pursued a minor political career (quaestor in 55, tribune in 52). He was expelled from the Senate in 50 and took service under Caesar in the Civil Wars. Elected praetor in 46 he was appointed governor of Africa (Numidia) but scandalized even his friends by his extortionate conduct. After Caesar's death, he retired to a life of leisured luxury in the country, where somewhat surprisingly he composed three historical works, an account of the conspiracy of Catiline (63 B.C.), a history of the war against Jugurtha, King of Numidia (112–105 B.C.), and a work, which no longer survives apart from fragments, on the events of the years 78–67 B.C. Nothing in Sallust's background or tastes would have suggested him to be a writer, let alone a philosophical historian. Retired statesmen, if they turned their hands to writing at all, usually penned memoirs to justify or extenuate their political actions. Now, however, in this new mood of questioning writers tackled more fundamental problems.

Sallust did not adopt Thucydides' view of causation completely. For him, although people behaved as they did because they were the sort of people that they were and although, therefore, a historian can discern a man's character from his actions and *vice versa*, there was a further principle at work – the moral degeneration of society. Rome's moral fibre had steadily decayed since the ancient days. Two factors in particular were hastening the process. The first was the removal of any counterbalancing power, such as Carthage, that would keep the Romans alert. The second was contact with the debilitating world of Greek culture. The combined result was that men came to be motivated by greed and ambition and sought personal advancement rather than the good of the state. This is how Sallust expresses it in the preface to the *Jugurtha*.

What guides and controls human life is man's soul. If it pursues glory by the path of virtue, it has all the resources and abilities it needs for winning fame, and is independent of fortune, which can neither give any man uprightness, energy, and other good qualities, nor deprive any man of them. But if the soul is enslaved by base desires and sinks into the corruption of sloth and carnal pleasures, it enjoys a ruinous indulgence for a brief season; then, when idleness has wasted strength, youth, and intelligence, the blame is put on the weakness of our nature, and each man excuses himself for his own shortcomings by imputing his failure to adverse circumstances.

(tr. S. A. Handford)

A true historian's first duty, however, must be to uncover the facts and then to make sense of them. As far as Catiline's conspiracy is concerned, Cicero, both in his writings of 63 B.C. and subsequently, presented his picture of what *he* thought happened (or ought to have happened). Sallust tried to remedy this bias by seeking out other sources, and he knew, of course, a number of other works by Cicero which dealt with the conspiracy but which are now lost. He also seems to have used the official records of the speeches delivered by Caesar and Cato on 5 December 63, when the question of the punishment of the conspirators was discussed. He quotes documents, including a defiant letter sent by Catiline to his friend Lutatius Catulus. And he must have questioned some of the survivors of those days as well as recalled for himself something of what happened. Despite all this, however, his judgement of the material is sometimes at fault and he presents in several respects a less accurate account than Cicero himself, although he does not in any way set out to correct Cicero. For the Jugurthine War, Sallust had the advantage of first-hand knowledge of Africa and of warfare. As written sources, he could have used the memoirs of Aemilius Scaurus (consul 115 B.C.), a leading figure at Rome through the period, and of his contemporary P. Rutilius Rufus, as well as those of Sulla. Others writers had also covered the period, including the Greek Posidonius (see p. 80), who evidently held an unfavourable view of the great general Marius, and the Roman annalist C. Sempronius Asellio; but there is little evidence of first-hand use of documentary evidence. Here again Sallust tries to perform his historical duty but can be shown to be guilty of errors of chronology and omissions and distortions of fact.

These mistakes arose from his shortcomings as a historian and not from any deliberate desire to misrepresent. He did conscientiously set out to discover what happened. Partly also they arose from his philosophical preconceptions. The desire to explain events in terms of people coupled with a desire to see in everything signs of the fatal decline of the aristocracy led Sallust to frame his narratives in an artificial, and sometimes misleading, way. This can be seen in the structure of the

Catiline. After the philosophical preface, Sallust gives a character sketch of Catiline (5):

> Lucius Catiline was of noble birth. He had a powerful intellect and great physical strength, but a vicious and depraved nature. From his youth he had delighted in civil war, bloodshed, robbery, and political strife, and it was in such occupations that he spent his early manhood. He could endure hunger, cold, and want of sleep to an incredible extent. His mind was daring, crafty, and versatile, capable of any pretence and dissimulation. A man of flaming passions, he was as covetous of other men's possessions as he was prodigal of his own; an eloquent speaker, but lacking in wisdom. His monstrous ambition hankered continually after things extravagant, impossible, beyond his reach. After the dictatorship of Lucius Sulla, Catiline had been possessed by an overmastering desire for despotic power, to gratify which he was prepared to use any and every means. His headstrong spirit was tormented more and more every day by poverty and a guilty conscience, both of which were aggravated by the evil practices I have referred to. He was incited also by the corruption of a society plagued by two opposite but equally disastrous vices – love of luxury and love of money.   (tr. S. A. Handford)

He follows it with a long digression on the decline of morality at Rome (6–13). He then launches straight into the events of 64 B.C. and carries on to the climax of the conspiracy and the ultimate dénouement, without giving more than the barest outline of the political events which had precipitated the crisis. So too his concentration on individuals in the *Jugurtha* is the cause of several serious dislocations.

There was also a further innovation which Sallust had to make. Just as Ennius had forged a vocabulary that was appropriate for epic poetry, so Sallust had to invent a historical language and style. History, as Cicero himself said, is very close to oratory, but it is not oratory, and a style which is intended to win over a large public meeting is too diffuse and emotional for the more sober analysis of events. There again

Sallust modelled himself on Thucydides, who had used unusual but carefully chosen words and who had delighted in
giving his sentences unexpected twists and turns, so that
the reader's attention was always held. Sallust looked back
to the writings of the Elder Cato as his linguistic model and
created a vocabulary which included a large number of
archaic or unfamiliar words or forms. He also cultivated the
short, abrupt, highly concentrated sentence that provokes
thought – and recollection. The flavour of such a style is
hard to convey in translation, but his summary of the state of
Rome in 63 B.C., which is modelled on Thucydides' account
of the situation in Corcyra, is a representative sample.

Never in its history – it seems to me – had the empire of Rome
been in such a miserable plight. From east to west all the world had
been vanquished by her armies and obeyed her will; at home there
was profound peace and abundance of wealth, which mortal men
esteem the chiefest of blessings. Yet there were Roman citizens
obstinately determined to destroy both themselves and their country.
In spite of two senatorial decrees, not one man among all the conspirators was induced by the promise of reward to betray their plans,
and not one deserted from Catiline's camp. A deadly moral contagion
had infected all their minds. And this madness was not confined to
those actually implicated in the plot. The whole of the lower orders,
impatient for a new régime, looked with favour on Catiline's enterprise. In this they only did what might have been expected of them.
In every country paupers envy respectable citizens and make heroes of
unprincipled characters, hating the established order of things and
hankering after innovation; discontented with their own lot, they
are bent on general upheaval. Turmoil and rebellion bring them
carefree profit, since poverty has nothing to lose.

(36.4–37.5; tr. S. A. Handford)

He can tell a story in a fast-moving and gripping fashion.
During the Jugurthine War Marius decided on an overland
attack on Capsa:

94

THE INFLUENCE OF GREECE

But when he heard that the king was far away and absorbed in other tasks, he judged that the time was ripe for bigger and harder undertakings. In the middle of a huge desert lay the important and strongly defended town of Capsa, the traditional founder of which was the Libyan Hercules. Under Jugurtha's rule its inhabitants were exempted from taxation and well treated. They were therefore particularly loyal to him, and the place was protected not only by its ramparts and a well-armed garrison, but still more by the difficulty of the surrounding country. For, except the immediate neighbourhood of the town, the whole district is desolate, uncultivated, waterless, and infested by deadly serpents, which like all wild animals are made fiercer by scarcity of food, and especially by thirst, which exasperates their natural malignity. Marius's mind was set on capturing this place, not only on account of its strategic importance, but also because he wanted to try his hand at what looked like a difficult enterprise, and because Metellus had won great renown by his capture of Thala, the situation and defences of which were similar, except that at Thala there were several springs of water near the walls, whereas the people of Capsa had only one never-failing supply – situated inside the town – apart from which they relied on rain water. This scarcity of water, both here and in all the comparatively uncivilized interior of North Africa, was rendered more endurable by the Numidian habit of living chiefly on milk and the flesh of wild animals and not using salt or other appetizers: they ate and drank to satisfy their hunger and thirst, not to indulge gluttonous cravings.

After making a thorough reconnaissance Marius decided – one must presume – to put his trust in heaven. For the difficulties that faced him were too formidable for human wisdom to provide against them unaided. He was even threatened by a dearth of corn, because the Numidians pay more attention to grazing than to raising crops; moreover, such grain as there was had by the king's order been conveyed into the fortresses, and the fields were parched and bare at the end of the summer. Nevertheless, Marius made such provision as his means allowed and his foresight suggested. The auxiliary horsemen were told to drive forward with the marching column all the cattle taken during the previous days. The lieutenant Aulus Manlius was sent with the light infantry to the town of Lares, where the wage-

95

money and reserve supplies were stored; and Marius gave out that he would come there himself in a few days in the course of a plundering expedition. This was said in order to conceal his real objective. He then advanced to the river Tanais.

Every day during this march he had distributed a ration of cattle to the men of each century and squadron, who were told to make water-containers out of the hides. In this way he made up for the short supply of corn and at the same time, without letting anyone discover his purpose, provided the utensils that he knew would shortly be required. By the time they reached the river, on the sixth day, they had a large stock of skins. There, after making a lightly fortified camp, he ordered the men to eat their dinners and be ready to march at sunset, abandoning their packs and taking nothing but the filled skins – as many as they themselves and their beasts could carry. In due course he set out, marched all night, and then halted. The same procedure was followed the next night; and during the third night, some time before dawn, he reached a hilly district not more than two miles from Capsa, where, with the whole army carefully screened from observation, he waited. At daybreak the Numidians, who had no reason to fear an attack, came out of the town in force, and Marius ordered all his cavalry and the swiftest of his infantry to run and occupy the gates. He was so eager for success that he hurried after them himself, to prevent the men from going after plunder. When the townspeople saw themselves thus taken by surprise, with a part of their number outside the walls and in the enemy's power, they were seized with such panic and dismay that they surrendered. Nevertheless, the town was set on fire, the adult men massacred, the remainder of the population sold into slavery, and the booty divided among the soldiers. This violation of the usages of war was not inspired by avarice or brutality on the consul's part: the fact was that the place was important to Jugurtha and difficult for the Romans to reach, and the inhabitants were a fickle and untrustworthy lot, whom neither kindness nor fear had ever been able to control.   (89.3–91.7; tr. S. A. Handford)

Sallust's influence was incalculable. He created history, something which Nepos believed only Cicero could have done in a way to rival the Greeks. Livy, although following a very different approach to style, acknowledges his debt to Sallust on every page, and his great successors, Tacitus and Ammianus Marcellinus, clearly derived their technique and much of their outlook from Sallust.

But Nepos himself, the friend of Catullus and Atticus and contemporary of Sallust, should not be forgotten either, even if his surviving works, which were once staple diet in schools, are now largely unread and neglected. For he, on a much less ambitious scale, showed this new-found interest in history for its own sake. He also possessed a related interest in antiquarian research, the chief exponent of which was the scholar Varro (p. 101). Cornelius Nepos was born in Cisalpine Gaul about 99 B.C. but at an early age settled in Rome, although his tastes remained literary rather than political. He lived through all the crises of the late Republic and died in the mid-20s B.C. His main work, *On Illustrious Men*, was first published in 34 B.C. but was revised and reissued after the death of Atticus, whose biography was included. It was an ambitious work, running to sixteen books and containing the lives of Roman and foreign generals, historians, kings, poets, orators and scholars. All that survives today are the accounts of twenty-three foreign generals and the *Lives* of the Elder Cato and Atticus, who qualify as Roman historians.

Nepos did not aspire to write history, as he makes clear at the start of his life of Pelopidas: 'I am afraid that I may appear to be writing history rather than giving an account of his life if I embark on a systematic account of his achievements.' But he was alive to the new-found curiosity of the Romans about the past and also to their desire to see the characters of historical figures revealed by their actions, such as the fairness of Aristides, nicknamed the Just. Like Sallust, he too had read Thucydides with enthusiasm but the inspiration for his own writing came not from Thucydides but from the long succession of Greek biographies begun by Xenophon and Isocrates and continued by Hellenistic writers, many of which were designed as philosophical examples, to commend or condemn patterns of behaviour. Nepos was perhaps not the first Roman to imitate the genre in Latin, but he was certainly the first to be popular and widely read.

The *Lives* are undemanding and uncritical. Although Nepos went to some pains to track down reliable authorities, he allowed numerous inaccuracies and misunderstandings to creep in. His style too, although one which serves his purpose, is unsophisticated. Nevertheless they read easily and well, reflecting the personality of their author, and contain passages of considerable feeling.

The aftermath of Caesar's assassination was a dangerous time for many, even if they had been neutral in politics. Nepos describes the plight of Atticus:

Suddenly fortune changed. Antony returned to Italy and everyone assumed that Atticus would be in great danger because of his friendship with Cicero and Brutus. So Atticus dropped out of public view when the generals arrived and, fearing that he would be proscribed, took refuge with P. Volumnius whom he had previously helped. (Such indeed were the ups and downs of the times that a man could be one day at the peak of success and another in desperate danger.) He brought with him his friend Q. Gellius Canus, who shared his tastes and interests. It is typical of Atticus' good nature that he lived on such happy terms with someone whom he had first known as a boy at school, that their friendship continued to grow until the end of his life. Antony was indeed embittered against Cicero, so much so that he hated him and all his friends, and his desire to proscribe them all was widely supported, but he remembered that Atticus had once done him a good service. So, after asking for his whereabouts, he wrote to him in his own hand to say that there was nothing to be afraid of and to ask him to call on him. He added that he had removed his name and, for his sake, Canus' as well from the list of proscribed. He sent an escort to ensure that no mishap should occur on the night journey. So Atticus, who had been in extreme terror, saved not only himself but his best friend. If you praise a helmsman who saves his ship during a storm in a rocky sea, should you not regard someone's foresight as remarkable who can steer his way to safety through so many, anxious political storms?

This is a straightforward account but one tinged both with personal feeling and political awareness. Nepos had lived through one of the most calamitous periods of Roman history.

5

INTELLECTUAL CURIOSITY

THE asking of questions, evidenced in the new popularity both of philosophy and of serious history, was accompanied by a parallel interest in facts. Facts are the prerequisite of any scientific inquiry, but earlier generations of Romans had been cheerfully casual about verifying their data whether historical, military or geographical. The late Republic saw a radical change in this respect. Greek advisers pioneered the way by compiling detailed briefs for leading generals, of the kind that, as we know, was later compiled by Demetrius of Tarsus for Domitian during Agricola's governorship of Britain. The whole governmental administration became more conscious of records and documents. This attitude was widely disseminated. Historians began to look for and to use archival material. As early as the 130s the consular Piso realized that the annual lists of dates and unusual events, preserved since time immemorial by the Pontiffs as precedents for their religious advice, were an important source of historical material. He was the first to incorporate them into a historical narrative. His example was widely followed. Licinius Macer, for instance, gained access to a linen roll which contained the name of magistrates probably from 444 to 367 B.C. and made effective use of it in his own *History*. Such research became a fashionable scholarly activity. Nepos, following the example of Hellenistic scholars like Eratosthenes and Apollodorus, undertook perhaps the first attempt to establish a definitive chronology of Rome. But his efforts were overshadowed by the greatest of all Roman scholars, M. Terentius Varro (116–27 B.C.), who in 47 B.C. completed a massive *Human and Divine Antiquities* in some forty-one volumes, and who also wrote a work entitled *Annales* – a chronological survey of history, on which all subsequent dates were based. We are still indebted to the Varronian chronology.

Varro's range was phenomenal. He did not confine himself to history but touched every area of human interest. One such field was religion. In addition to the *Divine Antiquities*, he wrote *Aetia*, modelled on Callimachus (see p. 135), which investigated a wide variety of Roman customs. He concerned himself with unearthing the background stories of cults and explaining the etymology of key names and terms. In this he was also following an established trend. Several Romans had written systematically about the gods, but the principal work that survives is Cicero's *On the Nature of the Gods*, published in 45 B.C., as part of the great philosophical programme which he undertook in those years (p. 88). In form it is a philosophical dialogue in three books, setting out the respective positions of an Epicurean (C. Velleius), a Stoic (Q. Lucilius Balbus) and an Academic (C. Aurelius Cotta, consul in 75 B.C.) on the question of 'what are "the gods"?' To that extent it resembles the structure of the dialogue *On Ends* (p. 88). In fact, however, like the companion dialogue *On Divination*, it is little more than a scholarly compendium of differing views on the subject, dressed up to be readable.

As for those who say that the world itself is a conscious intelligence, they have not grasped the nature of consciousness, or understood in what shape it can be manifest. I shall say something about this a little later. At present I would only express my astonishment at the stupidity of those who say that the universe itself is a conscious and immortal being, divinely blest, and then say that it is a sphere, because Plato thought this to be the most beautiful of all shapes. I for one find more beauty in the shape of a cylinder, a square, a cone or a pyramid.

What sort of consciousness do they attribute to this spherical god of theirs? They say that the sphere revolves with a speed which to us is inconceivable. In which case I do not see how it can be the abode of a constant mind and a life of divine beatitude. Any spinning movement affecting any smallest part of our bodies is unpleasant: so why would it not be unpleasant to a god?

Then again the earth, as it is part of the universe, would also be a part of this god. But we see vast expanses of the earth which are uninhabitable deserts. Some of these are scorched by the too near approach of the sun, others through its remoteness are frozen up with frost and snow. But if the world is a god, and these deserts are parts of the world, it must follow that god is roasted in one part and frozen in another.   (1.23–4; tr. H. C. P. McGregor)

There is virtually no positive or substantial contribution by Cicero himself. His own views on religion are to be sought elsewhere. He was, however, filling an evident need, and others followed suit. The poet Q. Cornificius wrote shortly afterwards a book 'On the Derivations of the Gods' and there was a spate of technical treatises on religious matters, by other contemporaries such as Nigidius Figulus ('On Thunderclaps'), Tarquitius Priscus ('The Prophecies of Vegoia') and, above all, A. Caecina on Etruscan science. They combined an interest in facts for their own sake with a fascination with antiquity.

Fortunately, two works out of the 620 volumes that Varro wrote do survive. One is his treatise on *Agriculture*, three books published in 37 B.C. when he was eighty and written for his wife Fundania. Varro was following a tradition started by the Elder Cato, who was the first person to write a handbook on farming in Latin. Cato's *De Agri Cultura* has come down to us but in a form which has suffered from successive additions and alterations. Yet the core of it is certain enough –

a sternly practical work, combining agricultural common-sense of a bluff kind with religious instruction. For the gods were at least as important as technology to the aspiring farmer.

The following is the Roman formula to be observed in thinning a grove: a pig is to be sacrificed and the following prayer uttered. 'Whether thou be god or goddess to whom this grove is dedicated, as it is thy right to receive a sacrifice of a pig for the thinning of this sacred grove and to this intent, whether I or one at my bidding do it, may it be rightly done. To this end, in offering this pig to thee I humbly beg thou will be gracious and merciful to me, to my house and household, and to my children.'   (139; tr. W. D. Hooper)

Cato was writing primarily for the new large landowner of the mid-second century who was interested in farming as an investment and not as a means of subsistence. Hence his focus is mainly on the capital-intensive enterprises – olives and vines – on farms of some 200 acres in size.

The work is a document of great historical interest but very elementary and undiscriminating. There is no doubt that others improved on it; we hear of the names of Sasena and Tremellius Scrota who wrote about advanced techniques which they exploited. But it is Varro who reduced farming to a systematic study. The three books deal with agriculture (soil, cultivation, seasonal work, plant nutrition), animal husbandry (especially horses and sheep) and stock-raising on the farm (including delicacies such as fieldfares, dormice and edible snails, and bee-keeping). Throughout Varro displays a forward-looking and experimental approach: 'In addition to inherited tradition, we should attempt by experiment to perform some operations in a new way, being guided by a systematic programme of research and not by chance.' He quotes fifty Greek sources in the Introduction, only to dismiss them in favour of first-hand experience.

The work was much imitated and quoted, deservedly,

because it has all the merits of a good text-book. It was certainly used by Celsus, who wrote a comprehensive work on agriculture in addition to his famous book of medicine (p. 109), and by Julius Graecinus, the father of Agricola, governor of Britain (A.D. 78–84), who wrote on the cultivation of vines. But the most attractive and skilled of all Varro's followers was L. Junius Moderatus Columella (c. 5 B.C.–60 A.D.), who wrote twelve books *On Agriculture* and at least two books (all that survive) *On Trees*. As will become apparent, it is significant that he came not from Italy but from Cadiz, in Spain, and had been a much-travelled soldier. So he brought to the study of farming a different background and new techniques. His works, unfortunately not easily accessible in translation, are a model of clear, sound and sensible advice on all aspects of farming, especially vines.

Farming in the last century of the Republic was a matter of topicality, not just because of fears of a drift to the city or hopes of the unification of Italy, but because of a more deep-rooted sense that peasant virtues were what had made Rome great. It is harder to explain the appeal of Varro's other surviving work – Books 5–10 of his twenty-five-volume *On the Latin Language*. The work, which was completed about 43 B.C., was evidently in three parts – etymology (2–7), inflexion (8–13) and syntax (14–25) – but Varro's preoccupation is with words, their forms and their meanings.

An *agnus* 'lamb' is so named because it is *agnatus* 'born as an addition' to the flock ... A *catulus* 'puppy' is named from its quick and keen scent [*catus*], like the names *Cato* and *Catulus*; and from this, *canis* 'dog': unless, just as the trumpet and horn are said to *canere* 'sing' when they give some signal, so the *canis* is named because it ... gives the signal with its voice.   (5.99; tr. R. G. Kent)

Above all Varro is concerned with an old Greek dispute as to whether linguistics is governed by analogy or by anomaly, that is whether there are certain immutable regularities or rules for the formation and inflexion of words or not. Varro was an analogist and went out of his way to explain apparent exceptions. 'If from *avis capere* "to catch birds" the *auceps* "fowler" is termed, ought there not to be a *pisciceps* "fisherman" from *piscis capere* "to catch fish"?'

Varro's emphasis is to be understood at least partly in the light of the philosophical importance which the ancients attributed to words. Words were the signs of reality, the means by which an entity was communicated. Therefore, the precise form of a word is closely related to what it signifies and *vice versa*. To know a word correctly is to comprehend what it represents. We cannot, for instance, have any idea about something we cannot talk about. The study of language had, as a result, always occupied a prominent place in Stoicism, and grammatical analysis was developed for the first time by a Greek Stoic, Crates of Mallos in the second century B.C. But the fascination with words went further than this. In religion, to know the name of a god enabled you to exercise some influence over him: if properly addressed, he had to listen. Hence the elaborate formality of Roman prayers. And in popular speculation the names of monuments and customs presupposed some underlying explanation. Why was Jupiter called, in one cult, Pistor 'The Baker'? What is the origin of the *sororium tigillum* 'the sister's beam'? At the furthest extreme the particles which comprise the universe are the sounds voiced by the creator (the Latin word *elementa* also denoted the letters of the alphabet). 'In the beginning was the Word and the Word was with God.'

Varro's etymologies are often fanciful and rash, such as *terra* 'earth' from *teritur* because it is 'trodden on', or *hiems* 'winter' from *imbres* 'showers'. But he ransacked early Latin literature for examples and parallels, and showed a keen interest in all details of Roman antiquities. The *On the Latin*

Language is a perfect example of a scholar's collection of facts for their own intrinsic oddity.

> The name 'Aventine' has been given several explanations. Naevius says it is from *aves* 'birds', because the birds flew there from the Tiber; others that it is from the Alban King Aventius; others that it is the Adventine Hill from the *adventus* 'coming' of people, because there was a temple of Diana there which was shared by all the Latins. I am decidedly of the opinion that it is from *advectus* 'transport by water', because originally the hill was isolated by swamps and streams. Therefore they *advehebantur* 'were conveyed' there by rafts. Traces of this survive in the name now called *Velabrum* 'ferry'.
>
> (5.43; tr. after R. G. Kent)

The sheer volume of Varro's output in fact defeated his purpose. His works were too difficult to consult in a hurry. It was not, therefore, a surprise that his successors, although equally interested in facts for their own sake, should have been concerned to present them in more manageable text-books. Verrius Flaccus was typical of the new age of Augustus. He was a freedman taken up by Augustus, who gave him a house, a pension and the oversight of his grandsons' education. Inspired by Varro, he wrote books on Etruscan matters and works on 'Notable Things', but the only two works which have partially survived are of special importance because they so exactly mirror the tastes of his time and society.

His longest work was a dictionary, *On the Significance of Words*, which adopted the unprecedented system of listing words alphabetically rather than treating them in groups by subject-matter. The system at once made the information, much of it taken from Varro, far more accessible; but even so its bulk (he devoted four books to the letter A and at least five to P) was so off-putting that it was abridged by Festus at the end of the second century. It is that abridgement which alone and partially survives, together with an abridgement made of the abridgement in the time of Charlemagne. Nevertheless one can form a very clear view of the scope of the work. It contained a wealth of information on early Roman literature and law, customs, myths and religious ceremonies.

The same interest in antiquities, especially those connected with religion, is evident in the calendar (*Fasti*) which Verrius set up in the market-place at Praeneste, giving explanations of major religious festivals month by month. The work was famous (Ovid drew on it: p. 178), but its precise nature was not known until the discovery of substantial fragments of the inscription itself in the nineteenth century. Thus 23 March, which is marked Q.R.C.F., carries this comment: 'Many scholars wrongly explain that this day is so termed because on it the king fled from the assembly-place. But King Tarquin did not depart from the assembly-place of the city and the same letters also occur in another month and mean the same thing. Therefore it is more likely that they indicate that law-cases can be heard once the assemblies are over.' Once again it is notable that Verrius produced something which, although scholarly (some of the explanations recur in his *On the Significance of Words*), was primarily intended to be of practical help. It was, after all, an age of religious revival.

Varro, therefore, who had actually compiled a handbook on senatorial procedure for the young Pompey when he returned fresh from his military success in the East but quite unversed in politics, was the man who set the precedent for definitive text-books in Latin. Such works were essential at a period when all sorts of technical advances were being made (in construction, engineering, decoration, as well as in military and medical matters), when the government required increasingly sophisticated information (on climate and ethnography, geology, astronomy or economic prospects), and when the wealthy classes at Rome had the leisure and opportunity to turn to other diversions than politics, whether they were breeding horses or building houses. From the hundreds of treatises that have disappeared three of particular interest have justly survived.

By far the most influential for European culture is Vitruvius, whose ten books *On Architecture* were read by Leonardo and Michelangelo when they were first printed in 1482. Details of his life are scanty and even his full name is uncertain, but Vitruvius had served under Julius Caesar and been appointed to a commission in the Engineers by Augustus. How far he played a part in Augustus's rebuilding plans as an architect we do not know, but he says of Augustus (1 *Praef.* 3): 'I see that you have built, and are now building, on a large scale. Furthermore, with regard to the future, you intend to devote so much attention to public and private buildings that they will correspond to our achievements and be a memorial to posterity. I have, therefore, supplied a detailed treatise so that by reference to it you may inform yourself about works already complete or about to be commenced.' This was written soon after 16 B.C. when Vitruvius was already an old man, but surprisingly the work contains in fact very little information about Augustus's own schemes of construction and reconstruction. It is a general handbook of architecture and related subjects, including water supply and machinery, written in a simple and unliterary style by a man of some taste and education, who had read not only Varro and the technical treatises of the Greeks but also Ennius and Lucretius. Since it was the first such systematic account in Latin it commanded a ready market at a time when great public works were being undertaken all over the Empire and when new men, rich and ambitious, were planning elaborate private dwellings of their own. It catered for that craze for architecture which the satirists were to attack, which Petronius parodies in his *Satyricon* (see p. 190) and which the Younger Pliny betrays in the tortuous account of his own house (*Letters* 5.6). Vitruvius deals with every aspect and provides specifications for theatres and temples, basilicas and baths, market-places and farms. He is well aware of the importance of functionalism, that buildings must be suitable for their purpose or the social status of their owners ('magnificent ante-chambers, alcoves and hall are not necessary for ordinary people because they pay their respects by visiting others and are not visited by others'). And he has strong views about some of the decadent standards of his time. Discussing wall-painting, he deplores the fashion for 'monsters rather than definite representations taken from definite things ... Candelabra support pictured shrines and on top of these clusters of thin stalks rise from their roots in tendrils with little figures seated upon them at random.' 'Such things', he concludes sternly, 'neither are, nor can be, nor have been', although they seem to have been popular enough among the citizens of Pompeii. Artistic degeneration accompanied that moral decline which Roman writers lamented.

Vitruvius's interests were not only architectural. He had a working knowledge of experimental science, discussing the poisonous qualities of lead or recommending a lighted lamp as test for foul air, and his last books display considerable expertise in geometry and engineering. It is against this background that the most authoritative medical text-book in Latin appeared. We know nothing of the life of A. Cornelius Celsus beyond the fact that he was probably writing under Tiberius and that, significantly (see p. 170), he came from Spain. He is known today simply for his eight books on *Medicine*, but he was not a practising doctor and the medical volumes were only part of a much larger encyclopedia which dealt with agriculture, warfare, rhetoric, law and philosophy as well. He was, therefore, very much following in the footsteps of Varro and providing a useful compendium of the present state of knowledge on topics relevant to a Roman man of affairs. Interestingly enough he also expresses the same prejudices of other Romans of his day about present society. He may indeed have read Sallust and Livy and his comment that 'idleness and luxury attacked the human body first in Greece and then with us' (1 *Praef.* 5) is in complete harmony with their attitude.

Celsus basically relied on literary sources, above all the works attributed to the great Greek doctors Hippocrates, Asclepiades and Erasistratus, and one can form a shrewd picture of contemporary medicine from his pages with their strange mixture of superstitious placebos (e.g. the powdered liver of a fox for asthmatic troubles) and practical advice (e.g. how to extract an arrow, or the value of a siesta in a Mediterranean climate). His scope is considerable. Book 1 gives advice on diet, Book 2 gives a summary of the principal symptoms to be watched, Book 3 deals with fever and Book 4 with internal complaints, Books 5 and 6 provide numerous pharmaceutical prescriptions and Books 7 and 8 outline some surgical operations ('Don't be influenced by a patient's screams into undue haste'). Above all he is aware of the limitations of the science and the need for further study, particularly of anatomy, which can be provided either by vivisection of condemned criminals or by examination of dying gladiators – a salutary reminder of the underlying brutality of the Roman world. To anyone interested in medicine and its history, Celsus is a most revealing and readable author.

If Celsus was one of the first Latin writers on medicine, Pomponius Mela, another Spaniard, from near Gibraltar, who was writing soon after Claudius's invasion of Britain in A.D. 43 (3.6.49), was the first serious Roman geographer. Nepos and Varro had indeed discussed geographical matters and Mela uses them as authorities, but the study of geography was

incidental to their wider interests and the field was held
almost entirely by Greeks even as late as the reign of Augustus,
when one of the greatest Greek geographers, Strabo, was
writing. But with the expansion of the Roman Empire there
was both a need for a reliable handbook and also an interest in
a *Roman* view of the known world. The three books of
Mela's *Chorographia* are not always reliable (the Danube does
not flow into the Adriatic) but they did give a detailed
coastal survey starting from Morocco and following the
shores of the Mediterranean and the Black Sea round to Spain,
and finishing with descriptions of the Atlantic coast of France,
the Baltic and the North Sea (up to the Orkneys), the Persian
Gulf and stretching to India and Africa. It is the kind of work,
later much more satisfactorily undertaken by the Elder Pliny,
which founded that fascination with strange corners of the
world which Tacitus played on in his *Agricola*.

Mela does not aspire to any great literary heights ('the
subject-matter is tedious rather than inviting', he admitted)
and, as is the way with all encyclopedists, most of his information is second-hand, but, like Herodotus, he enlivens
his book with his amazing eye for the marvellous and
bizarre, such as the island of hairy women (3.9) or the im-
measurable cave of Corycus (1.13.72).

Text-books are the natural outcome of the upsurge of
curiosity about facts which characterized the intellectual life
of the late Republic. There were even text-books on gastronomy, one written by Apicius (although the surviving
book which goes under his name is a much later compilation)
and another mocked by Horace (p. 146). One man, whose
work does not survive, is typical. C. Julius Hyginus (*c.* 64 B.C.–
c. A.D. 17) was a Spaniard and a freedman. Augustus appointed
him librarian of his new library on the Palatine. There,
inspired by the example of Varro, he wrote commentaries on
Latin poets, text-books on Italian geography, agriculture and

aviculture (used by Columella), families of Trojan descent and religion, and brief biographies of famous men. In conclusion, therefore, it may be appropriate to mention at this point one other work which seems to belong to this same movement. To the Roman, astrology/astronomy (for the two could hardly be divorced) was quite as relevant and technical a subject as medicine or agriculture. Varro and Nigidius Figulus had written technical works in the field. Moreover astrology was compatible with Stoicism. 'It was easy to suppose that in an integrated universe the position of the stars at a man's birth could be consistent with one set only of future events' (F. H. Sandbach, *The Stoics* (1975), p. 80). Horoscopes were in great demand, and the perpetual actions of the government in attempting to ban astrologers (as in 33 B.C. and A.D. 11) must be understood to have stemmed not from any disbelief in them but from fear of their excessive political power. Tiberius was guided throughout his life by the stars.

To serve this curiosity, M. Manilius wrote, between A.D. 10 and *c.* 16, a poem on astrology, stressing throughout Divine Providence and the role of Fate. Unlike Virgil's *Georgics* (p. 119), it is a true didactic poem, that is, it is meant to give a thorough and reliable account of the subject in an attractive format. In that sense it is the verse equivalent of a prose textbook. By an irony, Manilius is read today mainly for his 'poetical' passages, such as his digression on the legend of Andromeda (5.538 ff.) or his introductions, rather than for his content. In fact he wrote elegantly with considerable charm and variety, and he draws upon an enormous stock of learning, despite his claim to 'speak out of my own wisdom' (2.56). In Book 1 he gives an account of the creation of the sky, and then in the subsequent four books he goes on to discuss the signs of the zodiac, the horoscope, and the influence of the signs on men and children born under them. To the knowledgeable and credulous, Manilius offers invaluable treasures made readable by his poetry. 'They shall marvel unto whomsoever the stars have given it to know themselves and their holy motions.' But it is an arcane subject. 'Furthermore triangles as such move in opposition one to another. It is their alternate line that leads them to war along opposed paths: and thus the system of truth is harmonious in its every part. For Aries, Leo and Sagittarius, which are signs allied in one triangle, have no peace with Cheli and its whole triangle which Gemini and Aquarius complete . . .'

It is not recorded what reception Manilius met with. His life is unknown and the work is not elsewhere imitated or quoted. Yet in its own way it is typical of a generation that wanted detailed information and wanted it in Latin, not Greek.

6

BETWEEN REPUBLIC AND EMPIRE

CIVIL disorder had reigned at Rome since the 80s, with critical moments in 49 and 44 B.C. (Caesar's invasion of Italy and his assassination), and it was only brought to an end by the victory of Octavian (Augustus) over M. Antony at the Battle of Actium in 31 B.C. During that period a generation grew up which was disenchanted with politics and uncertain about the very future of Rome. The cynicism and despair that were already apparent in Sallust (p. 92) became increasingly marked in other writers.

> Which of the gods now shall the people summon
> To prop Rome's reeling sovereignty? What prayer
> Shall the twelve Virgins use to reach the ear of
>   Vesta, who grows each day
>
> Deafer to litanies?   (tr. James Michie)

So wrote Horace in the second ode of his first book, and the sentiment is matched by Livy's preface:

> I shall find antiquity a rewarding study, if only because, while I am absorbed in it, I shall be able to turn my eyes from the troubles which for so long have tormented the modern world, and to write without any of that over-anxious consideration which may well plague a writer on contemporary life, even if it does not lead him to conceal the truth.   (tr. Aubrey de Sélincourt)

Yet the same generation, which produced the finest of all Roman authors, was to live to see the restoration of security and calm. The transition from despair to confidence is mirrored by the evolution of the writers themselves, who move from a detached escapism to a commitment to the Roman ideal. This transition can be seen in the works of Virgil, who was born in Mantua in 70 B.C. and died in 19 B.C.; of Horace, who was born in Venusia in 65 B.C. and died in 8 B.C.; of Livy, who was born at Padua probably in 59 (or 64) B.C. and died in A.D. 17 (or A.D. 12); and even of their younger contemporary Propertius, who was born about 50 B.C. near Assisi and died before A.D. 2. The focus of this new commitment was the person of Augustus himself, who must have possessed rare qualities of inspiring affection and loyalty. But Augustus was also fortunate to have attracted to his side a colourful aesthete, Maecenas, who understood poets and writers and was able by his patronage and encouragement to give them every help. The new regime of Augustus gave men something worth writing for and believing in: they, in their turn, gave the regime an ideal.

VIRGIL

But it did not look like this in the 40s and 30s when Virgil began writing. His earliest work was a collection of short hexameter poems modelled on the *Idylls* of Theocritus. The collection of ten *Eclogues* which we possess was probably published after the triumph of Augustus, but the majority of the poems were written between 42 and 38 B.C. and published then in a first edition. Theocritus, from the Greek island of Cos (*c.* 300–270 B.C.), sensing that the old literary media – tragedy, epic, lyric – were worked out, experimented with other sub-literary genres. For example, he took the Mime and elevated it to a literary form by casting it in hexameters and in an artificial and self-conscious dialect. He is chiefly remembered as the father of pastoral poetry. One of the features of Mediterranean life is the spontaneous song-competitions between shepherds. Theocritus, perhaps during his years in Sicily, was impressed by this and created a new style of poetry. The essence of it is a poem which sets the scene for a song. Thus *Idyll* 7 tells of a country walk on Cos during which a goatherd Lycidas and Simichidas (Theocritus) exchange song for song about their loves. Lycidas' song is allusive and obscure, Simichidas' is bright with the most modern conceits of Alexandria. In *Idyll* 1 a goatherd describes a carved cup which he will give Thyrsis if he sings of the death of Daphnis. This he does in the most evocative tones. 'The eddies closed over him, a man beloved of the Muses and not unpleasing to the Nymphs.'

Virgil (P. Vergilius Maro) had been given a normal education and was destined for a public career, but, if we may believe the mythology that grew up round his life, his shyness proved his unsuitability, and he turned instead to poetry and philosophy – significantly the escapist philosophy of Epicurus as taught at Naples by Siro (p. 81). His family, like many others, had suffered losses and deprivations in the Civil Wars. We do not know what attracted him to the poetry of Theocritus, which had not enjoyed much acclaim at Rome, but he seized on it for the potential to create an imaginary world in which he could explore a wide range of emotions and ideas. Virgil's pastoral landscape is a curious blend of acute natural observation (*Ecl.* 1.47–8: 'Your land is enough for you even though the bare rock and the marshland with its mud and reeds encroach on all your pastures') and idyllic romanticism of the kind portrayed in so many frescoes at Pompeii – hills, lakes and the distant sea, cows and sheep quietly grazing, a small vegetable garden and a profusion of wild flowers (*Ecl.* 2.45–55: 'Ah, lovely youth, come here. Can you not see the Nymphs, laden with baskets full of lilies – all for you? See the white Naiad, plucking, for you, pale irises and poppy-heads, binding narcissus to the fragrant anise-flower, with cassia and other scented herbs twined in, and flaming marigolds to make the modest blueberries look their best. Myself I'll pick you quinces with their white and tender bloom, and the chestnuts Amaryllis loved when she was mine. And waxen plums'). He peopled it with country-men, like the elderly slave Tityrus and the Roman citizen Meliboeus in *Ecl.* 1 or the passionate shepherd Corydon in *Ecl.* 2 or himself as Menalcas in *Ecl.* 5. As the poems developed, the landscape became more and more idealized until it turned into the unlocalized Arcadia of *Ecl.* 10, and the people became more and more the mouth-pieces for Virgil's own thoughts. It is no matter that Corydon in *Ecl.* 2 grazed sheep in Sicily whereas in *Ecl.* 7 he appears to be a Mantuan goatherd.

Virgil started from the Greek originals of Theocritus. He is in fact very faithful to his models, but he gives them a twist that makes them peculiarly Roman and peculiarly his own. This can perhaps best be shown by *Ecl.* 2. It was inspired by Theocritus's *Idyll* 11, which opens almost as a letter from the poet to his doctor friend Nicias, saying that the only medicine for love is the Muses and illustrating this by the song which Polyphemus sang outside Galatea's cave. The *Idyll* is typical of Theocritus's 'song within a poem' composition and it is typical too of Theocritus's delight in transferring some feature of contemporary poetry into his pastoral world. Polyphemus's soliloquy is a parody of a familiar Alexandrine conceit – the serenade sung by a locked-out lover outside his mistress's door (*paraclausithyron*). Only here it is a cave, not a smart apartment, a one-eyed monster, not an elegant young Greek. It is that contrast which adds piquancy and humour. Superficially, Virgil's poem is very similar. Some lines are translated almost literally ('O Cyclops, Cyclops, where be your wits gone flying?'; 'O Corydon, Corydon, what is this madness that has got you?'). And Virgil adds other Greek elements, borrowing from a Greek elegiac poem of Meleager for his opening theme. But Virgil and Theocritus could not be more different. Polyphemus's love is heterosexual and treated at arm's length with irony and sophisticated humour. Corydon's love is homosexual and overpoweringly personal. This raises awkward problems. Scholars have argued that because Rome, unlike Athens, affected to be a heterosexual society, homosexual poems are therefore 'literary' and unreal – mere poetical exercises. Others, including ancient scholars, have inferred that Virgil had himself experienced the hopelessness of a homosexual affair. And certainly homosexuality flourished in ancient Rome, as in modern Europe. Yet it is always a mistake to try to interpret ancient poetry biographically. What can be said is that Virgil captures the tragedy and pathos of unrequited love with an intensity and an economy not matched elsewhere in the ancient world.

Love is one of the themes that Virgil explores against this pastoral background. *Ecl.* 8 deals with contrasting reactions to infidelity, and *Ecl.* 10 with the resignation of Gallus, the rejected lover, who sums up his attitude in the heart-rending 'Love conquers all and let us surrender to Love'. But other themes are heard – political themes like the dispossession of a farmer's land, or the death and deification of Julius Caesar (*Ecl.* 5). Nowhere are they more memorably expressed than in *Ecl.* 4, the so-called Messianic eclogue, which foretells the miraculous birth of a Wonder-Child and looks forward to the return of a Golden Age.

Time has conceived and the great Sequence of the Ages starts afresh. Justice, the Virgin, comes back to dwell with us, and the rule of Saturn is restored. The Firstborn of the New Age is already on his way from high heaven down to earth.

With him the Iron Race shall end and Golden Man inherit all the world ...

And it is in your consulship, yours, Pollio, that this glorious Age
will dawn and the Procession of the great Months begin.

(*Ecl.* 4.5–12; tr. E. V. Rieu)

Virgil here combines two different visions – the classical
ideal of a Golden Age and the Near Eastern image of the
Saviour Child. He did not, of course, have a particular child
in mind, whether Christ or a son of Octavian. He used the
visions as a means of conveying his distress at the present
world and of stating his own moral aspirations. Yet the myth
of Arcady, with, as Robert Coleman has written (*Vergil:
Eclogues*, p. 32), its 'simple way of life, contentment with
little, delight in natural beauty, manly piety, friendship and
hospitality, devotion to poetry and peace', was a myth. To
yearn for Arcady was to run away from the realities of
metropolitan life and from the burdens of Roman citizenship.

Virgil's intimate love of country life led him to follow the
Eclogues with a more elaborate and more ambitious poem in
four books on husbandry (the *Georgics*), which he composed
between 35 and 30 B.C. Once again he chose a Greek model.
About 700 B.C. Hesiod had written down a collection of Greek
hexameters which contained much traditional lore about
agricultural tasks and when they should be performed. The
poem was intended to be of practical value: poetry is much
more memorable than prose, and didactic advice can be
conveyed more easily to a wider audience by that medium.
The *Works and Days*, as it is called, survives, although there
is evidence that a good deal was added to it by subsequent
hands, and it enjoyed a special reverence in the classical world
both for its antiquity and for the charm of its language. Hesiod
provided Virgil with just the precedent that he needed. Yet
the similarity of style and purpose between Virgil and Hesiod
is much less than between Virgil and Theocritus. Hesiod was
using poetic language which was still basically oral rather

than literary and had a very definite factual message to convey. Virgil, on the other hand, was drawing on Ennius and, above all, on the recent didactic writings of Lucretius to refine a poetical Latin which had dignity and economy. And his intention was not to produce a farmer's manual. Such things were more readily available from the pen of Cato or Varro (p. 102). The plan of the work does indeed suggest a methodical treatise – Book 1 on crops and climate, Book 2 on trees, Book 3 on cattle, Book 4 on bees – but the suggestion is misleading, just as it is a mistake to interpret the work as a piece of conscious propaganda designed to encourage Romans to leave the city and return to the land. There are at least three vital themes which run through it. The first is Virgil's sheer love of the country. 'O happy, all too happy farmers, if only they knew their own blessings' (*Georg.* 2.458). That love is illustrated in countless little details – the technique of grafting or pruning, the building of a hedge, the quelling of a riotous hive. It is a love that could very readily become sentimental. The escapist notes of the *Eclogues* are sounded again in the description of the old man of Corycia (*Georg.* 4.125).

> I saw an old man, a Corycian, who owned a few poor acres
> Of land once derelict, useless for arable,
> No good for grazing, unfit for the cultivation of vines.
> But he laid out a kitchen garden in rows amid the brushwood,
> Bordering it with white lilies, verbena, small-seeded poppy.
> He was happy there as a king. He could go indoors at night
> To a table heaped with dainties he never had to buy.
> His the first rose of spring, the earliest apples in autumn.
>
> (tr. C. Day-Lewis)

But, secondly, that love is always balanced by an awareness of the harsh realities of nature. Country life is not always an idyllic pastoral. Cattle die, crops fail, swarms are decimated. So Virgil comes to see that man and nature are always in

tension and that man's duty is to cultivate his own awareness
so that he can live in harmony with whatever powers control
nature. Such a connection marks a switch from the idealizing
to the realistic, from the Epicurean to the Stoic point of view.
Man has to work and to struggle to earn his living from the
ground, as Virgil sums it up in that most poignant of all his
similes:

> For a law of nature
> Makes all things go to the bad, lose ground and fall away;
> Just as an oarsman, when he is sculling his skiff against
> The current, needs but relax the drive of his arm a little
> And the current will carry him headlong away downstream.
> (*Georg.* 1.199–203; tr. C. Day-Lewis)

Moreover, quite apart from the harshness of nature there is
the harshness of human nature. The horrors of war are still
ever-present. The Battle of Actium had only just been fought
and won, and Virgil captures the alarm and insecurity of the
times.

O Gods of our fathers, native Gods, Romulus, Vesta
Who mothers our Tuscan Tiber and the Roman Palatine,
At least allow our young prince to rescue this shipwrecked era!
Long enough now have we
Paid in our blood for the promise Laomedon broke at Troy.
Long now has the court of heaven grudged you to us, Caesar,
Complaining because you care only for mortal triumphs.
For Right and Wrong are confused here, there's so much war in the
    World,
Evil has so many faces, the plough so little
Honour, the labourers are taken, the fields untended,
And the curving sickle is beaten into the sword that yields not.
There the East is in arms, here Germany marches:
Neighbour cities, breaking their treaties, attack each other:
The wicked War-god runs amok through all the world.
So, when racing chariots have rushed from the starting-gate,

They gather speed on the course, and the driver tugs at the curb-
rein
– His horses runaway, car out of control, quite helpless.

(*Georg.* 1.498–514; tr. C. Day-Lewis)

There is, however, also a third new element. At *Georg.*
2.176 Virgil professes to 'sing Hesiod's song among the
Roman cities'. The latter phrase is startling. Until now Rome
and the Italian cities had co-existed in an uneasy relationship.
The Italians lacked the full privileges of Roman citizenship
and this was a source of constant friction in the first century,
when they were always ready to espouse some rebellious or
dissident cause. The unification of Italy was a major priority
and one to which Augustus addressed himself with patience
and perseverance. It was also an ideal which captured Virgil's
imagination, so that for the first time he adopted a constructive
role in contemporary affairs. In a famous passage, which precedes line 176, he writes of the glories of Italy:

But neither the Median forests, that rich land, nor fair Ganges,
Nor Hermus rolling in gold
Compares with Italy – no, not Bactra nor the Indies
Nor all Arabia's acres of spice-enriched soil.
This land of ours has never been ploughed by bulls fire-breathing
Nor sown with dragon's teeth;
It has never known a harvest of serried helmeted spearmen:
Rather is it a country fulfilled with heavy corn and
Campanian wine, possessed by olives and prosperous herds.
Here the charger gallops onto the plain in his pride,
Here the white-fleeced flocks and the bull, a princely victim
Washed over and over in Clitumnus' holy water,
Head our Roman trimphs to the temples of the gods.
Here is continual spring and a summer beyond her season.

(tr. C. Day-Lewis)

If such a dream of a united Italy was to be realized it
required men to work together for a common goal. Virgil's

selection of bees as the final subject for the poem was determined not only by his actual interest in them but also by their symbolic importance. Bees were seen to represent many things, such as poetic inspiration, but chiefly a highly organized community where each member worked for the good of all. And Virgil makes the comparison explicit when he uses the Roman term for citizens (*Quirites*) of the members of the hive: 'they themselves supply their sovereign and the tiny citizens of the realm.'

The *Georgics* then is a true poem but also a political poem. It contains many passages and episodes of great beauty, like the descent of Orpheus to the underworld, and many haunting lines ('But meanwhile time, irrecoverable time, flies' or 'suddenly she vanished from his sight, like smoke into the thin air'). It expresses Virgil's unusual sympathy with the natural world. But it also voices an important awareness. The days when every Roman aimed at personal pre-eminence and dignity were numbered. An autocracy which could unite classes and families and hold the empire together was as essential to Rome as the queen bee to her swarm. Augustus proved an exceptionally wise and skilful manipulator, and even as early as the 20s it is possible to detect a sense of relief, as life became more stable and purposeful. It was in that atmosphere that Virgil conceived of his ambitious project – the composition of a Roman epic that would rival Homer. We need not take seriously the stories that Virgil was pressed to write an epic about Augustus himself. Such stories are the stuff of romantic biographers, and Augustus and his confidant Maecenas were far too subtle patrons even to think of anything so crude. The theme had to be a heroic one that linked Rome and Troy, and it lay ready to hand in the legend of Aeneas, son of King Priam, who had escaped after the fall of Troy and settled in the West. It is not clear when the tradition was fixed that he landed in Italy and founded Alba Longa, near Rome, from where, two generations later, Rome itself was founded, but it is certainly a very old tradition. Statuettes of Aeneas carrying his father Anchises on his shoulder have been found in S. Etruria which date back to the sixth century B.C., and a nearby Latin town, Lavinium, claimed from the same period to be the home of Aeneas's father-in-law, Latinus, and to contain the 'tomb' of Aeneas. No doubt the story was much changed and embellished over the centuries, as scholars appreciated chronological problems (Troy fell, traditionally, in 1184 B.C., whereas Rome was not founded until 752 B.C.) or interpreted particular customs and monuments associated with Aeneas. It was also developed and extended in the Carthaginian Wars. Sicily was a cockpit of war, and Rome used the legend that Anchises had been buried in Sicily as a trick to win over the native Sicilians. But the most significant single factor was the claim of the ancient patrician family of the Julii to be descended from Aeneas's son Ascanius or Iulus – a claim which is asserted as far back as the third century B.C. This had a special relevance because Augustus was the adopted son of Julius Caesar and stood in direct descent from Aeneas.

Some time about 30 B.C. Virgil picked on this legend as the plot of a great epic. He was a slow and deliberate writer, often rewriting and casting the story in a prose synopsis before committing himself to full composition. Even so, when he died in 19 B.C., the *Aeneid* was unfinished, as the large number of incomplete lines and the inconsistencies between books (especially 4, 5 and 6) indicate. The story was to be told in twelve books, half the total of either the *Odyssey* or the *Iliad*, which were mechanically divided by Alexandrian scholars into twenty-four books corresponding to the twenty-four letters of the Greek alphabet. The first six books tell of the wanderings of Aeneas after the fall of Troy, partly recounted by him as a shipwrecked guest of Queen Dido of Carthage and partly narrated as his own experiences, especially the funeral games of his father in Sicily (5) and visiting the underworld (6). These books correspond to the Homeric *Odyssey*. Aeneas's fight to establish a bridgehead in Italy occupies the second six books and corresponds to the *Iliad*. But the differences from Homer are profound.

In the first place Aeneas is a hero in search of his soul. The *Aeneid* is very much of a spiritual quest, which makes it unique in ancient literature. Only Virgil admits of the possibility that a character can change, grow and develop. Aeneas in the early books is unsure of himself, always seeking instructions from his father or from the gods before committing himself to any course of action. In the underworld he sees a panorama of the future history of Rome down to the time of Augustus, and that vision gives him the self-confidence to act on his own initiative. He may still be a creature of emotion – indeed the epic ends with his succumbing to primitive passions of violence and killing his rival Turnus – but he accepts his role as the destined leader (*fatalis dux*) in a divinely planned enterprise. As he had said earlier, 'it is not of my will that I make for Italy', but now, whatever his misgivings, he carries out his mission with resolution. In other words, he is a man conscious of a religious vocation. The gods may often be hard, envious and inscrutable ('Stop believing that you can bend the fates of the gods by prayer'), it may be difficult to distinguish intractable fate from approachable gods, but a man's duty is to bring his own will into conformity with the gods', to achieve that equilibrium between human wishes and Divine Providence (*pax deorum*) which was the objective of Roman religion and the principle of Stoic philosophy 'to live according to Nature'. That is what is meant by *pietas*, the quality most often ascribed to Aeneas.

This was a logical development from Virgil's standpoint in

the *Georgics*, but the gods of the *Aeneid* are much more personal and less agricultural than in the *Georgics*. They supervise every aspect of man's life and not just the welfare of the farm. They are indeed the old Roman gods who ensured the success or failure of every activity in which human beings are involved, from childbirth to the prosperous workings of the stock exchange. They could not be less like the Homeric gods, who are simply Homeric heroes writ large, with the same pursuit of individual excellence at all costs. Take away the gods from the *Iliad* and the plot would remain the same, except that the heroes might lose stature, because their stature is enhanced by comparison with the frivolous omnipotence of the gods. But Jupiter and the other gods determine the underlying pattern of the *Aeneid*.

Virgil had come to this position by his own thinking, but it coincided with the views of the majority of his contemporaries.

> Roman, you may be innocent of guilt,
> Yet you shall pay for each ancestral crime,
> Until our mouldering temples are rebuilt
> And the gods' statues cleansed of smoke and grime.
>
> Only as servant of the gods in heaven
> Can you rule earth,

wrote Horace (*Odes* 3.6; tr. James Michie). Augustus himself had inaugurated an elaborate programme which comprised the reinstatement of numerous priesthoods and the reconstruction of a very large number of derelict temples. The programme worked and Roman religion survived to be a spiritual force that was more than a match for Christianity until the middle of the fourth century A.D. Part of the reason for this success was that the Stoics, unlike the Epicureans, talked the same language. Virgil, for all the Epicurean instincts of his youth, grew to adopt a Stoic viewpoint – that there is a Divine Providence and that all living things, from the humblest to the grandest, are part of that Divine Flame. As Anchises puts it in an apocalyptic passage of Book 6 (723 ff.):

> The sky and the lands, the watery plains, the moon's gleaming face, the Titanic Sun and the stars are all strengthened by Spirit working within them, and by Mind, which is blended into all the vast universe and pervades every part of it, enlivening the whole mass. From Spirit and Mind are created men and the beasts; and from Spirit and Mind the flying things, and the strange creatures which ocean beneath its marbled surface brings into being, all have their lives.
>
> (tr. W. F. Jackson Knight)

Secondly, there is no patriotism in Homer. It may be 'the one best omen to fight for one's country' but it is immaterial whether that country is Argos or Mycenae or Troy. But the *Aeneid* is, ultimately, about Rome, and Aeneas is never allowed to forget that dallying in Carthage is a betrayal of his mission to found Rome. The latent love of Italy as a country, first seen in the *Georgics*, becomes the over-riding concern of the *Aeneid*. It is mirrored in the account of the Trojans rowing up the Tiber to the site of Rome, where King Evander lived:

> Up the long loops of the river, under the shade of diverse Trees, through the green reflection of woods in the glass-calm water

or in some of the majestic similes:

> As when some stalwart oak-tree, some veteran of the Alps,
> Is assailed by a wintry wind whose veering gusts tear at it,
> Trying to root it up: wildly whistle the branches,
> The leaves come floating down from aloft as the bole is battered:
> But the tree stands firm on its crag, for high as its head is carried
> Into the sky, so deep do its roots go down towards Hades.
>
> (4.441–6; tr. C. Day-Lewis)

The mission of Rome is to provide peace and order for Italy and the rest of the world:

Let others fashion from bronze more lifelike breathing images –
For so they shall – and evoke living faces from marble;
Others excel as orators, others trace with their instruments
The planets circling in heaven and predict when stars will appear.
But, Romans, never forget that government is your medium!
Be this your art: to practise men in the habit of peace,
Generosity to the conquered, and firmness against oppressors.

> (6.848–53; tr. C. Day-Lewis)

Aeneas is the prototype of Augustus, and a vital element of the work is the foreshadowing of Roman history, which Virgil gives in different ways, in the catalogue of heroes in the underworld, in the prophecy of Father Tiber, on the shield of Aeneas, in the events at the funeral games of Anchises. The plan of divine providence for Rome is unveiled, just as Livy was later to trace the same story from Rome's beginnings to the present day to show 'through what men and by what policies, in peace and in war, empire was established and enlarged'. Octavia actually broke down when Virgil read her the lines on the vision in the underworld of her nephew and son-in-law Marcellus, who died in 23 B.C.

Alas poor youth! If only you could escape your harsh fate!
Marcellus you shall be. Give me armfuls of lilies
That I may scatter their shining blooms and shower these gifts
At least upon the dear soul, all to no purpose though
Such kindness be.

> (6.882–6; tr. C. Day-Lewis)

Thirdly, Aeneas is a very human hero, touched by love for his father and his friends and stirred to deep emotions. There are, of course, many affecting moments in both the *Iliad* and the *Odyssey* – Achilles' love for Patroclus, the parting scene between Hector and Andromache, the meeting of Odysseus and Nausicaa – but they are all larger than life, whereas

Aeneas's dilemma in *Aeneid* 4 is very personal and adds substance to his character. Shipwrecked at Carthage, demoralized and enfeebled on a foreign shore, Aeneas needed the protection and help of Dido: she, in turn, a solitary woman in a dangerous land, needed the strength and support of Aeneas. Thrown together in this way it was inevitable that they should fall in love, but the resultant misunderstanding was not the fault of either of them but of the gods. Dido believed that Aeneas had offered his hand in marriage and she, renouncing her pledge to remain true to the memory of her dead husband, Sychaeus, had accepted it. Aeneas admitted his love for Dido but denied that the affair was ever meant to have more significance:

> I'll never pretend
> You have not been good to me, deserving everything
> You can claim. I shall not regret my memories of [you],
> As long as I breathe, as long as I remember my own self . . .
> Nor did I offer you marriage
> At any time or consent to be bound by a marriage contract.
>
> (4.333–9; tr. C. Day-Lewis)

So Aeneas departs for Sicily and Italy, and Dido commits suicide; and even when they meet again in the underworld there is no reconciliation, only silence.

PROPERTIUS

It is the character of Aeneas that holds the epic together, especially during the more monotonous battle-scenes of the last six books. Unfinished though it was, the *Aeneid* was immediately acclaimed as the great masterpiece of Latin literature: it was read in schools and imitated and admired. One such admirer was Propertius, who acknowledged his debts to the *Eclogues* and *Georgics* and who, as early as 24 B.C., had heard something of the *Aeneid*. A generation younger

ROMAN LITERATURE AND SOCIETY

than Virgil, he came from a landowning family near Assisi,
where the Propertii were local magnates. Had he been a
contemporary of Cicero's he would no doubt have gone to
Rome and made a political career there but in fact he settled
in Rome and opted out, as many of his friends did. What is
fascinating about his literary output is that in a relatively
short spell (Book 1 of his elegies was published in 29 B.C.,
Book 4 in 16 B.C.) his attitudes undergo a radical transformation. Propertius never became an apostle of the Augustan
regime but he discovered a seriousness and commitment
which are analogous to the change in Virgil himself. He was a
pacifist. As late as 35 he could write: 'Peace has love as its
god, peace is what we lovers worship; my cruel persistent
battles are with my mistress.' Not for him the stern battles and
glorious triumphs of Augustus. He is quite prepared to mock
the 'god Caesar' in flippant tones and to undercut his efforts
at moral legislation and his attempts to subdue the world.
Even so, Propertius does recognize that there is a new, and
better, order.

It must be admitted that Propertius is not an easy poet for us
to follow, although he was called 'polished and choice' by the
ancients. His text has suffered great damage in transmission
(particularly in Book 2, which may in fact be a conflation of
two separate books and in which poems have been cruelly
mutilated and confused). As a poet, he also relied to a greater
extent than usual on a common cultural understanding among
his readers which enabled him to use a kind of literary short-
hand. Most readers today, for instance, meeting the name
'Ascanius' unawares might think of Aeneas's son: how many
would identify it with an obscure river?

Book 1 consisted of twenty-two poems, written in elegiac
metre (couplets of a hexameter followed by pentameter)
and almost exclusively concerned with the theme of love.
Roman love-elegy, substantial poems concerned with the

130

poet's emotions and involvement with his beloved, has no exact Greek counterpart but it grew out of two popular Greek genres. The first was the short epigram, usually in elegiacs and usually about love, wittily exploring some conceit or image. It had been perfected by Meleager (*c.* 140–70 B.C.). The type is reflected in a four-line epigram of his from the Greek Anthology.

Delicate Diodorus, casting fire at the young men, has been caught by Timarion's wanton eyes and bears, fixed in him, the bitter-sweet dart of love. This is indeed a new miracle I see; fire is ablaze, burnt by fire.

The epigrammatists built up a stock of conventional situations – the lover's serenade outside his mistress's locked door, the lover's complaint of infidelity, the attack on dress and cosmetics, the speeding of a loved one on a journey – and of conventional commonplaces about the disease, madness, fire, darts etc. of love. The second genre was the long narrative poem, again in elegiacs, usually on a mythological subject about the loves of gods and heroes. It should always be remembered that the ancients were surrounded with pictures, statues and reliefs that made mythological scenes and stories a part of their everyday experience. Catullus had already expanded the epigram to write a few subjective elegies about Lesbia (for the chief difference between an epigram and an elegy is in scale and subjectivity) and had drawn on the store of mythological precedents, but it was his successor, C. Cornelius Gallus, a friend of Virgil and Augustus, an unusually influential poet whose work is one of the greatest losses of antiquity, who seems to have established the elegy in its mature form.

In Book 1 Propertius writes with an audacity and brilliance that were not to be matched in Latin literature again. His poems revolve round his mistress Cynthia. The ancients believed that she was a real person, a free married woman of distinguished birth, called Hostia, and there is no reason to doubt that belief, since it reflects the tradition by which Catullus concealed Clodia under the pseudonym of Lesbia. Nor is there any reason to doubt that Propertius had an extended and tempestuous affair. But his poems do not describe different moments in that affair: rather, they analyse conflicting emotions and situations both of Propertius and of Cynthia through the unexpected adaptation of stock themes. For instance a well-known theme, found in New Comedy and epigram, dealt with a lover finding a girl asleep on her bed, who seizes his chance and ignores her reproaches when she awakes. Propertius takes this theme in his third elegy. He embellishes it with mythological examples (Ariadne, Andromeda and Maenads), but the twist, as Margaret Hubbard so well points out, is that Propertius does not rape Cynthia, and when Cynthia does awake she scathingly contrasts his supposed infidelity with her fidelity.

> Like Ariadne, who in languor lay
> On the lone shore, when Theseus sailed away;
> Or like Andromeda, unchained at last
> From the hard rock, and in the first sleep sunk fast;
> Or some dance-wearied bacchante, prostrate thus
> On grass-grown fringes of Apidanus –
> So Cynthia, breathing slumber, lay in bed
> With lax unconscious hands beneath her head,
> When I returned on tipsy feet one night
> With link-boys waving flares to give me light.
>   I tried, my senses not being wholly gone,
> To reach the bed she pressed so lightly on.
> Doubly inflamed, and urged, that side and this,
> By Love and Wine, two drastic deities,
> To slip an arm beneath the sleeper's back,
> To hold her, press her lips, and press the attack,
> I lacked the courage – having cause to know

And fear her biting tongue – to rouse her so.
I stood transfixed, like Argus in surprise
At Io's horns, with fascinated eyes.

    At last I loosed the chaplet from my head,
And set the flowers on Cynthia's brows instead:
Then put in place – with what delight! – the strands
Of straying hair; then cupping cautious hands
Gave apples, stealthy gifts, which one and all
Ungrateful slumber from her breast let fall.
Sometimes I heard her sigh, and as I read
Those cryptic signs, was numbed with baseless dread
That dreams had brought her fears till then unknown –
Some lover making her by force his own.

    The moon went by the window fronting her,
Resting its beams on eyelids slow to stir,
Which soon its mild persistence opened wide,
And rising on one elbow Cynthia cried:
'Back to my bed? From some rebuff, no doubt!
What other woman's door has shut you out?
Where have you spent long hours that should be mine,
Till stars are sinking, and your powers decline?
May you yourself pass nights of misery,
Such as your heartless whims impose on me.
Sometimes, to baffle sleep, I spun my thread,
Or turned, when tired, to play my lute instead;
Sighing at times, so often left to bear
Long hours of waiting, while you love elsewhere.
Till I succumbed to welcome wings of sleep,
This was the last sad thought that made me weep.'

                    (1.3; tr. S. G. Tremenheere)

The true power and originality of Propertius as a love poet
come out by comparison with Ovid (p. 168), but his first
book will have struck contemporary society ambivalently.
To his young friends, like Bassus and Ponticus, to whom he
addresses several poems, his obsession with such private
passions was exhilarating, but to Octavian (Augustus), already

anxious to try to safeguard marriage as an institution and encourage the raising of families, it must have seemed tasteless and provocative. And the insolent provocation is carried a stage further by one of the final poems in the book, in which one of Propertius's relations, a man named Gallus who was murdered near Perugia after escaping through Octavian's army, speaks his dying words.

It is idle to deny that the world which Propertius (and, before him, Catullus) portrayed was a real world. The poems are not mere literary efforts. When all allowances have been made for the licence allowed to orators and poets to invent discreditable anecdotes, there remains plenty of evidence to suggest that the social world of Propertius and his contemporaries was fast and immoral. Dissolute parties in high society were not uncommon, and were frequented by all sorts of women, from aristocratic debauchees like Augustus's daughter, Julia, through courtesans like Cytheris, the mistress of both Antony and Gallus with whom Cicero once had dinner, to the actresses and others who flocked to Antony's house. It was a continuation of a long tradition. Sulla's sex life was notorious, but not much less so than that of Verres or Catiline or a host of other prominent Romans of the late Republic.

Propertius's second book, published two years later, contains some of his best poetry although it is also the hardest to read, partly because the text is unusually corrupt and partly because Propertius was experimenting with new structural complexities that sometimes make it difficult to decide where a poem begins and ends, or what its logical unity is. But at the beginning of Book 3, written perhaps five years later, he sounds a completely new note.

Spirit of Callimachus and rites of Philetas, allow me, I pray, to enter your grove.

Callimachus, the leading poet and scholar of Alexandria, had indeed written epigrams on love, but Propertius is alluding not to them but to his great poem, the *Aetia*, which in highly sophisticated and witty language told of the origins of various practices and rites. And in Book 3 Propertius can be seen trying both to find a Callimachean style or technique in Latin and also to identify appropriate subjects. There are still love-poems but two of them are farewells to love and others deal less with personal experience than general topics (e.g. 'why do girls cost so much these days?'): in all, they only make a third of the whole, which is otherwise devoted to a medley of subjects: a hymn to Bacchus, a reproach to his kinsman Postumus for abandoning his wife to pursue glory, a lament for the death of Marcellus, studies of peace and war as ways of life, and so on. Propertius's poetry has changed direction, although he has not yet settled on a consistent or successful course. Yet grateful as he is for the encouragement of Maecenas (to whom 3.9 is addressed, a difficult poem on his poetic ideals), he has in no sense espoused the ideals of Augustus. Indeed 3.4, which opens 'the god Caesar is planning a war against the rich Indians', is thoroughly ironic in tone, making fun of Augustus's military pretensions and asserting, none too guardedly, that greed and ambition are the causes of war. Yet there is a respectability, a sobriety, about Book 3 which is not far far from the mood of the *Aeneid*.

The sadness is that Propertius never discovered a serious subject worthy of his talents or of his technique. The fact that his final book of elegies contains only half the number of poems in each of the earlier books and that it appeared after a lapse of at least five years is indicative in itself. So are the contents. Two of the poems (4.6, celebrating a four-year period of Augustus's reign, and 4.11, a lament for Augustus's step-daughter Cornelia) are blatantly official pieces. The poet's attempt to be Callimachean – 4.10 (the history of the temple of Jupiter Feretrius, a site of some contemporary topicality) or 4.2 (the statue of Vertumnus) – fails because Propertius, unlike Ovid in his *Fasti*, has no distinctive angle from which to write about them and lacks the humour and variety to make antiquarian matters interesting. Yet when he writes to Cynthia, all the old flair combined with new subtlety returns. 4.7 is a tragic elegy, based on a haunting episode of the *Iliad*. The dead Cynthia reproaches Propertius for forgetting her and reasserts her power over him. It is immediately followed by a comic poem in which Cynthia plays the role of vengeful Odysseus and Propertius that of an unfaithful Penelope, but the scene is a riotous festival in present-day Lanuvium. It is a poem full of surprises and wit.

TIBULLUS

Propertius never successfully adapted to the new spirit of the age. Another contemporary, Albius Tibullus, combined the pastoral quietism of Virgil's *Eclogues* with the anti-political eroticism of Propertius, but Tibullus's elegies possess a peculiar serenity and confidence which are very much in harmony with the sense of relief that followed the Battle of Actium. Tibullus may have been older than Propertius. He was probably born about 55 B.C., from a humbler but similar background to Propertius's, a country family in Latium. He tells us very little about himself in his poetry, and other sources tell us even less, but it is clear that, like Propertius, he renounced political or military ambitions and devoted himself to the life of poetry and the pleasures of town and country. His dislike of war is actively conveyed in a poem from his first book (1.10):

Who first introduced the terrible sword?
  What a brute he was, truly a brute-steel-hearted man!

From then on murder was hereditary in man, and war was born,
The shorter way was opened to the terror of death.

(tr. Philip Dunlop)

Unlike Virgil and Propertius he was encouraged not by
Maecenas or Horace but by one of Augustus's oldest associates, M. Valerius Messalla Corvinus. Messalla had fought
on the Republican side at Philippi but was one of the first to
join Octavian (Augustus), fighting with distinction in the
30s and being consul with him in 31 B.C., the year of the
Battle of Actium. He continued his career of service until an
old age: as late as 11 B.C. he was put in charge of Rome's
water supply. Messalla gathered a group of poets and artists
round him, some of whose work has been preserved in the
manuscripts which contain Tibullus's elegies.

Tibullus's output is very slight – a mere sixteen elegies. The
first book, containing ten, was probably published in 27 B.C.,
the second, perhaps posthumously, in 19 or 18 B.C. More even
than the poems of Propertius they are intended to be heard
and enjoyed by connoisseurs, at the readings or dinner-
parties which were the normal feature of social life (p. 13).
In the main they concern his love for Delia and (what should
no longer surprise us in such a milieu) a boy, Marathus. Both
were no doubt actual people (Apuleius claimed that Delia's
real name was Plania). Delia certainly is portrayed as a free
Roman woman and Tibullus envisages his relationship with
her as an enduring union. It was not a formal marriage (by
convention, passionate love was outside marriage, and Delia
already has a 'husband'), but it was certainly not a mere
affair. Promiscuity is roundly condemned.

And yet avoid promiscuousness through trust, not the stern grip of
 fear.   (1.6.75)

Constancy is seen as making for a dependable happiness and
for security in old age:

The girl who was true to nobody, when overwhelmed by age,
In her decrepitude shall draw with shaking hand the twisted
strands.   (1.6. 77–8; tr. Philip Dunlop)

In fact Roman law recognized cohabitation as a valid legal
bond after the lapse of a few years, so that Tibullus's dreams
for a lasting relationship were not all that far away from
Augustus's attempt to restore family life.

But he is also a deeply religious poet. His religion is
essentially the religion of the country, that pervasive Roman
belief that all processes of nature are in the control of supernatural powers whose co-operation can be won by the due
performance of traditional rituals – vows, prayers and
sacrifices. Tibullus's poem commemorating Messalla's Aqui-
tanian triumph in 27 B.C. opens with one of the finest descriptions of a festival in Latin.

All present, keep holy silence; we cleanse the fields and the harvest,
To re-enact the ceremony our fathers handed down.
Come, Bacchus, and down from your horns let there be dangled
Sweet grapes, and, Ceres, bind your forehead with ears.
Let there be rest for the ground this holy morning, rest too for the
ploughman;
Let the hard labour stop, and hang up the share.
Untie the traces from the yokes: the bullocks must now stand idle
By full mangers, with garlands on their heads.
All work that is done be for the god; let none of the women
Dare to lay her spinner's hand on her portion of wool.
You too must not be near us, must now draw away from the altar,
You, to whom Venus brought her joys last night.
Gods love what is pure and devoted: come then with clean clothing
And take the spring water up in clean-washed hands.
See how the dedicated lamb goes to the resplendent altars,
And the white-robed company, hair tied behind with olive-sprigs.
Gods of the land, we purify the fields, we purify the farmers;
Drive evil away from our borders, O you gods,

That the crop shall not mock the harvest with cheating grasses,
    Nor the loping wolves terrify the slower lamb.
Then shall the farmer, face shining, and confident in full furrows
    Pile up the broad logs on the glowing fire,
And the slave-born children, good sign of a well-filled settler,
    Will play in gangs and build lath-shelters by the fire.
I pray for things that shall be – look there at the good omens in the
    entrails;
    See how the filament proclaims the gods are mild.
                                    (2.1.2–26; tr. Philip Dunlop)

So in his first poem, he prays for the satisfaction of a country
life and promises that if his prayers are heard he will pay his
vows:

Never, my hopes, desert me, but always offer heaped-up harvest,
    And supply the rich must in brimming vats –
Because I am respectful of every lone tree-trunk in the ploughland
    That holds a wreath of flowers, and every old cross-roads stone;
And whatever the harvest that each new season produces,
    The first-fruits are laid up for the farmer-god.
                                        (tr. Philip Dunlop)

Such piety would also appeal to Augustus. And yet Tibullus
is not a true countryman. Although he came from the country
and, like his patron and others of his class, spent much time in
country villas, there is an air of unreality about the scenes he
paints:

I'll be a real farmer and sow the soft-stemmed vines in their season,
    And stout fruit-trees with a practised hand.   (1.1.7–8)

One doubts it. Tibullus is at home with the social side of
country life, the parties and entertainment and outdoor
sports. This is a townsman's countryside which serves as an
alternative to the real world of practical politics and hard,
unremitting business. But his escapism depends entirely on
the peace which Augustus had brought about (the Pax

Augusta): it would have been inconceivable a generation earlier.

The charm of his poetry lies not in its force or its wit but in its subtlety. There are all the mechanics and apparatus of Propertius: the stock situations – locked-out lovers, secret messages, reproaches, the beloved on the sick-bed and so on – and, to a lesser extent, the rhetorical elaborations – mythological parallels, comparisons and contrasts – are employed, but there is no straightforward theme or story in an elegy. Tibullus is perpetually shifting the subject and the argument, so that he presents not a coherent episode but a kaleidoscopic effect of images. 1.2. opens with a motif familiar from Alcaeus and Anacreon:

> Strengthen the wine, drown these fresh agonies.

Delia is being kept under lock and key and we are to imagine Tibullus at home, telling his slave to bring more wine for him to drown his sorrows. He curses the door-keeper and makes prayers to the door. But the illusion is not followed through. At line 15 he apostrophizes Delia and tells her to invoke Venus's well-known skill in aiding lovers' escapes and deception. Equally suddenly, at line 25, he switches to the theme that lovers have a charmed life and that he can roam safe at large and even penetrate her house undetected. This idea leads on to a conventional account of the witch's magic art (Medea's herbs etc.), which Delia is supposed to employ to guard her lover. Yet why should he trust Delia's powers, because she claimed she could free his heart from love, but his prayer was only that she should love too? Another abrupt transition leads to a dramatic contrast between the ambitious soldier, greedy for glory and gain, and the unwarlike Tibullus, who will outdo the soldier's hardships:

> If but with Delia I may yoke my pair ...
> Softly I'll sleep even on the naked ground.

Has he gone too far? Has he blasphemed Venus?

> I've seen a man who mocked young love's distress
> Bowing, when old, to Venus' stern duress.

The poem ends with a prayer to Venus.

> Venus, be kind; to you my heart is bound;
> Why burn in rage the fruits from your own ground?

These transitions correspond to natural modes of thinking. They require a different appreciation from a clear-cut narrative but they are singularly effective. Tibullus is the most accessible of all the Augustan poets, because what he writes is very much the product of a single personality.

HORACE

The three poets so far considered have much in common, although their output differs greatly, in quantity, quality and variety. Horace (Q. Horatius Flaccus), however, who knew them (he refers in his poetry to all three) and was a protégé of Maecenas, is in a slightly different category. In the first place he was the son of a freedman and, therefore, did not belong to the same social class as the others. True, his father had given him the best possible education and he had fought on the side of Brutus and Cassius at Philippi, but he did not have the prospect of a real political career to espouse or to renounce. The summit of his ambition was a minor clerical post in the Treasury, given him by Octavian in 39 B.C., and a small Sabine farm, donated by Maecenas in 34 B.C., which secured him independence and an adequate competence. Secondly, his active and creative life spanned a longer period than any of the others – from the earliest epodes and satires of the 30s to the last book of odes in 13 or 12 B.C. Finally, although he does not aspire to the great heights of epic, his range is extraordinarily diverse – epodes, satires, odes and epistles.

Satire was a peculiarly Roman genre. The Latin word *satura* meant a 'medley' and had nothing originally to do with what we call 'satire' or 'satirical' (which is a purely derivative meaning): still less with the wanton monsters called satyrs (see p. 191). It was a medley or hotchpotch of poems in various metres on a variety of subjects of topical interest. Ennius and his son-in-law Pacuvius are said to have been the earliest writers of satire, but nothing of their work remains to enable us to form any picture of it. The man who gave it character and substance was a friend of Scipio Aemilianus, C. Lucilius. Lucilius, a wealthy knight from Suessa Aurunca in Latium, wrote prolifically between 133 B.C. and his death in 102 B.C. on a wide spread of topics – travel, politics, gastronomy, philosophy, sex – but his principal topic was the shortcomings of his political enemies, on whom he heaped, with a ribald gusto, every kind of scorn and ridicule. As he developed, he abandoned other metres, such as the trochaic, in favour of a loose, powerful hexameter which had become established as the appropriate metre of the genre. There was no direct Greek model for satire. Lucilius certainly owed much to the uninhibited outspokenness of Aristophanes and to the popular writings (diatribes) of Greek philosophers, but the style and the content were very much his own, as the surviving fragments show. Their hall-mark is their dramatic and conversational tone.

At first sight it might seem strange that Horace should have chosen such a *public* medium for his earliest compositions. He was always painfully conscious of his social position and his lack of political ambition.

Now I revert to myself, a freedman's son, carped at by everyone because I'm a freedman's son,

he says in *Sat.* 1.6.45, and he goes on to recall his first interview with Maecenas.

The excellent Virgil previously told you what I was; then Varius did the same. When I came before you I gulped out a few words – for shyness struck me dumb and prevented me from saying more. I didn't make out that I had a distinguished father or that I rode round my estates on a Tarentine nag.

Yet Horace had something serious that demanded to be said. He had seen life and thought deeply about it. He became an Epicurean because he valued human happiness, and, although in no sense a strict or professional philosopher, he remained one all his life. His concern was to try to bring home to people the follies and the vices of the age. So he adapted the Lucilian satire from a personal weapon of attack to an informal, indirect way of moralizing, so much so that his satires are often named *sermones* 'conversations'. Unlike Lucilius, Horace never attacks living people, only trends or movements, and he attacks dead people only as representative of common faults or vices. He tempers Lucilius's violent verbosity by creating a rich style which moves from colloquialism to parody and allusion. Above all he avoids any appearance of systematic argument and slides from topic to topic with a half-deprecating inconsequence. At the same time he commands attention by his subtle reworking of Greek themes and ideas, just as Propertius created an elegy out of an epigram.

The first satire of Book 1 (which consists of ten pieces written between 39 and 35 B.C.) deals with two different faults – job-dissatisfaction and envious greed for money. It opens disarmingly:

How is it, Maecenas, that no one is content with his own way of life?

and goes on to give examples, familiar from many Greek writers, of the lawyer who yearns for the country life and of the farmer who yearns for the bright lights of the city. But the theme imperceptibly switches to acquisitiveness, with examples of how money is wrongly thought to bring prestige and attention. Throughout the tone is anecdotal and conversational. Horace never sermonizes, but the subjects which he selected were both ones that had been regularly and conventionally treated by Greek authors from the fifth century onwards and also ones which were all too relevant to his own day – the dissatisfaction with public life and the financial rat-race, highlighted by both Virgil and Propertius in their early writings. But Horace would tackle them only in this discursive way, because he lacked the social standing to make authoritative pronouncements of his own.

Something of his preoccupations at this time can be seen in the range of subjects reflected in Book I. *Sat.* 2 deals with sexual immorality, especially the folly of courting society ladies, who are dangerous prey and hard to get. *Sat.* 3 stresses the importance of forbearance in dealing with the foibles and eccentricities of men, as contrasted with the rigidity of Stoic perfectionism.

> In practice we turn good qualities upside down and love to throw mud at a white fence. If one of our acquaintances is a decent, genuinely unassuming chap, we nickname him 'Slowcoach' or 'Fathead' . . .
> If a friend in a drunken moment . . . feels hungry and snatches up some chicken that has been served to me, shall I like him any the less for that? What would I do if he stole something or betrayed a trust or broke his word of honour?

Sat. 4 and 10 are literary and defensive, justifying Horace's adaptation of Lucilius and indicating the improvements in language, style and tone which he has introduced. To modern tastes Lucilius was too coarse, too personal, too flamboyant and too prolix. 'He was a muddy river from which you would wish some things removed.' *Sat.* 6, deliberately situated in the centre of the book, faces up to the poet's situation as being, on the one hand, a humble man dependent on Maecenas's patronage and, on the other, an independent person with the courage of his own convictions ('I go wherever I like on my own'). Horace claims that because he has had a good, moral education and has been picked out by Maecenas as deserving support, because he is in no position either to desire or to seek public honours, he 'can enjoy life more fully than if my grandfather, father and uncle had all been quaestors'.

The other poems are vignettes of social life: the bore who buttonholes Horace on a walk in Rome and frustrates all attempts at escape (*Sat.* 9), a dramatized anecdote of repartee (7), an amusing tale of a wooden statue of Priapus in the garden of Maecenas accidentally scaring off some old hags bent on witchcraft (8), and the entrancing account of Horace's journey with Maecenas to Brundisium in 38 B.C. for a conference with Mark Antony (5). This latter, perhaps suggested by a Sicilian journey of Lucilius, is one of Horace's most realistic and evocative poems, with all its details – the barge-trip across the mosquito-infested marshes, the ball-games played by Virgil and his friends, while Horace suffered from eye-trouble, the girl who did not keep her midnight assignation, and so on.

Not perhaps a very drastic analysis of Rome's troubles, or a very constructive prescription for their cure. There is no suggestion that a new moral order is going to be initiated, that the civil disorders are at last nearing their end or that Octavian will introduce a new epoch. Yet compared with the strident impotence of Lucretius, Horace's gentler and more home-spun common-sense did spark off a response in his audience. The book was appreciated not only by his patrons (its reward was his Sabine farm) but by a wider audience. It certainly helped to influence Roman attitudes to the blind materialism that had motivated previous generations.

The secret of satire is its easy, offhand immediacy, which is difficult to maintain. Horace attempted a sequel, eight satires published in 30 B.C. Any reader, however, will at once notice a change. The subjects are no longer, in the main, autobiographical, snatches of Horace's own experience, but have a distinctly bookish flavour – discussions of Stoic paradoxes (3, 7: 'all fools are mad' and 'all fools are slaves'), praises of rustic simplicity (2, 6), ridicule of gastronomy (4, 8). The subjects are handled with great lightness and variety. Horace deploys all his skills of allusion, metaphor, humour, anecdote and dialogue. Yet perhaps only *Sat.* 4 is really successful, if rather foreign to modern tastes, for the Romans took their food seriously and wrote elaborately about it. An Epicurean, Catius, gives a disquisition on food and drink which manages to combine the way-out and the ordinary (Mignonettes de Poulet petit Duc and boiled potatoes) and at the same time to show up the bogus Epicurean who mistakes good living for happiness. Catius is wrong both in his ideals and even in the basics of cooking.

I long for the chance to approach those secluded springs and to draw therefrom the rules for a life of blessedness,

he says, travestying Lucretius; but the rules amount to little more than

Remember to serve eggs which are long in shape, for they are superior in flavour to the round, and their whites are whiter.

The essence of satire is to say the truth while making people laugh, the truth not about physics or metaphysics but about the actual day-to-day problems of ordinary folk. About 30 B.C. Horace turned from the composition of satires (and epodes, a trivial genre of artificially vitriolic attacks on individuals, pioneered by Archilochus in the seventh century) to the imitation of the odes of Alcaeus and Sappho. Alcaeus (*c.* 600 B.C.), an aristocrat from the island of Lesbos and a victim of a political revolution which replaced the aristocratic government with a popularist tyranny, wrote a series of intense poems, usually built up of four-line stanzas and intended to be sung to musical accompaniment, on a variety of subjects – war, love, politics, drinking. They are immediate reactions to immediate situations. Alcaeus's contemporary Sappho adopted a similar style and technique, the majority of her poems are more intimate, centred on the emotions of her own circle. The poems had always enjoyed great celebrity in the classical world, and Catullus had experimented with at least one imitation of Sappho in the original metre, so that Horace's claim to have been the first to 'naturalize' the poets of Lesbos is somewhat overstated. Nevertheless his decision to write in their genre was significant, especially in view of the timing (the first three books of the *Odes* were completed and published in 23 B.C.). It reflects something of the change of mood inspired by Actium.

The *Odes* range widely. There are love-poems and party-poems, poems on politics and poems on religion. And Horace employs an extensive variety of metres. Because of the extreme economy and precision of his language, the *Odes* are peculiarly difficult to translate into English, and in recent years they have been criticized as being artificial and 'literary'. What is Horace, a professed Epicurean, doing writing a hymn to Mercury (1.10) or Bacchus (2.19; as R. G. M. Nisbet commented, 'Horace's shouts of "Euhoe" are embarrassing, and though he claims to have seen the god singing in the mountains, posterity has remained incredulous')? Are not all his girls – Lydia, Lalage, Pyrrha and the rest – simply poetical figments inspired by Greek examples? And, when in the first six odes of Book 3 he tackles great patriotic themes of Roman history, is not his commitment to Augustan ideals too simple and too complete to be sincere? Such criticism is misplaced and misdirected. Like Virgil and Propertius, Horace builds a Graeco-Roman construct which he uses to say something personal. To isolate the Greek element or the conventional elements is to destroy the totality of the conception. The Augustan world was a Graeco-Roman world, and Horace and his readers were conscious of living in such a world of the imagination. It is as wrong to ask for precise biographical details about Pyrrha as it is to go to the other extreme and deny 'her' any validity. The eighteenth century understood this: real life does not have to be realistic. In almost all the poems, Horace is talking through a mask about himself, his emotions, beliefs, hopes and fears, but the mask is a sophisticated and complex one.

Nothing shows this better, perhaps, than 1.9, which is modelled on a drinking-song of Alcaeus:

> Look how the snow lies deeply on glittering
> Soracte. White woods groan and protestingly
>   Let fall their branch-loads. Bitter frost has
>   Paralysed rivers: the ice is solid.
>
> Unfreeze the cold! Pile plenty of logs in the
> Fire-place! And you, dear friend Thaliarchus, come,
>   Bring out the Sabine wine-jar four years
>   Old and be generous. Let the good gods
>
> Take care of all else. Later, as soon as they've
> Calmed down this contestation of winds upon
>   Churned seas, the old ash-trees can rest in
>   Peace and the cypresses stand unshaken.
>
> Try not to guess what lies in the future, but
> As Fortune deals days enter them into your
>   Life's book as windfalls, credit items,
>   Gratefully. Now that you're young, and peevish

Grey hairs are still far distant, attend to the
Dance-floor, the heart's sweet business; for now is the
   Right time for midnight assignations,
     Whispers and murmurs in Rome's piazzas

And fields, and soft, low laughter that gives away
The girl who plays love's games in a hiding-place –
   Off comes a ring coaxed down an arm or
     Pulled from a faintly resisting finger.

                      (tr. James Michie)

Thaliarchus (a Greek name) may be as unreal as the Sabine wine (Cockburn '35 port), but the overall picture is not, and nothing could be more convincingly suggested than the winter of old age. This is Epicureanism at its finest – detached, objective and humane.

Horace was a true countryman and his feeling for the countryside is one of the most personal aspects of his poetry, shown sometimes in a turn of phrase (e.g. the boar lurking in its brambled hiding-place) or an observed glimpse (as of Mount Soracte in winter), and sometimes in a complete poem like the spring of Bandusia (3.13).

Throughout the *Odes* one can sense a growing sympathy with the ideals of Augustus. The love-poems have none of the amorality of Ovid, even if they cover the same topics:

What slim youngster, his hair dripping with fragrant oil,
Makes hot love to you now, Pyrrha, ensconced in a
   Snug cave curtained with roses?   (1.5)

The young bloods come round less often now,
Pelting your shutters and making a row
And robbing your beauty sleep. Now the door
Clings lovingly close to the jamb – though, before,
   It used to move on its hinge pretty fast.

            (1.25; tr. James Michie)

Horace knows what it is to be in love but he pities the lover: he does not encourage him. So too the religious poems (whatever Horace's theoretical philosophy may have told him) reveal an awareness of the social value of religion:

> Thunder in heaven confirms our faith – Jove rules there;
> But here on earth Augustus shall be hailed as
>   God also, when he makes
> New subjects of the Briton and the dour
> Parthian.   (3.5)

Belief in the gods and common decency could help to bring back peace:

>   Our fields are rich with Roman
>   Dead and not one lacks graves to speak against our
>   Impious battles.   (2.1; tr. James Michie)

So it is no surprise that Horace should write some overtly political poems. After all, it was in the tradition: Alcaeus had done so. Nothing in them suggested that Horace felt he had to write them or even that he was told to write them. It is true that he displays considerable naivety (the position of the Roman soldiers who went native after being captured by the Parthians in 53 B.C. was both understandable and unimportant, and no Roman politician can ever seriously have debated moving the capital from Italy to Troy) but, as with Livy, this only reflects his lack of practical experience of affairs. What comes across is his positive involvement:

> Only as servant of the gods in heaven
> Can you rule earth. The seed of action is
> Theirs, and the fruit. Slighted, have they not given
> Suffering Italy multiple miseries?

And with it all a note of pessimism:

> Time corrupts all. What has it not made worse?
> Our grandfathers sired feeble children; theirs

Were weaker still – ourselves; and now our curse
Must be to breed even more degenerate heirs.

(3.6; tr. James Michie)

Barely five years before, Livy had written of 'our modern day when we can neither endure our vices nor face the remedies needed to cure them'.

The *Odes* met with a surprisingly lukewarm reception. In a later poem Horace, after reasserting his originality as a Latin lyric poet, asked:

You want to know why the ungrateful reader praises and loves my pieces at home but unjustly criticizes them in public? I am not one to chase after the vote of a fickle public for the pride of a supper or a gift of worn-out clothes. I am not one to court professional critics. Hence these tears. (*Epist.* 1.19.35–41)

He implies that, apart from his own acquaintances, the public was hostile. It is difficult to see why, and Horace offers no enlightenment. Perhaps the medium was too novel, perhaps the language too spare (he was, after all, writing in competition with Virgil, Propertius and Tibullus), perhaps Horace is being disingenuous. The fact remains that he abandoned the ode-form until first he was invited officially by Augustus to compose the *Carmen Saeculare* for the Secular Games of 17 B.C., and then, as a result of his growing recognition as the doyen of Roman poets, was encouraged to complete a fourth book of *Odes* some time after 13 B.C. But Book 4 is very different from the three earlier works. There is no longer the intimacy between the poet and the person he is addressing in the poem. Horace is more detached, more withdrawn. And there is missing, too, the engaging personality of Maecenas, who drops out of the poems, no doubt because of the break in his relationship with Augustus (p. 162). The themes are predominantly serious and political (such as the odes on the victories of Drusus and Tiberius), reflecting the greatness of Augustus's achievement in restoring peace and morality. But the old tone is gone. There is no longer the spontaneous enthusiasm that coloured the years immediately after the Battle of Actium.

At least ten years passed between *Odes* 1–3 and *Odes* 4 and in that period Horace, who was forty-two in 23 B.C., became an old man. It needs to be remembered that the average expectation of life for a Roman was forty-five years, so that it is natural that at that age Horace should turn again to some of the fundamental questions of life – 'what is of benefit to rich and poor alike' (*Epist.* 1.1.24). In order to explore some of these problems, both grave and trivial, he created yet another form – the imaginary letter in verse. As usual he looked to Greek precedents. Plato and Epicurus had used letters as a means of conveying philosophical speculations, and verse-letters in Greek are not uncommon, such as Theocritus's *Idyll* 11 (see p. 117). But the combination was new and unique in Latin. To some extent it was fostered by the enormous success which Cicero's *Correspondence* enjoyed.

The form had the advantages of satires and more. It could be informal and allusive, passing lightly from one train of thought to another. It could be, as Pope was to exploit, indirect, not analysing a topic systematically but hinting at a point or going round it. Above all it could be personal. All Horace's *Epistles* have real addressees who are sharply characterized, like Manlius Torquatus to whom *Epist.* 1.5 is addressed. It is an invitation-poem, and begins:

> If you do not mind reclining at dinner on inexpensive furniture and eating nothing but vegetables on cheap dishes, then about sunset at my house, Torquatus. I shall expect you.

Torquatus came from an old and distinguished family, and Horace goes on to allude to a famous victory which his ancestor had won in 340 B.C. The invitation is to a party in honour of Augustus's birthday; but, although Torquatus is real enough, the invitation is not. Such poems were an old literary convention which recurs in elegists. Horace uses it as a means of repeating some of his favourite beliefs – in the simple life, the futility of money and extravagance, the value of friends.

Book I of the *Epistles*, published in 20 B.C., contains some of Horace's most attractive poetry. It is hard to catch in translation the conversational warmth and the home-spun common-sense which pervade them. So to Tibullus:

> Dear Albius, impartial critic of my *Satires*, what will you be doing in the country at Pedum? Writing something to outdo Cassius? Or strolling quietly among the healthful woods and thinking wise and beautiful thoughts? You were never a body without a soul. The gods gave you beauty, wealth and the art of enjoyment. What more could a nurse pray for her charge than fame and favour, health and wealth, and clean living?
>
> Amid hopes and cares, amid fears and passions, believe that every day that has dawned is your last. Each unexpected extra now will be doubly welcome. As for me, when you want a laugh, you will find me in fine fettle, fat and sleek, a hog from Epicurus' herd.
>
> (*Epist.* 1.4; tr. after H. R. Fairclough)

The letter is full of gentle allusions (e.g. Odysseus's criticism of Antinous that he did not have wits as well as looks in *Odyssey* 17.454) and quiet humour, which Tibullus must have welcomed from an older man; but the point of the epistle is general not particular, not any special dilemmas of Tibullus but the old question of affluence stifling creativity.

More than any of his other works, the *Epistles* give a picture of Horace, his friends, his society and his interests. They have the same intimacy as the writings of Robert Frost or the later Auden. So congenial and flexible did the verse-letter prove that Horace extended its scope to write three much longer epistles (2.2 to Florus, about 19 B.C.; 2.1 to

Augustus, after 15 B.C.; and the so-called *Art of Poetry*, a letter to Piso and his sons, of uncertain date). All of them are concerned with the views of Horace as an old man on literature. What he writes barely reflects the extraordinary contribution which he himself had made to the development of Latin literature. He depends heavily on the traditional theories of Aristotle and his successors, and treats of genres, such as drama, which had long since ceased to play a prominent role at Rome, except in revivals. But in the letter to Augustus he does touch on a theme which was to prove of crucial importance in the next generation – namely the relationship of poetry to government. The poem opens with praise for Augustus's achievement and then switches to an attack on contemporary taste which rates archaic poetry higher than modern. Modern poets should be read, and modern poets should write on real issues such as the ideals of Augustus's government. The poem closes with Horace's elegant and polished refusal to write such a poem himself. The letter to Augustus is, of course, much more delicate and complex than such a bald summary might indicate, but the problem at the heart of it became more urgent the longer the Principate survived.

LIVY

It may seem strange to consider a historian in the company of four great poets but Livy dealt with the same themes as Virgil or Horace and dealt with them in a very similar way. There is much of the poet about him, especially in the early books. And he was acquainted with the same circles, although he seems never to have been intimate with the current literary scene. Various anecdotes connect him with Augustus, and he certainly advised the youthful Claudius in his writing, but a revealing story shows that his recitations of his history were not popular or fashionable. He seems always to have remained the detached provincial, and was criticized for it by a contemporary, Pollio.

Livy was born at Padua, according to ancient sources in 59 B.C. but possibly as early as 64 B.C. We know little about his family background, so we cannot judge whether his evident failure to attend a Greek university and his certain avoidance of a public career were due to humble circumstances or, more probably, personal disinclination. He came to Rome and devoted his life to the composition of a history of Rome from the foundation of the city to the present day. It was a mammoth task which he began in 30 or 29 B.C. and left probably incomplete on his death in A.D. 17 (or A.D. 12). Although only thirty-five books survive, there are summaries of the whole work which show that 142 books in all were published, bringing the story down to 9 B.C.

The date (30/29 B.C.) when Livy began is in itself significant. The Battle of Actium was seen to be a turning-point. Peace was now in prospect and it was possible for a writer to look back over history from a secure base and not feel that he was going to be overwhelmed at any moment by new disorders. 'Augustus Caesar brought peace by land and sea to the world' (1.19.3), and Padua, like Assisi, had been the scene of some bitter episodes in the Civil Wars. Livy's approach was close to Sallust's. His search for an understanding of history assumed that human character was the determinant factor. 'I invite the reader's attention to the consideration of the kind of lives our ancestors lived, of who were the men and what the means by which Rome's power was acquired and expanded.' But whereas Sallust wrote only short monographs concerned with the recent past and approached his subject with all the practical experience of an ex-praetor, Livy was tackling a much broader canvas that reached back beyond records to prehistoric times and he tackled it with a scholarly

detachment which resembled that of the young Virgil or
Propertius. As he himself wrote: 'I shall find antiquity a
rewarding study, if only because, while I am absorbed in it,
I shall be able to turn my eyes from the troubles which for so
long have tormented the modern world' (*Praef.*; tr. Aubrey
de Sélincourt). Elsewhere he said 'when I am writing about
antiquity, my mind somehow is cast in an antique mould'.
Unlike Sallust, again, Livy was not trying to re-create a Greek
historian in Latin. Indeed he is almost unique among Roman
writers in not being directly inspired by a Greek original. He
did, of course, use the great historian Polybius as a major
source for the Carthaginian Wars, and indirectly he owed
much both to other Hellenistic historians and to the classics,
Herodotus and Thucydides; but Livy's knowledge of Greek
language and literature, no doubt as a result of his limited
education, compares unfavourably with that of all his contemporaries. Nor was he interested in research for its own
sake. Sallust had tried to verify the facts about Catiline and
Jugurtha, but Livy was content to take over a narrative at
second hand from an earlier chronicler and reshape it according to his own artistic aim. It rarely crossed his mind that that
narrative might be tendentious and largely fictitious.

Livy's preoccupation with individual personality, in fact,
also provided him with the mechanism to overcome the
scrappy nature of annalistic history. Instead of a barren list of
unconnected events Livy constructs scenes of moral episodes
which are designed to bring out the characters of the leading
figures. Tullus Hostilius, the third king (1.22–31), is fierce
(*ferox*) and the events of his reign are tailored to display that
ferocity. The triumphant Horatius stabs his sister, Mettius
Fufetius is torn apart by two chariots, the population of Alba
Longa is forcibly evicted. Camillus is *pius*, respecting his
duties to gods and men. So the narrative in Book 5 covering
both his capture of the rival city of Veii and his rescue of Rome

from the Gauls revolves round a number of episodes showing piety in action – the winning over of Juno, the protectress of Veii; the draining of the Alban Lake; the exploits of Fabius Dorsuo and L. Albinius in safeguarding religious rites; the self-sacrifice of the aged senators – and culminating in a great speech in which he calls on the Romans never to desert their religious traditions. In the later books, the pattern is the same. The Hannibalic War is told in terms of the persons of Hannibal, Scipio, Flaminius and Fabius Cunctator. And no doubt Livy used the same technique even in writing about modern history. Certainly we can see his interest in the characters of Caesar and Pompey through Lucan's poem on the Civil War, which used Livy as a primary source.

This technique had a further advantage, besides giving unity and shape to the narrative. It helped Livy to bring the tale alive. The climax of almost every moral episode is a short speech or dialogue uttered by the principal characters. It was a device used, for example, by Horace in his *Odes* to highlight the key moment of the story. But ancient literary criticism insisted that where an author composed a speech either in history or in oratory it should fit the character of the speaker. Thucydides was often criticized for the sameness of his speeches. To achieve the right effect Livy deployed the whole range of the Latin language, but the subtlety of his tones is inevitably lost in any translation, however good. Sometimes he sets out to re-create the great rhetorical effects of the orators of his youth, such as Cicero or Hortensius. When we read the speeches of T. Quinctius (3. 67–8), C. Canuleius (4.3–5), Ap. Claudius (5.3–6) or Camillus (5.51–4) we can hear the thundering periods, the political clichés, the emotive vocabulary of the late Republic. For those men were statesmen and that is how statesmen speak. On other occasions Livy favours brief utterances, with colloquial, archaic or poetical language as the situation demands. The coarse impetuosity of Turnus Herdonius is caught in a single vulgar exclamation (1.50.9). Coriolanus's mother addresses him in tragic language with tragic thoughts (2.40.5):

I would know . . . before I accept your kiss, whether I have come to an enemy or to a son, whether I am here as your mother or as a prisoner of war. Have my long life and unhappy old age brought me to this, that I should see you first an exile, then the enemy of your country? Had you the heart to ravage the earth which bore and bred you? When you set foot upon it, did not your anger fall away, however fierce your hatred and lust for revenge? When Rome was before your eyes, did not the thought come to you, 'within those walls is my home, with the gods that watch over it – and my mother and my wife and my children'? Ah, had I never borne a child, Rome would not now be menaced; if I had no son, I could have died free in a free country! But now there is nothing left for me to endure, nothing which can bring to me more pain, and to you a deeper dishonour, than this. I am indeed an unhappy woman – but it will not be for long; think of these others who, if you cannot relent, must hope for nothing but an untimely death or life-long slavery.

(tr. Aubrey de Sélincourt)

The list could be multiplied indefinitely, and it is important to remember, while reading a translation, that to a Roman's ears Livy's characters would have sounded real because each was made to speak in a distinctive and fitting way.

Livy made history comprehensible by reducing it to familiar and recognizable characters, and his literary versatility made the work such a success that it was accepted as a classic within a generation and underwent the fortune of numerous abridgements and anthologies. Yet, for all his detachment, he could not avoid revealing something of his attitude to his own times and his vision of the future. Unfortunately, because the last 100 books are lost, we cannot tell whether there was a significant shift in Livy's views over the years as he came nearer to contemporary events. What we can see, however, is that even in the early books, written in the 20s, there is a marked tension. On the one hand there is a deep pessimism. In the preface he talks of 'the dark dawning of our modern day when we can neither endure our vices nor face the remedies needed to cure them'. Later on he comments: 'Fortunately ... in those days authority, both religious and secular, was still a guide to conduct, and there was as yet no sign of our modern scepticism which interprets solemn compacts, such as are embodied in oath or a law, to suit its own convenience' (3.20.5). Part of this can be put down to a literary convention; Livy was following in the footsteps of Sallust, for whom everything was steadily deteriorating, although Livy saw the cause as the pernicious infection of foreign cultures, while Sallust blamed the disappearance of external threats which had forced the Romans to maintain their moral discipline. But it is more deep-seated than that. Augustus once teased Livy for being a 'Pompeian'. The term meant not so much someone anxious to put the clock back politically and restore the party warfare of the Republic; it meant someone of independent, but essentially nostalgic and unrealistic, views. On the other hand, Livy is proud of Rome, proud of her greatness and achievements and conscious of her mission in the world and he feels that, given the right leadership and attitude, the old virtues could return. As Camillus, rejecting a proposal that Rome should be rebuilt on a different site after its destruction by the Gauls, said:

Not without reason did gods and men choose this spot for the site of our City – the salubrious hills, the river to bring us produce from the inland regions and sea-borne commerce from abroad, the sea itself, near enough for convenience yet not so near as to bring danger from foreign fleets, our situation in the very heart of Italy – all these advantages make it of all places in the world the best for a city destined to grow great.   (5.54; tr. Aubrey de Sélincourt)

Like Virgil, Livy found inspiration in the ancient stories of Rome – in Aeneas, Romulus, Camillus or the Decii – to illumine the present.

This unresolved tension is balanced by another. Livy claims in his preface that history can help you to improve your behaviour by offering you clear precedents to follow or avoid. But if behaviour is dependent on character and character is innate, how can you change your behaviour patterns, particularly if the gods intervene (in so far as they intervene at all) only in the natural processes – disease, war, disaster and the like? The dilemma can be resolved by supposing that you can be educated to act *against* your instinctive character, as Tacitus seems to have believed that Tiberius did (see p. 254); but that is perhaps too sophisticated a solution for Livy, who was not a thinker but a superbly gifted story-teller. Augustus could mount an elaborate campaign to change people's conduct, using every propaganda medium to promote *virtus*, *clementia*, *iustitia* and *pietas*, but Augustus was a realist. It may, rather, be that Livy never (at least so far as can be judged from his surviving work) really adapted to the changed circumstances. He had grown up a confirmed pessimist in the troubles of the 40s and 30s, yet he could not but scent the optimism in the air of the 20s. It is the dilemma of Virgil all over again.

In retrospect, the 20s were a decade almost unparalleled in literary history, and we know the names of many other writers besides the five whom chance (or merit) has enabled to survive. But creativity and curiosity cannot co-exist with absolutism.

7

THE EARLY EMPIRE

AUGUSTUS tried to combine autocratic government with the appearance of Republican forms. He claimed to have restored the Republic. At first he maintained his power by being elected consul annually, but this was patently against Republican tradition, so that from 23 B.C. onwards he was content with the grant of consular and tribunician powers. The tribunician power, as well as conferring personal sacrosanctity, theoretically enabled him to veto any measure and to introduce proposals personally to the Senate and to the people. The consular power, modelled on the power given to ex-consuls when they went to govern a province, was defined as being superior to that of any of his colleagues and valid in any province. In practice, however, it was not Augustus's legal powers that mattered but his authority. And that, as the years went by, grew and grew.

In the early years of his reign we hear of riots and opposition, but gradually, as the survivors of the Civil Wars dropped away, Augustus was left – alone and undisputed. He gradually built up an effective administration – a civil service, run largely by Greeks like Nestor, Pompeius Macer, Theon or Athenaeus, and a cabinet of selected senators who acted as political advisers. The prominence of Greeks in the imperial household reflected not only their superior capabilities but also the fact that they were loyal, having no other allegiance except to the emperor. It also signified the continuing culture of Hellenism. Much was achieved. The empire was fundamentally reorganized, the frontiers were secured and a major attempt was made to put the economy on a sound footing. Augustus undertook massive public works in Rome and throughout the empire. Above all he restored confidence in the national future and in the institutions. The great programme, which he launched, of rebuilding temples and reinvigorating religious ceremonies, like the Secular Games held in 17 B.C., caught the imagination of the people, who uneasily sensed that their past calamities were a direct consequence of their neglect of the gods. He also attempted to regulate behaviour by a series of measures culminating in the Lex Julia *de adulteriis coercendis* of 18 B.C. which made adultery a serious crime.

At the same time, however, Augustus had to endure a succession of bitter personal blows. As we have seen, his favourite nephew, Marcellus, died in 23 B.C. He became estranged from his old friend Maecenas, who died in 8 B.C. His most loyal and effective general, Agrippa, died in 12 B.C. There seemed to be a curse on his family. His stepson, Drusus, a young man of evident charm and ability, died as a result of an accident in 13 B.C. and his two grandsons, Gaius and Lucius Caesar, died in A.D. 2 and 4. His surviving stepson, Tiberius, ultimately to be his successor, retired in dudgeon to Rhodes in 5 B.C. and continued to live there for many years. Not only death soured Augustus's life. His daughter Julia, who had been married to Agrippa and then to Tiberius, openly defied the moral crusade which Augustus was trying to conduct and flaunted her lovers, a young Gracchus and a son of Mark Antony. In 2 B.C. Augustus was forced to banish her to the island of Pandateria, and only eleven years later her daughter, also Julia, suffered the same fate for similar reasons. Her case, however, is particularly relevant, because the poet Ovid was in some way involved in the scandal and himself was banished to the Black Sea.

Ovid (P. Ovidius Naso), the last of the great classical poets, is unique in giving us his own autobiography, in an elegiac poem (*Tristia* 4.10) which he wrote from exile. In it he tells how he and his elder brother were brought up at Sulmo in a prosperous equestrian family. His brother pursued a normal career as an orator, while Ovid himself preferred a more dilettante life:

> But I, a child, the Thespian sweets did savour
> And more and more did win the Muses' favour.
> 'Leave, leave these fruitless studies, son,' oft cried
> My father. 'Homer but a poor man died.'

He was appointed to a minor magistracy. However,

> Both mind and body were unapt for labour
> And vexed ambition I could never favour.
> And still the Muses did entice me still
> To their calm sweets, which e'er had my good will.
>
> (tr. John Gower, *c.* 1645)

He read poetry, he made the acquaintance of Horace and Tibullus and set eyes on the great Virgil, and he began to make a name for himself at Rome as the successor of Tibullus and Propertius.

Ovid, then, closely resembled Tibullus and Propertius in background, career and tastes (he was invited to be the first senator from his part of Italy, Paelignum), but he was a generation younger, born in 43 B.C. and so only a boy at the time of the Battle of Actium. It can, I think, fairly be claimed that had his poetry been written earlier in the reign it would have escaped censure. It is not really any more shocking than Propertius's, although as will become clear, it may be less serious. As it is, Ovid's first work, the *Amores*, which he began writing in the 20s, appeared in 14 or 15 B.C. (a second edition was perhaps issued in 1 B.C.), followed by the *Art of Love* and a poem on cosmetics; and although at the time of his banishment he was, ironically enough, engaged on two substantial and sober works, the *Metamorphoses* and the *Fasti*, it was too late and the damage had been done. Augustus's biographer Suetonius records numerous proofs of Augustus's clemency and considerate behaviour, even the fact that he was unmoved by lampoons about himself, but as his reign went on he tightened the laws on criminal libel and indecency. In A.D. 9, when Ovid and Julia were banished, Augustus was a lonely saddened old man, who used to quote a line of the *Iliad*:

> Ah, never to have married, and childless to have died.

A far cry from the high-spirited and fast young man who shared wild escapades with Mark Antony.

The effect of this change was far-reaching. It greatly inhibited free speech and writers more and more preferred silence or sycophancy. Ovid indeed continued to write prolifically until his death at Tomi in A.D. 18 but his output consists mainly of verse epistles (*Tristia* and the *Letters from Pontus*) commenting on his life in exile and his misfortune.

But the vital thing is to appreciate precisely what it is about the *Amores* that made Ovid more than a latter-day Propertius. A reader coming to the work for the first time might be forgiven for thinking that Ovid had simply exhausted a well-worn seam. Here is the lover, here is his girl-friend Corinna and here all the familiar, stock situations – secret letters, serenades, clandestine assignations at parties, ecstasy and despair and so on. Yet the more one reads, the clearer the impression becomes that this is no passionate exploration of emotion. Ovid is making fun, clever, brilliant fun but fun none the less. Corinna is no real person and, whatever Ovid's own expertise as a lover, the events recorded in the *Amores* are all delicate leg-pulls of events related in Propertius, Tibullus or Catullus, or other lost elegists.

Perhaps this can best be understood by a direct comparison between two poems, Propertius, 2.15 and Ovid, *Amores* 1.5:

What bliss is mine! Oh! Glorious night!
Oh! little bed of great delight!
What talks we had by candle flame!
When it was dowsed what struggles came!
At times she lay with breasts exposed
The while in lusty bouts we closed;
Anon she made me sober down
And sought the shelter of her gown.
When drowsy eyelids downwards slid
She laid her lips on either lid,
And when they opened at her kiss
Said 'Should a lover laze like this?'
How various were the ways we clung!
How long my lips on her lips hung!
Darkness the lover's work impedes;
In love it is the eye that leads.
'Twas seeing Helen, nude, 'tis said,
Arise from Menelaus' bed
That desperate love in Paris bred.
Naked Endymion, they say,
With Phoebus' naked sister lay.
If you persist in lying dressed
My hands shall tear away your vest;
Nay more, if still you anger me,
A bruised arm shall your mother see,
A girl who has a mother been
May blush to have her bosom seen:
Your breasts are firm and you may claim
To wanton with no sense of shame.
The long, long night is drawing near
When never more will dawn appear;
While therefore we are spared by fate
My loving eyes with beauty sate,
And may your favour bind us two
With ties that time can ne'er undo,
Just like the male and female dove
Completely one in mutual love.

Mad passion passes, some suppose;
When it is true no end it knows.
As well could earth the farmer cheat
By growing weeds from grains of wheat;
Or Phoebus drive his dazzling car
With horses black as midnight are;
Or rivers start to run up hills;
Or fish to live in dried up rills;
As I could let my longing stray:
In life, in death, I'm hers alway.
If she should grant me nights like this
A year would seem a life of bliss,
If many such she deigned to give
I in the seventh heaven should live.
Nay, with one night the veriest clod
Would deem himself a demigod.
If all the world were but agreed
To imitate the life I lead
And, heavy after draughts of wine,
Each by a woman's side recline,
No sword a-thirst for blood there'd be,
No battleships upon the sea,
Nor would by Actium's tides be tossed
The bones of Roman sailors lost,
Nor Rome so often beat her breast
By her own victories obsessed,
In mourning for her triumphs won
By Mother Rome o'er Roman son.
Justly forsooth will history praise
The civil discords of these days!
The battles in which I contend
Nor god nor goddess can offend.
Now, Cynthia, while as yet 'tis day
Throw not the fruit of life away.
Not all your kisses are enough;
See how the scattering petals slough
From brows with withering garlands dressed

And in the winecups float at rest.
So, though today so sweet prevails
The fragrance that our love exhales,
Tomorrow's dawn, it well may be,
Will seal the fate of you or me.

(Propertius, 2.15; tr. S. G. Tremenheere)

A SHADY AFTERNOON

A humid day: a shady afternoon:
my limbs fell where the couch sank to embrace me.
The blinds drawn fast – except
one that swayed open, and in poured false light,
light of green forests,
half-light that falters, fades as Phoebus leaves us,
or as Night turns to Dawn:
the kind of light that should hide timid girls –
if they're undressed and hope that no one's near.
Yet look! Here comes Corinna
in her chemise that flutters as she moves:
her hair floats to her shoulders –
in that brave style Semiramis was dressed
to cross the threshold to her wedding bed.
And so was Lais dressed –
that pretty queen who pleased so many men.

I ripped her shift; so very thin it was
it scarcely flawed the beauty under it,
and she fought hard to gather it around her,
to win a foolish battle –
then she gave in – which was her self-betrayal!
Her frail chemise had vanished:
she stood before me more than beautiful.
How could I fail to praise her arms, her shoulders!
And O her waiting breasts
erect for kisses . . . And that fair field below them!
What long and lovely flanks, what girlish thighs!

167

But why say more? All that I saw
was in my arms, was perfect. I took her naked.
And what did we do next? Who does not know?
Worn out, we had a brief, but deep siesta.
O give me many afternoons like this!

(Ovid, *Amores* 1.5; tr. Horace Gregory)

Certain features of Propertius's poem need to be singled out. In the first place it is not a straight, linear narrative of the concise kind that Ovid's is. Secondly, Cynthia (assuming that she is the girl, although in the original text her name is not actually mentioned) is given at least as much importance in the poem as Propertius himself: her reactions and feelings are powerfully conveyed. Thirdly, there is throughout a strong sense of pessimism. It is significant that the mythological examples which Propertius gives of making love in the light are doom-laden. We don't need to be told what happened to Paris and Endymion. By contrast Ovid's examples of Semiramis and Lais are little more than deliberately offensive. And Propertius's poem ends with the poignant image of the dying flower-garland drooping into the abandoned wine. We may be on top of the world today but, who knows? tomorrow may be our last. Ovid, on the other hand, ends with the complacent and banal 'I hope that there will be many days like this'. In other words he has taken Propertius's poem and undercut it, producing a neat and witty episode devoid of any emotion except cynical self-satisfaction. 'What was Propertius making such a fuss about?'

The *Amores*, therefore, is an essentially frivolous collection of poems designed to amuse and shock, and it displays, perhaps for the first time in Latin literature, the use of rhetoric purely for its own sake. With the end of genuine political life, rhetoric became an end in itself rather than a means to persuading an audience to adopt a certain course of action. The point was well put by the historian Tacitus, who wrote a

Dialogue in which one of the speakers, Maternus, explaining the current decline of orators, says:

At Rome too the eloquence of our forefathers owed its development to the same conditions. For although the orators of today have also succeeded in obtaining all the influence that it would be proper to allow them under settled, peaceable, and prosperous political conditions, yet their predecessors in those days of unrest and unrestraint thought they could accomplish more when, in the general ferment and without the strong hand of a single ruler, a speaker's political wisdom was measured by his power of carrying conviction to the unstable populace. (*Dial.* 36)

The effect of this was that the teaching of rhetoric, still by far the most important element in Roman education, became more and more divorced from reality. Encolpius, the leading character of Petronius's *Satyricon*, put his finger on it when he said:

Our professors ... are hag-ridden, ... surely, when they shout 'I got these wounds fighting for your freedom! This eye I lost for you. Give me a hand to lead me to my children. I am hamstrung, my legs can't support me.' We could put up with even this stuff if it were a royal road to eloquence ... I'm sure the reason such young nitwits are produced in our schools is because they have no contact with anything of any use in everyday life. All they get is pirates standing on the beach, dangling manacles, tyrants writing orders for sons to cut off their fathers' heads, oracles advising the sacrifice of three or more virgins during a plague – a mass of sickly sentiments: every word, every move just so much poppycock. (1; tr. J. P. Sullivan)

This unreality is equally confirmed by Juvenal (*Sat.* 7.150 ff.; see p. 248):

Or do you teach declamation? You must possess iron nerves
To sit through a whole large class's attack on 'The Tyrant'. Each boy
Stands up in turn, and delivers by rote what he's just

Learnt at his desk: all gabble off the same
Stale old couplets and catchphrases – bubble-and-squeak
Rehashed without end.   (tr. Peter Green)

And we are fortunate enough to possess some of the works
of one of the most influential of these teachers.

Annaeus Seneca was born about 54 B.C. at Cordoba in
Spain. He made rhetoric his profession, spending some time
at Rome and being one of the first provincials from outside
Italy to make his mark as a writer. This is in itself an interesting social phenomenon: for just as the major Republican
authors came not from Rome but Italy, so in the early Empire
they came from the Romanized provinces like Gaul or Spain,
reflecting the increasing number of natives who were adopting Roman citizenship and taking an active part in the administration of the empire. In addition to Seneca and his
family, especially his second son (p. 202) and his grandson
Lucan (p. 216), one can point to Pomponius Mela, the geographer (p. 110), and Columella (p. 104), both from Spain,
Julius Graecinus from Gaul (p. 104), and M. Manilius, the
poet (p. 112), from Antioch.

In the course of a long life of some ninety years, Seneca
wrote numerous rhetorical works, of which two, the *Con-
troversiae* and the *Suasoriae*, survive in large measure. *Con-
troversiae* were dramatic exercises in forensic skill. An imaginary case was proposed and pupils took sides as accusers,
defenders or advocates. The cases were often as ridiculous and
far-fetched as Petronius and Juvenal suggest. A sick man asks
his slave to give him poison; the slave refuses; in his will he
orders that his slave be crucified; the slave appeals to the
tribunes. A young man, who has fallen into the hands of
pirates, in vain beseeches his father in a letter to ransom him.
The daughter of the pirate chief makes him take an oath to
marry her if he gains his freedom. He swears; she elopes with
him, he returns home and marries her. The marriage of his

son with a wealthy orphan is proposed to the father, who calls upon the son to consent and repudiate the pirate's daughter. The *Suasoriae* were show speeches, again on artificial themes, e.g. the reward of the Regicides, or Cato deliberates whether he should commit suicide. Such speeches became especially popular in the Greek world during the second century, and 'sophists' as the practitioners of the cult called themselves, became among the most celebrated figures of the Empire, as the careers of Herodes Atticus or Aelius Aristides show. But they also had a great vogue in Latin. To succeed in his field a speaker had to dazzle his audience: truth or seriousness was irrelevant:

Our young men, still at the malleable stage of their education, who hang round our public speakers in order to improve themselves, are eager not only to hear but also to take home with them some striking and memorable utterance; they pass it on from mouth to mouth, and often quote it in their home correspondence with country towns and provinces, whether it be the flash of an epigram embodying some conceit in pointed and terse phraseology, or the glamour of some passage of choice poetical beauty. (Tacitus, *Dial.* 20)

Rhetoric, therefore, that quest for verbal brilliance, had been instilled into Ovid from his earliest years. There were plenty of gems in the *Amores*, but it is not as purely a rhetorical work as the *Heroides*, a collection of fifteen letters written in elegiac verse by distraught heroines and completed about 5 B.C. Oenone to Paris or Phyllis to Demophoon are truly artificial themes typical of the classroom, and Ovid handles them with a mixture of ingenuity and epigram. So Phaedra writes to Hippolytus:

I mingled bashful shame with love
 till love surpassèd shame:
Where the words I blushed to speak
 in writing read the same.

Once again Ovid has taken over an idea of Propertius. The model of the *Heroides* is the letter of Arethusa to her husband (Prop., 4.3), but there is a sameness about them which no verbal brilliance can redeem. The most amusing and successful of all Ovid's works is the *Art of Love* (2 B.C.–A.D. 2). The poem is a take-off of the solemn Greek didactic poetry already represented in Latin by Lucretius and Virgil's *Georgics*. Hunting and fowling were favourite subjects for didactic verse but Ovid gives them a nice twist in making girls not animals or birds the object of pursuit. The first two books instruct the young lover how to find and how to win a girl; the third book (evidently an afterthought) gives advice to girls. The mock-pompous note is never far away:

> The several places where choice beauties be
> Thus far hath Thalia sung to thee.
> The fair one which thou most does fancy, how
> To obtain – the top of art – I'll teach thee now.
> Whoe'er you be, your docile minds incline
> And everyone observe my discipline.

And the poem is full of humorous parodies of earlier writing. Hesiod's *Works and Days* is gently mocked.

> He errs that thinks he may at pleasure plough
> Or that the seas at all times ships allow;
> Times are appointed when to sow and reap
> And times when sailors venture on the deep.
> So in your courting be not overlong:
> For love there is a right time and a wrong.
>
> (tr. F. Wolferston)

So too the tragic complaints of Ariadne abandoned on Naxos, 'Alas, what will happen to me?' (a popular theme rhetorically developed at length by Catullus and Virgil), are answered by the unexpected arrival on the scene of Bacchus and his ardent attendants. A passage from Callimachus's learned

Aetia on an obscure and mythical king of Egypt, Busiris, is brought in as a straight-faced illustration that bad girls come to a bad end. Ovid also draws on his earlier *Amores* for many of the conventions of love – letters, maids, parties and so on. But the poem is chiefly memorable for the graphic view it gives of Rome, with the temples, colonnades and great theatres where a man can always be sure of picking up a girl.

> Hither they come to see and to be seen.

Ovid does not actually advocate adultery. Indeed he claims that the poem is not concerned with married women. He also includes a long, possibly over-fulsome, reference to Augustus's naval games of 2 B.C. and to C. Caesar's impending departure on a military expedition to the East. And in a notorious passage he stresses the value of religion to society:

> 'Tis fit there should be gods: then gods there be;
> In wine and incense let us pay their fee.
> Be sure they do not bind themselves in sleep,
> All seeing they; your life then harmless keep.

Yet the tone of the whole poem is utterly, disarmingly cynical and amoral. When Ovid was involved in scandal, it was this poem that Augustus held against him.

Like Propertius, as he grew older Ovid moved to more sedate, or at least superficially more sedate, themes. The major work of the five years leading up to his exile in A.D. 9 was a long mock-epic poem, in fifteen books, relating some 250 stories of people who were transformed from human beings into animals, flowers, springs, mountains and so on. The mere idea of the project staggers the imagination. Both the subject and the scale of the work pose, to our minds at least, the most daunting challenge. But it must be remembered that the subject at least was, once again, one that had been made respectable, indeed interesting, by earlier Greek authors. Metamorphosis is as old as Homer, who wrote finely about

Niobe, and it was a subject which, with its converse, metempsychosis or transmigration of souls, had preoccupied philosophers and poets from classical Greece to Hellenistic times. Latterly there had been limited collections of tales, such as the *Ornithogonia* of Boios, translated into Latin by Aemilius Macer, which dealt with humans who turned into birds (e.g. Philomela); and Parthenius, a Greek who had helped Virgil, is said to have composed a *Metamorphoses*, but we know nothing of its contents. Moreoever it was a subject which obviously exercised a popular appeal, as we can see from pictures and sculptures. In essence it is the taste of a leisured and uncommitted society.

Whatever the attractions of the subject for Ovid (and it afforded him the opportunity of recounting many humorous and risqué anecdotes about the loves of gods and women as well as of culminating in a patriotic outburst on the apotheosis of Julius Caesar as a star), it called for a technical *tour de force* to handle the transitions between so many stories, to provide some overall unity and to keep monotony at bay. Twentieth-century readers, unlike their counterparts in the twelfth to fourteenth centuries, when the *Metamorphoses* was probably the most popular secular work of antiquity, are apt to underestimate Ovid's achievement, although it is significant that a leading modern composer recently attributed his inspiration for a flute sonata to constant rereading of the Penguin translation. For a great achievement it certainly is, but an achievement essentially of rhetoric rather than feeling. If Ovid had had anything of substance to say, technique would have been dispensable. As it was, technique was of the essence, and that Ovid had more than mastered.

Of the three main technical problems facing Ovid, unity was the most difficult and the one not wholly resolved. Apart from the phenomenon of metamorphosis itself there is no single unifying theme, such as the wrath of Achilles or Aeneas's

Italian destiny. There is a certain sweep of history from pre-historic stories, such as Deucalion and Pyrrha, through the heroes of ancient Greece and ancient Rome to the present day, but there is no development and no coherent thread. Yet it is difficult to see the poem as anything other than a species of epic. It certainly has all the hall-marks of epic – catalogues, similes, speeches etc. – and if the subject-matter called for a less elevated style than Virgil's, the use of the hexameter, as in the *Art of Love*, rather than elegiacs, as in the *Amores*, gives the tone. For the hexameter was the metre of didactic and epic poetry.

But Ovid gives the illusion of unity by the sheer ingenuity with which he links story to story. In Book 10 Orpheus consoles himself for the loss of his wife Eurydice by singing of other unhappy loves which ended in metamorphosis, such as Hyacinth or Myrrha. So in Book 4 one of the daughters of Minyas suggests that they while away the night-watches by telling stories and considers four stories which she will *not* tell (the familiar rhetorical device of *praeteritio*) before picking on the exquisite tale of Pyramus and Thisbe. The variety of transition is endless.

Even so, 250 tales of metamorphosis would pall but for Ovid's constant changes of mood and tempo. No two stories are told in the same way. One may be in the grand manner, as Orpheus begins:

Since all things bow before Jove's might, begin my song with Jove, O Muse, my mother;

another in a familiar, almost conversational tone, as Lelex outlines the background to the story of Philemon and Baucis (*Met.* 8.621 ff.):

In the hill-country of Phrygia there is an oak, growing close beside a linden tree, and a low wall surrounds them both. I have seen the spot myself . . .

There is much of the verbal dexterity so apparent in the *Amores* and the *Art of Love* (notably in the account of Echo and Narcissus); there can also be passages of impressive solemnity, especially when Ovid uses the rhetorical device of three clauses building up to a climax but essentially repeating the same point (*tricolon*) – (1) the crops are laid flat, (2) the farmers' prayers are vain and (3) the long year's toil has gone for nothing. Even in the actual description of the transformation itself, Ovid manages to avoid any note of monotony or sameness:

Philemon and Baucis looked after the temple of Jupiter as long as they lived. Then, one day, bowed down with their weight of years, they were standing before the sacred steps, talking of all that had happened there, when Baucis saw Philemon beginning to put forth leaves, and old Philemon saw Baucis growing leafy too. When the tree-tops were already growing over their two faces, they exchanged their last words while they could, and cried simultaneously: 'Goodbye, my dear one!' As they spoke, the bark grew over and concealed their lips. (tr. Mary M. Innes)

It is Ovid's descriptions that stay in the memory, descriptions of people, often impressionistic and mobile, like that of Daphne ('she was graceful to see, as the wind bared her limbs and the gusts stirred her garments, blowing them out behind her. Her hair streamed in the light breeze, and her beauty was enhanced by her flight'), and descriptions of places, sometimes formal and idealized but more often characterized by an Italian's sharp appreciation of nature:

There was a valley, thickly overgrown with pitchpine, and with sharp-needled cypress trees . . . Far in its depths lay a woodland cave, which no hand of man had wrought: but nature by her own devices had imitated art. She had carved a natural arch from the living stone and the soft tufa rocks. On the right hand was a murmuring spring of clear water, spreading out into a wide pool with grassy banks. (*Met.* 3.155 ff.; tr. Mary M. Innes)

The *Metamorphoses* is a rich tapestry, one of the most purely enjoyable works of literature from any civilization and one that matches the culture and complexity of Augustan Rome. At the same time Ovid was working on another project, equally challenging but much more committed in intent – the *Fasti*. Inspired by one of Propertius's attempts to re-create in Latin Callimachus's *Aetia* (see p. 135), he planned an elegiac poem on the Roman calendar, taking the festivals as they occurred day by day and month by month and giving an account of their origins and ceremonies.

Augustus had taken great trouble to resuscitate the practice of Roman religion, but the average Roman, as a result of long years of neglect, had forgotten the significance of the various cults and ceremonies. In a memorable phrase Varro had once gone so far as to write that many gods were actually dying of neglect. The Roman people, therefore, needed to be re-educated, just as Verrius Flaccus had educated the people of Praeneste by setting up an annotated calendar in their market-place (p. 107). The subject had attractive possibilities because there were many quaint and dramatic legends to be told in association with the individual festivals, from the rape of Lucretia to the story of Ceres and Proserpine. It was also a field whose possibilities Propertius had already broached in his search for congenial but serious themes for his art but which he had only tentatively and unsuccessfully explored. Moreoever there is no doubt that Ovid was genuinely intrigued by the obscure oddities of Roman religion. He constantly refers to his own experience. He had asked the priest of Quirinus about the significance of the sacrifice of a dog to Mildew (Robigo); he had drunk of the sacred spring in the grove of Aricia; he had questioned the priestess whether his daughter should marry in May; he had jumped over the three bonfires at the feast of Parilia.

The subject-matter was, therefore, attractive. It enabled him to re-create yet another Greek genre in an original and distinctly Latin form. Callimachus had written a calendar, and his *Aetia* was precisely such a collection of explanations of old rites. It could also be handled with the maximum variety. Each month was to occupy one volume (some 1,000 lines) but the individual festivals could be treated on different scales. Indeed the success of the *Fasti* lies precisely in the avoidance of monotony, by varying the tone and the dimensions of each account. Some are brief, almost perfunctory, some are humorously burlesque (such as Faunus or Anna Perenna), some contain entrancing mythological digressions or exotic oddities (such as the Lemuria), while others strike a grand and solemn note.

Yet the work which we have contains only six books, covering the first six months of the year, and was left incomplete when Ovid was exiled in A.D. 8. Evidently he restarted work on it again towards the end of his life, since our version contains a dedication to the young Germanicus, from whom he seems to have hoped for a pardon. But it was never finished. It may have been published posthumously. Or did Ovid lose interest in it? That is, at first sight, odd. The *Fasti* allowed him plenty of scope for the praise of Augustus and his deeds, and he took his chance in both hands. He reworked such old panegyrical themes as the comparison between the splendour of modern Rome and its primitive origins, already used by Virgil, Propertius and Livy:

> Shall not these slopes give way to halls immense
> And every nation justice seek from thence?
> (1.515–16; tr. L. P. Wilkinson)

He celebrates Augustus's victories as the guarantee of lasting peace, symbolized by the dedication of the Altar of Peace in 13 B.C.:

> Thy braided tresses wreathed with Actian bay,
> Come, gentle Peace, in all the world to stay.
>
> (1.712–13)

He praises Augustus's clemency, bravery, justice, even divinity. But none of it saved him from Augustus's inexorable displeasure. He was banished, never to return. Perhaps his offences hurt Augustus too nearly. The facts are unclear. Perhaps too Augustus, like any reader today, could see through the clever superficiality of Ovid's tributes. Just as Horace's last *Odes* are magnificent but do not ring true, so Ovid's commitment to Augustus's administration springs from necessity, not from conviction. The distance between subject and sovereign has already become too great. Ovid himself summed it up once for all in a phrase that evokes Louis XIV – *res est publica Caesar*, 'Caesar is the state'.

There remained only silence or sycophancy. Ovid's poems from exile, the *Tristia* and *Letters from Pontus*, are the poems of a broken man. They are full of nostalgia, tenderly recalling past occasions in Rome or a youthful grand tour with a friend. They are full of self-pity, dramatizing the horrors of his new surroundings:

> Snow lies, and ere it melt in sun or rain
> Comes Boreas and hardens it again.
>
> (*Trist.* 3.10.13–14)

> In youth I shunned all horrid martial fray,
> Nor ever handled arms except in play;
> Now, middle-aged, a shield and sword I bear,
> And press a helmet on my grizzled hair.
>
> (*Trist.* 4.1.71–4; tr. L. P. Wilkinson)

Above all they are full of sycophancy, pleading with Augustus for a pardon that never came.

It seemed as if originality had died. As Tacitus was to write

179

after the end of Domitian's despotism: 'out of their prime have been blotted fifteen years during which mature men reached old age and old men the edge of decrepitude, and all without opening their lips'. The Principate of Augustus and Tiberius was not as bad as that, but it was dangerous to touch on matters affecting recent history or current policy. There are simply no poets of comparable outspokenness to Propertius or Ovid. After Livy, historians, with one exception, were wary of tackling contemporary affairs and kept to safe topics. Even Livy did not publish his later works in Augustus's lifetime. Two of the more notable historians, little more than names to us, were L. Arruntius (consul in 22 B.C.), who wrote on the Punic Wars, and Fenestella (died in A.D. 19, aged seventy), whose *Annals* dealt with ancient customs and constitutional history. In a later period, probably under Claudius, Q. Curtius Rufus wrote ten books on Alexander the Great, most of which survive. The history is valuable for the information it gives about Alexander and is readable in a 'bookish' way, but it lacks depth or conviction. The rather rhetorical picture painted of Alexander as a tyrant favoured by fortune never suggests that the author had stopped to ask many questions about the Julio-Claudian emperors under whom he lived. Alexander was a safe and fashionable subject. Orators had degenerated to the cultivation of rhetoric for its own sake, as the Elder Seneca's efforts reveal (p. 170). Literature was left to the more prosaic compilers of text-books (p. 111) – a task more in keeping with the utilitarian spirit of the age.

One man who did not choose silence was C. Velleius Paterculus (*c.* 19 B.C.–*c.* A.D. 31). His family, of S. Italian stock, had long enjoyed the patronage and support of the Tiberii Claudii Nerones. He himself served under the future Emperor Tiberius in Germany and Pannonia with sufficient distinction to become praetor in A.D. 15, the first full year of Tiberius's reign. His career, in sharp contrast to some of those that have just been considered (such as Ovid's), exemplified Roman traditions of service, ambition, loyalty and deep national pride. Presumably in his retirement from active military life, he embarked on a summary history of Rome from the foundation down to the present day. Most of the first book is missing, so that we cannot form any clear impression of its character; but the second book contains a valuable account of more recent times, from the late second century down to the accession of Tiberius. Its main emphasis is on the Principate and it is natural that it should give most space to Tiberius, who had served as commander-in-chief during the latter years of Augustus's reign and to whom Velleius himself was obviously personally devoted. He dedicated the work to M. Vinicius, consul in A.D. 30 and son-in-law of Germanicus, Tiberius's nephew.

Velleius was not the first to write a summary history or compendium. The genre had a tradition at Rome going back to the time of Sallust and Nepos. But his was certainly the first that secured a substantial public. This fact is, as will be seen, of cardinal importance, for it is symptomatic of a new movement closely akin to the growth of the text-books, the production of manuals for ready reference (see p. 198). Nor was Velleius's concentration on particular characters, such as Tiberius or Augustus, novel. This had always been the fundamental basis of Roman historiography: Livy had constructed his history round leading individuals. What was new was the abandonment of critical standards. Velleius, as his references show, had certainly read widely and is at pains to impress his knowledge, for instance, of the *Annals* of Hortensius or 'the longer volumes of others about the Civil Wars'. Yet he has no philosophical approach to his subject. Because he was personally committed to the royal house, history is seen as culminating in the achievement of Tiberius. Tacitus's picture of Tiberius was equally distorted in the other direction

(p. 254), but Tacitus was writing 'without passion or prejudice' (*sine ira et studio*) and had formed his impressions, however false, without personal preconception. Velleius is not a good historian because he is not interested in weighing the evidence. It may be too harsh to accuse him of sycophancy, but a passage such as his final judgement of Tiberius makes nauseating reading, even if Tiberius had deserved the compliments.

> With what honours did he send his beloved Germanicus to the provinces beyond the seas! With what effective diplomacy did he force Maroboduus, who had clung, like a serpent to his hole, to his territories, to emerge like a serpent under the spell of his charms (a simile which means no disrespect to Caesar)! With what wonderful swiftness and courage did he repress the formidable war stirred up by Sacrovir! ... What public buildings did he construct in his own name or that of his family! With what pious munificence, exceeding human belief, does he now rear the temple to his father!
>
> (2.129; tr. F. W. Shipley)

Not even Ovid went as far as that, and Ovid did not aspire to being a historian. And it is ironic that, for all his admiration of Tiberius, Velleius probably perished in the downfall of the emperor's chief minister Sejanus in A.D. 31.

8

PRINCIPATE AND PROTEST

THE preceding chapters have suggested certain definite trends. The competitive nature of Roman Republican society put a premium on the ability to speak and write well. The rise of Rome to world-power and the resulting contact with other civilizations, such as the Greeks, the Celts and the Egyptians, encouraged a wide-ranging curiosity which led to an interest in philosophy, history and antiquarianism. These interests were developed in a context of affluence, individualism and, essentially Greek, culture, which naturally promoted the subjective exploration of human emotions. Late Republican Rome was a passionate society that took delight in analysing its passions. Ultimately the competition for individual supremacy in the state brought Rome to anarchy and civil war, and led many of her natural leaders, in politics and the arts, to opt out.

That Rome did not disintegrate was due to the ruthless skill and imagination of one man – Augustus. After the Battle of Actium his contemporaries sensed that a new order had begun – an order under which the old political free-for-all had no place and under which the state not the individual was ultimately important. So in the 20s there was a spontaneous mood of patriotism and seriousness, what may be called *Romanitas*, to be discerned in one way or another in the works of all the surviving writers. Maecenas, and after him Augustus and Tiberius, did all they could to promote this. Augustus's patronage cannot be under-rated. In addition to the great new library on the Palatine which he completed in 27 B.C. and put under the charge of Hyginus (p. 111), he extended his support to every promising writer. It was not just Virgil or Horace who benefited. It must never be forgotten that the authors whose works do survive are only a fraction of those who were writing at the time. Vitruvius (p. 108) or Phaedrus (p. 188) and a score of others were just as willingly encouraged. Some, like Livy, rejected the proffered advances.

Augustus's motives were no doubt not entirely disinterested. We know that he wanted literature to act as a unifying and reforming force at Rome. But we know equally that he had a genuine taste for literature itself. As the years passed, however, and Augustus himself grew older and more lonely, the problem of state patronage became greater. 'The state is Caesar.' Just as, in the interests of public well-being, forensic oratory or legal science were subordinated to the central administration, so writers had either to serve the state, as historians or poets or compilers of useful text-books, or to play safe, by silence or an escapist interest in the remote past. Tacitus summed it up: 'the principate and liberty were incompatible' (*Agricola* 3.1). Free-speaking was by its very nature divisive and anti-social. It was not only Ovid who suffered. The works of T. Labienus and Cassius Severus were publicly burned and Cassius was exiled. Literature under the early Principate was in an exactly analogous plight to literature in the modern Soviet state.

Yet old traditions die hard. Two factors in particular kept literature alive during the first century A.D. – opposition and education – and, although it is obviously hazardous to comprise fifty or more years in a single survey, since the regimes of different emperors varied so markedly and since the world changes so greatly in half a century, nevertheless such an analysis may prove helpful, because it was not the personality of the emperor that mattered but the system. Tiberius (A.D.

14–37) was embittered and vindictive; Caligula (A.D. 37–41) was mad; Claudius (41–54), a cranky scholar and painstaking administrator, was unassertive and invalid; Nero (54–68), in principle a great patron of the arts, became jealous and suspicious; Vespasian (69–74) was a man of action rather than culture; Domitian (81–96) was a ruthless and uncivilized tyrant.

The opposition was essentially reactionary in character. It looked back to the good old days of the Republic, when liberty enabled men to achieve their own position (*dignitas*). It might sometimes be little more than romantic nostalgia of the kind which Livy evidenced. It might sometimes be jealousy or pique on the part of aristocrats who felt that they had been cheated of their inheritance. Most of the revolts against the emperors in the first century were motivated not by democratic ideology but by personal rivalry. Senators in particular were in a great dilemma. If they voiced their real views, they were suspected of treason; if they did not, they were accused of docllity, as is shown by a surviving speech of Claudius complaining that senators simply listened to an official proposition, exclaimed 'Hear, hear' and left the chamber congratulating themselves on an excellent debate. There were some redoubtable figures, like the lawyer Antistius Labeo under Augustus, who refused to be cowed, but what sustained the tradition of opposition was Stoicism. At first sight this is curious. Stoic doctrine recognized kingship as the ideal form of government, but the crucial distinction which Stoicism made (and which is in fact, ultimately, unreal) was between kingship and tyranny. Kingship admits of individual liberty, tyranny does not. Stoicism upheld the basic natural rights of man. As Seneca was to write, 'man is inviolable' (*homo res sacra homini*). It also encouraged martyrdom; a man's duty was to stick to his principles whatever the cost, as Cato did at Utica.

So in the early Empire a number of Stoic senators gained publicity for their obstinate intransigence. The most notable was Thrasea Paetus, consul in A.D. 56, who registered a protest against Nero's government by deliberately abstaining from attending the Senate and compounded the insult by writing a eulogy of Cato and celebrating Brutus's birthday. Paetus was no republican but an old-fashioned individualist who justified his stand by his philosophy. When forced to commit suicide in A.D. 66 on Nero's orders he died with the words 'it is better to die like a free man than degrade myself to no purpose and then perish like a slave'. His example was followed by his son-in-law Helvidius Priscus, whose uncompromising Stoicism (an ancient commentator remarked that 'he behaved as if he lived in a free state') ended in his death at the hands of Vespasian in A.D. 75. Later still Arulenus Rusticus and Herennius Senecio were to suffer the same fate. If Paetus and Priscus were the most celebrated martyrs, it is clear that there were many others, and the first act of most emperors wanting to crack down on any opposition was to suppress the philosophers; that meant primarily the Stoics, as Domitian did with severity in A.D. 93, when Epictetus was one of the victims. The same effect of Stoic conviction can be seen in Seneca (if only fitfully at the end of his life: see p. 206) and, spectacularly, in his nephew Lucan (p. 217).

Opposition, however, was not only philosophical or theoretical, nor was it only the outcome of injured pride. The Empire had brought dramatic changes to Rome. The make-up of the society had altered. We have already noticed the great influx of provincials who made their mark as writers (the Elder Seneca, Columella etc.; see p. 170), which was matched by the increasing number of non-Italians who found their way into government service. The imperial administration in particular employed freedmen and Greeks both because they possessed professional skills and because they had no ulterior loyalties. Under Claudius the government was virtually run by Pallas and Narcissus, both Greeks. Places in the Senate were increasingly occupied by Gauls and Spaniards and even easterners. Indeed, by the end of the century, such were the ravages of civil wars, conspiracies and vendettas that barely half a dozen families could trace their descent from the old aristocracy of the Republic, and by the second century perhaps only the Acilii Glabriones still survived. Rome was becoming a cosmopolitan centre. Seneca, trying to comfort Helvia in her exile, assured her that foreigners in Rome made up more than half of the city's population. Could Augustus have anticipated that within a century a Spaniard, Trajan, would be emperor?

In addition, at an appalling cost of human suffering, Rome entered upon a period of unparalleled opulence and extravagance, which no imperial legislation could inhibit. There is no need to spell it out. Supported by a slave economy and the spoliation of the resources of the known world, Romans were able to indulge their tastes in luxury of every kind – art, architecture, jewellery, dress, perfume, food and wine, music, spectacular entertainments, sex. One has only to look at the splendours of a small suburban town like Herculaneum, destroyed in A.D. 79, to gain an idea of how sumptuous Rome must have been for the rich. Such luxury went hand in hand with the degradation of the poor and under-privileged, the slaves who provided the labour, the gladiators and others who provided the amusement, the peasants who provided the means of existence. Life was cheap and the Romans held it cheap. Yet in a society of that kind, flattery, corruption and graft can bring fortunes to even the most lowly placed, and all the evidence, not just that of satirists, suggests that at every level men used whatever unscrupulous methods they could to improve their lot. If that is the dark side, there was also scope for true service. Loyalty and competence were rewarded in the army, on the land and in business. Men like Velleius or Agricola could make their way to the top in the same way that a hard-working bailiff or centurion could, as countless inscriptions reveal.

The first person to voice this opposition, however covertly, whose works have come down to us is one of the most under-rated of Roman writers. C. Julius Phaedrus (c. 15 B.C.– c. A.D. 50) was by origin a Thracian slave but, after a Roman education, became a freedman of Augustus, who must have detected his promise. He wrote five books of fables, modelled on the traditional fables of Aesop, and it is to him, more than anyone else, that we owe the stories of King Log or the Fox and the Sour Grapes. His fables did not become widely popular in the ancient world (there are very few references or allusions to them) and as a result his surviving work is evidently very incomplete and truncated. All the same, a total of ninety-three fables, written in Latin iambic verse, survive.

A man named Aesop may once have existed, perhaps a Greek slave in Samos in the sixth century; but Aesopic fables, that is, short moralizing tales whose main actors are animals, go back beyond history. They were certainly used by early Greek poets such as Archilochus and Pindar. A collection of them was made around 300 B.C. at Alexandria which was consulted and expanded by later writers and which was the basis of Phaedrus's own adaptations. Romans were, of course, familiar with them. Horace, for instance, was fond of their homely wisdom and introduced the story of the town mouse and the country mouse into his *Epistles*. Phaedrus, however, was a creative and ambitious man. Rather than try his hand at genres, such as satire, which were already well established, he aimed to pioneer a new Greek genre which had not yet been naturalized in Rome. Though he sometimes labours the point of a tale, he writes neat and lucid poems, in an elegant and conversational style, which almost always have real topicality; it is this that gives them an added piquancy. The topicality may be social. He mocks the vices of money-makers (4.20, The Wolf and the Dragon), of corrupt advisers (1.25, The Dogs and the Crocodiles), of drunkards (3.1, The Old Woman and Her Wine-Jar) and so on, vices which were to feature in other satirists as well but which were real enough at the time. The topicality may also be political. Indeed Phaedrus himself says that he was prosecuted by Tiberius's minister Sejanus. We do not know what the outcome was but Phaedrus seems to have continued to publish fables as late as the reign of Caligula (Book 3 is dedicated to Eutychus, a prominent charioteer under Caligula). Quite apart from attacks on informers (a class which is rife in any absolutist state and was particularly so under Tiberius), such as 1.17 (The Sheep, the Dog and the Wolf), and opportunist upstarts (like Sejanus, The Jackdaw in Peacock's Feathers), no reader could fail to detect the political message in King Log (1.2):

In the days when Athens flourished under a democracy, freedom grown rank disturbed the civic calm and licence relaxed the reins of old-time discipline. Then diverse factions formed a common plot and soon a tyrant rose and seized the citadel, Pisistratus. The Athenians now bewailed their dismal state of servitude, not that their ruler was unkind, but any load is hard to bear for those unused to it. When they began to murmur, Aesop told them this little tale:

'The frogs, while enjoying at large the freedom of their marshes, called with loud cries on Jupiter to grant them a king, one who should forcibly restrain their lax morality. The father of the gods laughingly bestowed on them a little piece of timber; he hurled it, and when it fell with sudden splash and noisy dashing of the water it filled the timid tribe with awe. Time passed as it lay there sunk in mud, till one frog chanced to thrust a stealthy head above the pool and, having by reconnaissance learned all about the king, called forth the whole assembly. The frogs, no longer awed, raced through the water to his side. Then the saucy crowd played leap-frog on the plank. With every insult they defiled it, then sent an embassy to Jove to get another king; for, said they, the one he gave them was no good. Thereupon Jupiter sent them a water-snake, who took to snapping them up one by one with cruel teeth. In vain they tried to flee from death; they were too sluggish. Fear even took away their power of speech. On the sly, therefore, they made Mercury their messenger to Jove, beseeching for help in their affliction. Then quoth the Thunderer in reply: "Since you are unwilling to put up with the god you had, you must put up with this evil." Likewise, you citizens of Athens,' said Aesop, 'must bear the evil that you have lest a greater one befall you.'

(*Fab*. 44; tr. B. E. Perry)

It was courageous of a Greek and an ex-slave to write so openly about Augustus and Tiberius, and there can be few more penetrating lines than the couplet:

> Amid a change of government in states
> Poor folk change nothing but their master's name.

(1.15.1–2)

PETRONIUS

A much more important and controversial figure is T. Petronius, who was probably consul in A.D. 61 and almost certainly Nero's 'Master of Elegance' whose death is recorded by Tacitus in A.D. 66:

... He spent his days sleeping, his nights working and enjoying himself. Others achieve fame by energy, Petronius by laziness. Yet he was not, like others who waste their resources, regarded as dissipated or extravagant, but as a refined voluptuary. People liked the apparent freshness of his unconventional and unselfconscious sayings and doings. Nevertheless, as governor of Bithynia and later as consul, he had displayed a capacity for business.

Then, reverting to a vicious or ostensibly vicious way of life, he had been admitted into the small circle of Nero's intimates, as Arbiter of

Taste: to the blasé emperor nothing was smart and elegant unless Petronius had given it his approval ... [Falsely accused by his rival Tigellinus and unable to defend himself before Nero, he decided on suicide.] He severed his own veins. Then, having them bound up again when the fancy took him, he talked with his friends – but not seriously, or so as to gain a name for fortitude. And he listened to them reciting, not discourses about the immortality of the soul or philosophy, but light lyrics and frivolous poems ... He appeared at dinner, and dozed, so that his death, even if compulsory, might look natural ... Petronius wrote out a list of Nero's sensualities – giving names of each male and female bed-fellow and details of every lubricious novelty – and sent it under seal to Nero. Then Petronius broke his signet-ring, to prevent its subsequent employment to incriminate others. (*Annals* 16.17–20; tr. Michael Grant)

It is idle to speculate about Petronius's biography and background. What we have are some fragments and one substantial portion (dealing with a vulgar dinner given by an ex-slave called Trimalchio) from Books 14–16 of a work entitled *Satyricon*. The title means 'the goings-on of satyr-like people' and the plot, so far as it can be reconstructed, certainly bears this out. Basically it is the story told by a young man called Encolpius (= 'embraced'), who has offended the sex-god Priapus and is punished by him with impotence, about his adventures in S. Italy with his boy-friend Giton (= 'neighbour') and his companion Ascyltos (= 'indefatigable'). They undergo a series of adventures (theft, murder, sacrilege and so on), all of which are the staple fare of romantic novels, and which probably culminated in Encolpius's rejection of his unnatural tendencies in favour of more normal heterosexual ones. That, however, is very much a matter of conjecture. What we have to go on is the one substantial section – their presence at Trimalchio's banquet. Various other characters flit across the scene – Agamemnon, a professional rhetorician at Puteoli; Eumolpus, a homosexual poet; Lichas, a ship's captain; and other guests at the banquet such as Habinnas, a mason and local worthy, Echion, a rag-collector, and so on.

The book itself, which must have run to some twenty (or perhaps twenty-four) volumes, was a very loosely constructed farrago of prose and verse through which the plot traced only a very tenuous thread. Such a genre had a long history: indeed, as has been seen (p. 142), satire at Rome was in origin just such a medley, and Varro had apparently written work in this style. It gave the author scope for endless self-indulgence – digressions in the forms of poetical parodies, picaresque (Milesian) anecdotes, songs and so on. One such traditional theme was the dinner-party. Dinner-parties (and their Greek equivalent, drinking-parties or symposia) were the regular occasion for social intercourse in the ancient world. As such it was natural that they should be written about in themselves as well as be used as the setting for other literary essays (as Plato's and Xenophon's *Symposia*). In his second book of *Satires* (2.8), Horace draws an exquisite picture of a dinner-party given by one Nasidienus in honour of Maecenas and others. The piquancy of the satire lies in the fact that everything which Nasidienus gives them is a little too exquisite – pregnant lamprey, wings of hare, male crane, breasts of pigeon and so on, served on maple-wood tables and washed down by the very best vintages of Caecuban and Chian – and a little too proudly explained by the host himself. Horace doubtless had literary precedents (Lucilius seems to have written on the subject) and he was followed by Juvenal, who wrote a much less subtle, much more vitriolic satire on Virro's dinner-party (see p. 243).

Petronius took the topic, but the dinner-party which Encolpius and his friends gate-crashed was very different. The host, Trimalchio, can tell his own story. He wanted his epitaph to be

HERE SLEEPS
GAIUS POMPEIUS TRIMALCHIO
MAECENATIANUS
ELECTED TO THE AUGUSTAN COLLEGE IN HIS ABSENCE
HE COULD HAVE BEEN ON EVERY BOARD IN ROME
BUT HE REFUSED
GOD-FEARING BRAVE AND TRUE
A SELF-MADE MAN
HE LEFT AN ESTATE OF 30,000,000
AND HE NEVER HEARD A PHILOSOPHER

(tr. J. P. Sullivan)

According to his own (rather drunken) account he had made his fortune this way: As the slave-boy of a senator called Pompeius 'I came from Asia as big as this candlestick. In fact, every day I used to measure myself against it, and to get some whiskers round my beak quicker, I used to oil my lips from the lamp. Still, for fourteen years I was the old boy's fancy. And there's nothing wrong if the boss wants it. But I did all right by the old girl too. You know what I mean . . . Well, as heaven will have it, I became boss in the house, and the old boy, you see, couldn't think of anything but me. That's about it – he made me co-heir with the Emperor and I got a senator's fortune. But nobody gets enough, never. I wanted to go into business. Not to make a long story of it, I built five ships, I loaded them with wine – it was absolute gold at the time – and I sent them to Rome. You'd have thought I ordered it – every single ship was wrecked. That's fact, not fable! In one single day Neptune swallowed up thirty million. Do you think I gave up?' He did not give up. He made his wife sell her clothes and jewellery, tried again and made a profit of 10,000,000. As a result he invested it in land and real property. 'I built this house. As you know, it was still a shack, now it's a shrine. It has four dining-rooms, twenty bedrooms, two marble colonnades, a row of boxrooms up above, a bedroom where I sleep myself, a nest for this viper [his wife], and a really good lodge for the porter. The guest apartment takes a hundred guests.' As for his estates, each day a special messenger read the latest news.

26 July: Births on the estate at Cumae: male 30, female 40. Wheat threshed and stored: 500,000 pecks. Oxen broken in: 500.

On the same date: the slave Mithradates crucified for insulting the holy spirit that watches over our dear Gaius.

On the same date: Deposits to the strong-room ... 10,000,000 sesterces.

What distinguishes Trimalchio's dinner-party is its extravagance, vulgarity and tastelessness. The food is a mixture of the ordinary and the exotic, all ostentatiously served up. 'Spartan hounds began dashing everywhere, even round the table. Behind them came a great dish and on it lay a wild boar of the largest possible size ... From its tusks dangled two baskets woven from palm leaves, one full of fresh Syrian dates, the other of dried Theban dates.' The wine is bogus ('Falernian, Consul Opimius, One Hundred Years Old'). The implements are vulgar and brash: 'Now I'm very keen on silver. I have some three-gallon bumpers ... showing how Cassandra killed her sons [in fact she did not have any], and the boys are lying there dead – very lifelike. I have a bowl my patron left – with Daedalus shutting Niobe in the Trojan Horse [neither Daedalus nor Niobe had any connection with the Trojan Horse]. What's more, I have the fights of Hermeros and Petraites [current gladiators] on some cups – all good and heavy.' The company is low-class – rag-collectors, masons, bad rhetoricians and the like. The relays of slaves are dirty, noisy and impudent. And the whole proceedings degenerate into a noisy, drunken, bawdy brawl culminating in the final scene where Trimalchio rehearses his own funeral only to be disturbed by the local fire-brigade, who have mistaken the row for a fire. In the confusion Encolpius and his friends escape.

The dinner-party has provoked lively controversy, indeed some of the finer flights of Freudian lunacy. At first sight it is natural to see it as a bitter attack on the ignorance ('Diomede and Ganymede were the two brothers. Their sister was Helen. Agamemnon carried her off and offered a hind to Diana in her place. So now Homer is describing how the Trojans and Tarentines fought each other. Agamemnon, of course, won and married off his daughter Iphigenia to Achilles. This drove Ajax insane . . .') and vulgarity of the *nouveaux riches*. Some of Trimalchio's traits, such as his preoccupation with his digestion and his fondness for playing dead, can be precisely paralleled. But it is not as easy as that. The story is told by Encolpius who himself comes across as equally ludicrous and contemptible. Like his two companions, he talks with the glib artificiality of a declaimer, exuding 'spurious emotions and false drama'. Just when a satirical blow is about to be struck home, it misfires because the narrator himself is satirized. Critics therefore have claimed the work is not so much a protest against Petronius's time as a creative novel, autonomous in its own right. Yet in all its detailed incidents it is perpetually parodying the situations of Greek novels. With so little surviving, a final judgement is impossible, but when one considers Petronius's own career one sees a man who was capable of laughing at Nero and at the same time laughing at himself for so doing. Such is surely the truly pessimistic satirist. And the character of the *Satyricon* is much the same, fundamentally negative and bankrupt but wickedly observant of life and manners.

EDUCATION

The second main factor that kept literature alive was education, with its conservative bias towards the acquisition of the art of fine expression. The vitality of rhetorical education can be judged not only from its influence on writers, which will be considered later, but also by the spate of technical or semi-technical monographs which it inspired. As any reader of the papers poured out by the Schools Council of Great Britain will know, education is a productive industry in itself. We hear of many writers on rhetoric during the period. Some of them, like the pupils of Apollodorus and Theodorus, are mere names, or not even that; others are more substantial, like the Elder Pliny, who composed a practical manual in three volumes entitled *Students*. From this plethora of rhetorical discussions, two of particular interest survive, both of which reflect the conditions of the latter part of the century. The first is a professional handbook in twelve books by Quintilian. M. Fabius Quintilianus (*c.* A.D. 33–*c.* 100) came from Calagurris in Spain. He made his mark at Rome as a young man and later became a distinguished teacher of oratory, being the first rhetorician to be paid an official salary and numbering most of the up-and-coming young men, like the Younger Pliny, among his pupils. By nature primarily an academic and theoretician, although he practised for many years as an advocate, he had no qualms about accepting the patronage of Domitian, whose wayward tyranny drove others to exile or silence. Indeed he became tutor to Domitian's heirs. From A.D. 88 onwards he devoted himself to the composition of his *Oratorical Institutions*, which deals in detail with the technical education of an orator. It updates Cicero's writings and brings them more into line with the tastes and needs of the later first century. It covers an enormous range, from minute specifications about the planning, division and construction of orations, the figures of speech, ornaments and rhythms that should be employed, to the finer points of physical delivery. Incidentally it contains much of interest about the comparative criticism of Greek and Latin writers and about the ideal of the perfect orator.

For the modern reader, however, a much more attractive work is the *Dialogue* written by Tacitus about A.D. 105 but set at a dramatic date of A.D. 75. It is a dialogue on the alleged decline of oratory between Curiatius Maternus, a poet, Marcus Aper, an advocate, Julius Secundus, a historian, and Vipstanus Messalla, a Roman aristocrat. Although, as might be expected, Tacitus reaches no firm conclusions, he does bring out very clearly the awareness that genuine eloquence (that is, eloquence which is concerned with saying something and not merely with saying it well) is incompatible with an absolutist state. 'Eloquence is the child of Licence' and 'the emperor's discipline had calmed eloquence as it had everything else' (38.4). To demonstrate this he allows Messalla to give a fascinating synopsis of the merits and demerits of orators of earlier days. A work of outstanding charm, written in an easy, flowing style very different from the cryptic concision of Tacitus's historical books, the *Dialogue* is the best possible introduction to the intellectual and educational climate of the early Empire, when men were taught to speak but had nothing to say.

As things are, since it is impossible for anyone to enjoy at once great renown and great repose, let everyone make the most of the blessings his own age affords.

Such a well-ordered education depended upon convenient short-cuts. What was needed was not thorough text-books which went into the subject in depth but potted aids that provided the answers. An orator required amongst other things a store of historical examples which he could draw upon to illustrate some particular point; he required a stock of epigrams which would put an end to an argument (see p. 168). He required convenient logical syllogisms. Above all, who could be expected to work his way through the great volume of Greek and Latin literature? As Velleius had already shown, the public wanted summaries and compendia that were easy to consult.

These needs were quickly met. Publilius Syrus, who had come to Rome as a slave from Antioch in the time of Julius Caesar and made a name for himself as an author of mimes, had a gift for composing epigrammatic sayings and apophthegms. This was recognized by the Elder Seneca, to whom, probably, is due the surviving collection of one-line maxims. In keeping with the new demand for ready reference, they are arranged alphabetically, e.g.:

F   When *fortune* flatters, she comes to ensnare ...
M   The *master* is valet when he fears those he orders.

Hardly inspiring or original, but certainly useful for a would-be speaker. More blatantly practical is the *Memorable Deeds and Sayings* compiled by Valerius Maximus, a work which enjoyed the success of no fewer than two epitomes. Valerius's background is unknown but he was a contemporary of Velleius and as devoted an admirer of Tiberius, to whom his nine volumes are dedicated, although Valerius had the hindsight to disclaim any connection with Sejanus, whom he roundly denounces. Valerius's purpose is simple. He ransacks the historians, especially Livy, Varro and Cicero and the Greek historians, for historical anecdotes, Roman and foreign. These are set out in a neat, well-written form, which could immediately be quarried by an orator seeking for some appropriate precedent to illustrate his case. Valerius preserves much that is interesting and valuable, but he is a classic case of an author who has sold his soul to the sycophancy of his times and to the quick rewards that can be gained by writing a 'pot-boiler'.

> And so, Caesar, the sole salvation of our country, I invoke you at the beginning of this work. Gods and men have agreed that you should have dominion over land and sea. It is thanks to your divine providence that the virtues, which I am to speak of, are championed and the vices most vigorously punished. (1 *Praef.*)

The first century has left many traces of similar works – an anthology of Livy's speeches in the time of Caligula and an abridged version of the whole work by the time of Martial. One that survives is the *Epitome* by P. Annius Florus, a book which used to be much read in English schools as a source of both Roman history and Latinity. Florus, an African born about A.D. 70, studied at Rome and then lived in Spain, where he produced his *Epitome*. It is a major source for the lost works of Livy dealing with late Republican affairs, but Florus also utilized Sallust and Cicero.

One man, however, unites the two worlds of the serious text-book and the convenient manual, and his career is a perfect example of the force of education stimulating the itch to write. Besides, there are few more attractive figures in the ancient world than Pliny the Elder (C. Plinius Secundus; *c.* A.D. 23–A.D. 79).

> Thank you [wrote his nephew to the historian Tacitus] for asking me to send you a description of my uncle's death so that you can leave an accurate account of it for posterity ... It is true that he perished in a catastrophe which destroyed the loveliest regions of the earth ... and one so memorable that it is likely to make his name live for ever ... The fortunate man, in my opinion, is he to whom the gods have granted the power either to do something which is worth recording or to write what is worth reading, and most fortunate of all is the man who can do both. Such a man was my uncle, as his own books and yours will prove.
>
> (Pliny the Younger, *Letters* 6.16.1–33; tr. Betty Radice)

Pliny's background was not unlike Catullus's; they both came from well-to-do provincial families in northern Italy. Pliny went early to Rome and, in the conventional way, pursued a legal and military career, seeing service in Germany over a period of years beginning in A.D. 47 and then holding, with exemplary efficiency, administrative posts in Gaul, Africa and Spain. Ultimately he was admiral at Misenum when he met his death investigating the eruption of Vesuvius. What was remarkable about him was his capacity for work and his eye for detail. He reproached his nephew for walking when he could have been working; at all hours he had a slave to read to him or take dictation; and, by his account, he was able to make do with four or five hours' sleep at night. In addition to the *Natural History*, thirty-one books of which survive, he had written, as could have been anticipated in his times, text-books on rhetoric (p. 196) and javelin-throwing, twenty books on the history of the German Wars, which were used by Tacitus, and a life of his patron, Pomponius Secundus. He bequeathed to his nephew 160 volumes of handwritten notes, which, the latter discovered, amounted to twice that size because they were so compressed. Nothing escaped his notice. He could recall the dress worn by Claudius's wife Agrippina, the colour of five emperors' eyes or the ship that brought the Egyptian obelisk to Rome. Every page contains some curiosity culled from reading or observation.

The *Natural History* is a vast encyclopedia, the logical succession to all the pioneering researches of Varro. The structure is, to us, rather shapeless, and that cannot be put down to the fact that it was published posthumously. After an introductory volume, Pliny deals with the universe (Book 2) and physical geography (3–6). He then turns to anthropology (7), zoology (8–11, land, sea, birds, insects) and botany (12–19). After that he discusses the medical products from botany (20–27), zoology (28–32) and mineralogy

(33–8, digressing on the fine arts). He estimated that he had assembled 20,000 facts from 100 authors. 'There is no book so bad that one cannot glean something of value from it.'

Pliny was a genuine scientist, fascinated by facts for their own sake. Yet in his desire to synthesize all his knowledge he was bringing to a logical conclusion the fashion for anti-quarian research, for text-books and for convenient reference books which has already been noted. Although he makes the customary noises about decadence and luxury, he very con-sciously avoids asking basic questions about politics or society or morality. He documents the world as he saw it without passing any searching judgement on it. He accepted the limitations of the Principate and found his own outlet for expression and his own satisfaction in its service.

9

WORDS AND TRUTH

THE pressures on intelligent men under the Julio-Claudian emperors and their immediate successors were intense. On the one hand the acquired art of saying *anything* well entailed equally a disinclination to go into the true rights and wrongs of anything. Even when a writer had a cause which he seriously championed, his efficiency was lessened precisely because the cause became smothered in mere words. This is evident in Lucan. On the other hand political realities equally encouraged men not to face up to actual facts and to salve their consciences by taking refuge in eloquent generalities. This, which was so tragically to come to pass in Nazi Germany, is brought out by the Younger Seneca and, in a very different way, by Persius.

Seneca is, by any standards, one of the great figures of Roman literature. His influence in many fields – on the development of Renaissance drama, of the essay, of Christian philosophy and of the English language in the sixteenth century – is incalculable. Yet the more one studies his life and work, the more his practice seems to fail to live up to his ideals. In the end moral cowardice and verbal dexterity win. This is not to judge him harshly. Few, even with his talents and opportunities, could have achieved so much in the peculiar climate of his time.

The details of his life are reasonably secure. He was born in Spain about 4 B.C., the second son of the rhetorician Seneca (p. 170). His elder brother, adopted by Junius Gallio, became the governor of Achaea in A.D. 51–2 who 'cared about none of these things' (Acts 18.11–17); his younger brother was the father of the poet Lucan. Educated by the best teachers in Rome, he early developed great facility in writing and speaking, and, what was to be his ruling passion in life, he fell in love with philosophy, that is, with Stoicism. Philosophy was for him something almost mystical and it exercised great influence on his personal life; he was abstemious, austere, devout and studious throughout his career. His family already had powerful connections at Rome, so that the foundations of a political career were laid for him by obtaining the quaestorship about A.D. 31; but during the later years of Tiberius's reign and under that of Caligula he preferred to opt for the safer, dilettante paths of literature and research, as so many others did. Nor did he fare any better under Claudius. For some not wholly understood reason he was required to live in Corsica from A.D. 41 until, in 49, on the death of Messalina and the ascendancy of Agrippa, he was brought back to court to become praetor and tutor of the young Nero. During this period of exile he wrote enough to secure for himself a very considerable literary reputation, but it was his influence over Nero that was the most important single fact in his life. After Nero succeeded in A.D. 54, Seneca and the army commander Burrus, although not technically holding any political posts, effectively ran the government for the first five years. Modern historians have questioned just how enlightened that *quinquennium* was (it certainly saw the introduction of some much-needed reforms); but there is no doubt that it was a paradise compared with the wilful eccentricity that characterized the latter part of the reign, when Nero took power firmly into his own hands. In A.D. 59 Nero murdered his mother. At the same time Seneca was subject to a great deal of jealous criticism which centred chiefly on his enormous wealth. Increasing awareness of the weakness of his position led Seneca to withdraw more and more from politics until in A.D. 62, on the death of Burrus, he went into voluntary retirement. Not even that could keep him safe. In A.D. 65 he was accused, with his nephew and others, of complicity in a conspiracy against Nero and ordered to commit suicide.

Unperturbed, Seneca asked for his will. But the officer refused. Then Seneca turned to his friends. 'Being forbidden', he said, 'to show gratitude for your services, I leave you my one remaining possession, and my best: the pattern of my life. If you remember it, your devoted friendship will be rewarded by a name for virtuous accomplishments.' As he talked – and sometimes in sterner and more imperative terms – he checked their tears and sought to revive their courage. Where had their philosophy gone, he asked, and that resolution against impending misfortunes which they had devised over so many years? 'Surely nobody was unaware that Nero was cruel!' he added. 'After murdering his mother and brother, it only remained for him to kill his teacher and tutor.'

These words were evidently intended for public hearing. Then Seneca embraced his wife and, with a tenderness very different from his philosophical imperturbability, entreated her to moderate and set a term to her grief, and take just consolation, in her bereavement, from contemplating his well-spent life. Nevertheless, she insisted on dying with him, and demanded the executioner's stroke. Seneca did not oppose her brave decision. Indeed, loving her wholeheartedly, he was reluctant to leave her for ill-treatment. 'Solace in life was what I commended to you', he said. 'But you prefer death and glory. I will not grudge your setting so fine an example. We can die with equal fortitude. But yours will be the nobler end.'

Then, each with one incision of the blade, he and his wife cut their arms. But Seneca's aged body, lean from austere living, released the blood too slowly. So he also severed the veins in his ankles and behind his knees. Exhausted by severe pain, he was afraid of weakening his wife's endurance by betraying his agony – or of losing his own self-possession at the sight of her sufferings. So he asked her to go into another bedroom. But even in his last moments his eloquence remained. Summoning secretaries, he dictated a dissertation.

(Tacitus, *Annals* 15.61–2; tr. Michael Grant)

If that were all, it would be an imposing record of an able man trying to keep afloat in dangerous times. But Seneca was also a prolific writer. There have come down to us nine tragedies, a collection of 124 philosophical letters, seven books of *Natural Questions* (i.e. on science, including earthquakes and comets), twelve philosophical essays and a satirical pamphlet about Claudius (the *Apocolocyntosis* or 'Pumpkinification'). It is these writings which raise the awkward questions about Seneca's consistency, indeed integrity. During his years of exile, for instance, he wrote three *Consolations*, formal essays based on Greek models, offering advice and comfort in times of distress or bereavement. In one he comforts his mother, Helvia, for the loss of her exiled son and rehearses eloquently such arguments as that exile is merely a change of scene which cannot affect one's goodness and is a disgrace only in the eyes of man. It is a noble and moving plea. Yet at much the same time he wrote a similar piece to Claudius's freedman Polybius on the death of his brother which, for all its professed high-mindedness, is little more than a cringing appeal for his own recall.

O how blessed is your mercy, Caesar, which makes exiles live more peacefully under your rule. They are not uneasy, nor do they fear the sword hour by hour, nor cower at the sight of every ship; through you they possess not only a limit to the cruelty of fortune, but also the hope of her being more kindly and peaceful even as she is. One may know that those thunderbolts are indeed most just which even those they may have smitten worship.

When he was eventually recalled, he was happy to accept preferment at Claudius's hand; but after Claudius's death he composed a speech for Nero to deliver to the Senate of such malicious ingenuity that it reduced the audience to helpless laughter and he published the *Apocolocyntosis*, a wicked satire in mixed verse and prose: Claudius attempts to take his seat among the gods but, after an Irreverent Council, the gods decide that he should be deported to Hell. There he is judged by Aeacus (on Claudian principles: that is, only the case for the prosecution is put) and condemned for all eternity to shake dice in a bottomless shaker (the genuine Claudius was an addict) and then to remain an assistant law-clerk in Hades.

Again in A.D. 55 Seneca composed the *On Mercy*, dedicated to the young Nero. He argues the need for clemency in a sovereign: 'Cruelty makes a tyrant; but the affection of subjects is a stronger defence for a prince than their fear.' 'To save life', he writes, 'is the peculiar privilege of exalted station which never has a right to greater admiration than when it has the good fortune to have the same power as the gods, by whose kindness we all, the evil as well as the good, are brought forth into the light.' Very high-minded, but Seneca, even if he was not actually an accomplice, certainly condoned the murders of Britannicus, of Nero's mother in A.D. 55 and of Agrippina in 59. In the *On Peace of Mind*, written perhaps about A.D. 59, he can discourse on the virtues of poverty: 'If you compare all the other ills from which we suffer – death, illness, fear, desire, pain – with the evils which our money brings, the latter will far outweigh the former' (8.1). Yet Seneca's wealth was notorious, and his business interests worldwide. It could even be plausibly alleged that it was his threat to call in some loans to Britons that sparked off the revolt of Boadicea.

Such contradictions could be multiplied over and over again in a man who wrote 'Philosophy . . . moulds and builds the personality, orders one's life, regulates one's conduct, shows one what one should do and what one should leave undone, sits at the helm and keeps one on the correct course as one is tossed about in perilous seas' (*Letters* 16.3; tr. Robin Campbell). Seneca's formulation of his philosophy is seen at its best in his letters addressed during the last three years of his life to a young friend, Lucilius. They are more informal and intimate than his treatises, although they are no less carefully designed to cover all the principal topics of Stoicism. Seneca is following the example of Cicero's published correspondence, though more self-consciously. The letters are real enough but they are, as it were, the instalments of a book. Seneca humanizes Stoicism without retreating from its fundamental principles of living self-sufficiently according to nature, of accepting whatever happens without excessive emotion as part of the divine plan and of treating all men as fellow-men.

The first thing philosophy promises us is the feeling of fellowship, of belonging to mankind and being members of a community ... it is quite contrary to nature to torture one's body, to reject simple standards of cleanliness and make a point of being dirty, to adopt a diet that is not just plain but hideous and revolting ... Philosophy calls for simple living, not for doing penance, and the simple way of life need not be a crude one. (*Letters* 5)

I'm glad to hear, from these people who've been visiting you, that you live on friendly terms with your slaves. It is just what one expects of an enlightened, cultivated person like yourself. 'They're slaves,' people say. No. They're human beings. 'They're slaves.' But they share the same roof as ourselves. 'They're slaves.' No, they're friends, humble friends. 'They're slaves.' Strictly speaking they're our fellow-slaves, if you once reflect that fortune has as much power over us as over them. (*Letters* 47; tr. Robin Campbell)

But what makes Seneca's letters so attractive is his gift of observation. He can take some little scene and use it as the text for a piece of philosophizing:

Today we saw some boats from Alexandria – the ones they call 'the mail packets' – come into view all of a sudden. They were the ones which are normally sent ahead to announce the coming of the fleet that will arrive behind them. The sight of them is always a welcome one to the Campanians. The whole of Puteoli crowded onto the wharves, all picking out the Alexandrian vessels from an immense crowd of other shipping by the actual trim of their sails, these boats being the only vessels allowed to keep their topsails spread.   (*Letters* 77; tr. Robin Campbell)

This forms the opening of a long letter on the subject 'at whatever point you leave life, if you leave it in the right way, it is a whole'. A plea for inner tranquillity is inspired by an unpleasant experience:

Here am I with a babel of noise going on all about me. I have lodgings right over a public bath-house. Now imagine to yourself every kind of sound that can make one weary of one's ears. When the strenuous types are doing their exercises, swinging weight-laden hands about, I hear the grunting as they toil away – or go through the motions of toiling away – at them, and the hissings and strident gasps every time they expel their pent-up breath. When my attention turns to a less active fellow who is contenting himself with an ordinary inexpensive massage, I hear the smack of a hand pummelling his shoulders ... But if on top of this some ball-player comes along and starts shouting out the score, that's the end.
                                     (*Letters* 56; tr. after Robin Campbell)

Seneca, in fact, far more than Petronius or Juvenal, gives us a precious series of vignettes of Roman social life – the horrors of the games (*Letters* 7: 'I happened to go to one of those shows at the time of the lunch-hour interludes ... murder pure and simple. The combatants have nothing to protect them; every thrust they launch gets home ... In the morning men are thrown to the lions and the bears; but it is the spectators they are thrown to in the lunch hour'), the perils of a crossing from Naples to Puteoli (*Letters* 53: suffering from seasickness, 'I dived into the sea ... in my woolly clothes. You can imagine what I suffered as I crawled out over the rocks'), the charms of a seaside town (*Letters* 51) or the ordinary farming routine in the country (*Letters* 86). He aimed at an easy-going style, as if he were conversing with a friend at home or on a walk; but in fact all the time he strained after neatness. The endless search for the clever *mot* reduced his prose to a stream of epigrams, some memorable, some merely pretentious. The letters tend to become disjointed and intermittent, a string of self-contained sentences, like the writing of his admirer Bacon or, even more so, Sir Thomas Browne. As Macaulay not unjustly wrote, 'I cannot bear Seneca ... his works are made up of mottoes. There is hardly a sentence which might not be quoted; but to read him straightforward is like dining on nothing but anchovy sauce.' Take the last paragraph of Letter 91: 'how can those who have a bad name rob you of a good one?'; 'it is rash to condemn something one knows nothing about'; 'no one has power over us when death is in our power'. And so on. Although it is no doubt true that philosophy is more effective when it is memorable, Seneca had become the victim of the rhetorician's passion for 'point'. The audience, as Aper had said in Tacitus's *Dialogue*, only listened to a speaker in order to glean some impressive quotation to repeat at home.

So strong is this impression when one reads Seneca's letters that it undermines the more important element – his humanity, courage and generosity. For all his reputation in the ancient world, there is no evidence that anyone was ever induced to follow a particular course of action as a result of reading his philosophical works. His real influence was to come in the Christian era when apologists were glad to clothe his doctrines in Christian dress. St Paul and Seneca were contemporaries; credulous Christians believed that they had even corresponded.

If, then, the effect of the letters, which were obviously intended seriously, is impaired by their presentation, a rather different judgement has to be made of Seneca's tragedies. It is not certain when they were written, perhaps during his years of exile in Corsica, perhaps after his recall in A.D. 49.

Whenever they were written, Seneca brought to them first-hand experience of political life. Tragedy as a dramatic art had more or less died with the poet Accius (c. 85 B.C.), and although there were revivals of the old tragedies of Naevius and Livius Andronicus, popular taste in the late Republic favoured less serious spectacles. Authors who wanted to treat the old themes in a tragic way tended to write plays which were meant not for stage production before a large and indiscriminate audience but for recitation before a more select one, a literary and cultivated one. Ovid, for instance, wrote a *Medea*, which was highly acclaimed, and the names of several other playwrights are known. It would, however, be a mistake to think that the shift was from plays which were to be acted to plays which were to be read. Public recitation was, as has been seen (p. 12), a sort of dramatic performance in itself, involving a great deal of action, illusion, 'business' and delivery.

One consequence of the change, however, was that the tragedian was no longer able to influence the wider public on important issues, whether moral or political. Aeschylus aimed to use the myth of the Oresteia to say something about justice, and Athenian justice in particular. Euripides' war-plays, like the *Trojan Women*, are an explicit commentary on the sufferings brought about by the Peloponnesian War. Even revivals of Roman tragedies had their impact. In 59 B.C. at the Games of Apollo in July, an unknown tragedy was revived and the actor Diphilus was forced to give a dozen encores of the line 'To our misfortune art thou Great', the allusion being taken to apply to Pompey. Even so, an author who wanted to express his inner beliefs could do so in a veiled and generalized way, as Phaedrus had done in his fables and as Mamercus Scaurus did (although to his cost) in his tragedy *Atreus*, which appeared under Caligula.

No such temptation assailed Seneca. His tragedies are devoid of anything that could be even remotely regarded as critical. His choruses, mere literary interludes, sometimes contain commonplace moralizing of a philosophical kind, as in the first chorus of his *Agamemnon* on Fortune, but for the most part they are mere padding, indulging in mythological and similar decoration for its own sake. In the *Thyestes*, a play of unmitigated gruesomeness whose model is unknown, the chorus, before the final blood-curdling act, launch into a long ode about the impending dissolution of the universe:

That belt of constellations that marks out the passage of the years,
The highway of the holy stars that lies oblique across the zones,
Will fall away, and see the stars fall with it.
The *Ram*, at whose approach, even before the spring's full warmth,
Ships may spread sails to balmy zephyrs – he who once
Carried the frightened Helle over the sea,
Into the sea himself will fall.
The *Bull*, who holds the Hyades between his shining horns,
Falling will bring the *Gemini* down, and down will fall
The bent-armed *Crab* . . . [etc., etc.]
(Thyestes 845 ff.; tr. E. F. Watling)

The fatal instinct to produce an exhaustive list of instances where one would serve is all too present. What could be more grotesque than the climax to the ode on the universal power of love?

> The Punic lion shakes his mane,
>   And speaks his passion with a roar.
> Love moves, and the whole forest roars again.
> Love moves the monsters of the senseless sea,
>   And the bull elephant in Luca's fields.*
>   All nature is his prey.
(Phaedra 345 ff.; tr. E. F. Watling)

* Elephants were first used in Italy as a weapon of war by Pyrrhus campaigning against the Romans in Lucania.

The plots, also, all taken from the Greek, lack any finesse. There is no balancing of good against evil or good against good. It is a straightforward path to calamity, marked by the constant repetition of emotive words (anger, fear, catastrophe, blood, tears, death etc.). Seneca had known plenty of bad men and witnessed plenty of disasters, but he makes no attempt to explore the motivation of men or the causation of events. Theseus, miraculously restored to earth after four years in the Underworld aiding his friend to kidnap Persephone, is confronted with planted evidence that his son Hippolytus has slept with his wife Phaedra. Even allowing for the convention of ancient drama, what could be less appropriate than his reaction?

> Whence came this foul infection, this corruption
> Into our blood? Could this man have been bred
> On Grecian soil, or in the Scythian Taurus,
> The Colchian Phasis? Every stock returns
> To its ancestral type, degenerate blood
> Retains the nature of its primal source.
> This is that warrior people's [*scil.* the Amazons'] native vice –
> To abrogate legitimate love, and sell
> Chaste women's bodies in the public market.
>
> (*Phaedra* 906 ff.; tr. E. F. Watling)

Instead of analysing human character, Seneca relapses into the most hackneyed common-place. Every speech reads like one of his father's declamations, divorced from context and reality.

There are moments when the rhetoric does rise to heights that justify it, especially in his version of the *Trojan Women*, and there are lines which are memorable in themselves (e.g. *Trojan Women* 869: 'to die, without the fear of death, is easy death'). There are also passages where Seneca does set out well some of the tenets of Stoicism, for example *Thyestes* 344 ff. on true kingship, or *Trojan Women* 378 ff. on death:

Is it the truth, or but an idle tale
   To give false comfort to our fears,
That the soul lives on when the body is laid to rest?
                                    (tr. E. F. Watling)

Nevertheless, given Seneca's active desire to be a philosopher in politics and given the unique opportunity which tragedy offered for exploring the human condition, one can only conclude that the man and the writer are two different creatures. Reading Seneca's plays one has some sympathy with Juvenal's complaint at being forced to attend dramatic recitations:

                              Is there
   No recompense for whole days wasted on prolix
   Versions of *Telephus*? And what about that *Orestes* –
   Each margin of the roll crammed solid, top and bottom,
   More on the back, and *still* it wasn't finished!
   I know all the mythical landscapes like my own back-room.
                              (*Sat.* 1.5 ff.; tr. Peter Green)

No such criticism can be levelled at Persius, who is perhaps the most original of all the early imperial writers, although not in any sense a major one, or an easy one. A. Persius Flaccus (A.D. 34–62) came from a well-to-do Etruscan family. His father died when he was young and he was taken to Rome, where he was educated under the best teachers of the day, such as Palaemon. He was related by birth to Arria, the wife of the Stoic martyr Thrasea Paetus (p. 186), so that it was natural that he should move in Stoic circles. At the age of sixteen he became a pupil and friend of L. Annaeus Cornutus, the leading Stoic philosopher, whose name indicates that he was a freedman of a relation of Seneca's. Certainly Persius knew (although he did not like) Seneca and was a close friend of Lucan, who greatly admired his poetry. As his satires show, Persius himself was a whole-hearted adherent of Stoicism.

Persius, therefore, was at the centre of a highly articulate and critical group, and from an early age displayed a talent and liking for writing. When he died, from natural causes, at the young age of twenty-seven, his executors destroyed his juvenilia and published only the six *Satires*, not 700 lines in all, on which his reputation rests. In them he makes his own profession of what his aims were. Anxious to avoid the meaningless glibness of his contemporaries (a criticism that could certainly be levelled against the tragedies of Seneca), he wanted to produce 'something rather more boiled down' (*aliquid decoctius*). At the same time he wanted to expose the vices of contemporary society (5.15–16: 'you show your art by the way you scrape at vicious morals and nail a fault with well-bred banter').

Certainly no author is more compact than Persius. He wrote slowly and carefully, compressing his thoughts to the point of obscurity and making widespread use of the art of allusion. The opening of his first satire, a programmatic one on the state of current literature in which he attacks and parodies a wide range of authors, betrays this conversational 'tele-graphese':

The toils of man! The emptiness of life! [a grandiloquent quotation from Lucilius]. 'Who's going to read that?' Are you talking to me? Nobody, of course. 'Nobody?' Well, two at the most. 'That's a bad business.' Why? Because Polydamas and the Trojan Women [in Homer, notoriously reproachful] may prefer Labeo [a bad poet] to me? Rubbish.

Such composition is a work of refined art. Indeed Persius prefaces the third satire with an entertaining argument between his higher and his lower self, which likes to lie in bed in the morning and makes all sorts of obstacles when it eventually gets down to writing. But once one has recognized the allusions and sensed the transitions of thought (both of which would have been much easier for an educated Roman), few authors give so much pleasure and satisfaction.

'I can do it tomorrow just as well.' All right, do it tomorrow. 'What? Do you mean you regard a day as a big concession?' But when another sun shines, already we have used up yesterday's tomorrow: see, another tomorrow ladles the years away, and always keeps a little ahead.   (*Sat.* 5.66 ff.)

The trouble is that the contents of the satires do not live up to Persius's stated intention. They deal with Stoic problems but not with problems that have any relevance to real life. Neither the political stituation under Nero (which Lucan was to grapple with) nor the social evils (which Petronius, however anonymously, held up to view) figures at all in his work. The second satire, for instance, in honour of the birthday of an old family friend, Macrinus, is on the subject of prayer. Although philosophers had often discussed how one should pray and criticized the hypocrisy of many worshippers, with public protestations and secret thoughts, Persius is one of the first to stress that it is purity of mind rather than purity of hand which matters and that one should not equate the divine with the human:

Souls stooped on the ground and void of the divine, what use is it to introduce our own morals into the temples and infer the gods' good from this sinful flesh?   (*Sat.* 2.61 ff.)

Yet, full of humorous and cynical touches as it is ('Do you think you have bought God's ears by a bribe of greasy intestines?'), the satire never tackles equally important issues such as whether the gods are just and compassionate or whether there is a meaning in the evident injustice and squalor of modern life. The fourth satire, which is concerned with the right knowledge of oneself, a Stoic theme, opens promisingly with Socrates reproving young Alcibiades for presuming to run Athens while his own thoughts are set on more personal enjoyment. There surely was the chance for political allegory, however discreet; but Persius declines it and the satire veers off into reflections that we often recognize other people's faults rather than our own. When in his last satire he considers the right use of wealth, it is in terms, which were almost commonplace among satirists, of the legacy-hunter and not in practical terms of investment, charity, thrift and so on.

Persius's interests were in philosophy, not life; or rather – for this would be fairer – Persius, like other Stoics, had been so conditioned by his education that he could not look at life except as philosophy. What to us seem bookish subjects such as 'every fool is a slave and only the wise man free' (*Sat.* 5) were to him the real subjects. And his contemporaries were not slow to acclaim his remarkable gifts – his learning, his polish and his wit.

LUCAN

Chief among these admirers was Persius's younger contemporary Lucan. M. Annaeus Lucanus (A.D. 39–65), a pupil of Cornutus, was an infant prodigy whose literary talents as a student drew him to the attention of Nero. He was made quaestor unusually young and in A.D. 60 won the prize at the games of Nero. The friendship did not last long, partly because Lucan was evidently of independent mind, only too aware of his own gifts, partly because his uncle was already out of favour at court and partly (so the ancient sources allege, and there is no reason to doubt them) because Nero, for all his genuine interest in the arts, was jealous of anyone who might outshine him. What is certain is that Lucan was hot-headedly involved in the conspiracy of A.D. 65 and was forced to commit suicide.

At the age of twenty-five he had already achieved much. The titles of numerous works, now lost, are recorded. What does survive is the unfinished epic *Pharsalia* or *Civil War* in ten books (twelve were planned), the only Latin epic to challenge Virgil in power and dignity. Lucan chose as his subject the civil wars between Caesar and Pompey which culminated in the decisive Battle of Pharsalus in 48 B.C., and he used as his sources the accounts of Livy and Caesar himself among others. The choice of subject is highly significant. It represented a conscious decision to break with the traditional 'safe' subjects of myth, legend and early history (such as Silius Italicus's *Punica*: see p. 221) and to bring epic into the modern world. It also represented a desire to explore publicly the consequences of Caesarism, of that absolutist government which had replaced the old republicanism as a consequence of Caesar's victory, and of Augustus's at Actium. It is perhaps not easy for us to realize just how bold and defiant an innovation Lucan was making. It was a brilliant protest, based on clear and unequivocal Stoic principles, not only against Nero as a person but against the oppressiveness of the totalitarian regime. The actors are human; perhaps for the first time in ancient epic, the gods, so prominent in Virgil and Homer, have no role. Lucan achieved what his admired friend Persius failed to achieve – an influential Stoic assertion of human rights.

The tone is set at the very beginning with a panegyrical dedication to Nero.

However, if the fates could not prepare for Nero's advent by any other means – if eternal empire may not be bought except at a heavy price, as when of old a War of the Giants was needed to secure Jupiter's throne – then I naturally abstain from further complaints

... Rome has greatly profited from her Civil Wars: were they not fought, Caesar, that you might reign today?

And O, great prince, when your watch among men ends, and you finally rise skywards, the celestial palace of your choice will receive you amid the loud acclamations of heaven. I cannot venture to prophesy whether you will assume Jupiter's sceptre or prefer to mount Apollo's fiery chariot and survey the earth from it as you drive along ... And, if you put too much weight on any single portion of the limitless aether, you will endanger its balance; it would be best to take up your stance in the very centre of heaven and thus preserve universal equipoise.   (1.45 ff.; tr. Robert Graves)

These lines were apparently actually published, together with the first three books, before Lucan's disgrace. How he got away with it beggars imagination. Nero prided himself upon being a charioteer and was grossly overweight: and to make him a denizen of heaven when Lucan expressly eliminated the gods from any direct function was a staggering piece of satirical audacity. After the contorted sophistication of Persius and the verbiage of Seneca, these lines still read as a breath of fresh air.

But it is not until Book 7, the battle itself, that Lucan gives voice to his deepest feelings about the plight of his generation. 'It was the struggle, which continues today, between freedom and Caesardom' (7.698). In two eloquent passages, in his own words and not put into the mouth of any character, he comments:

The goddess of freedom, banished from Italy by the Civil War, has long since fled beyond the Tigris and the Rhine, and refuses to return, though we may cut our throats in wooing her. Germans and Scythians bask in her blessed presence, but she does not deign to glance back at this country. If only Rome had never known who she was! We Romans, in fact, deserve to be slaves: we deserved it when Romulus killed his brother Remus ... And we deserved slavery ever afterwards until the fratricidal Battle of Pharsalus.

I even regret that Brutus drove out the Tarquins. What advantage is it to us now that we enjoy a few centuries of constitutional government and learned to let consuls rather than kings name the years? The Arabians, Medians and other orientals who have lived continuously under tyrants are far more fortunate than we; they need not feel ashamed of being slaves, as we must. It is most false to say that gods rule this world and that Jupiter rules the gods: nothing but blind chance makes the world go round.   (7.432 ff.)

The world suffered an irreparable disaster, because what we lost at Pharsalus was more than life and property; Roman liberty lay prostrate and Caesar's swords sufficed thereafter to cow generation after generation. But do we great-grandchildren of the combatants really deserve to be born slaves? Are we cowards that we fear to die? No, this is a punishment for our fathers' fears: fortune who gave us tyranny should also have given us a chance to take the field against our tyrants.   (7.638–46; tr. Robert Graves)

The overall effect is, however, diminished by Lucan's youthful exuberance. The poem has certain very serious shortcomings, even allowing for the fact that it is incomplete and unrevised. A good plot is the essence of epic, and the Civil War does not really offer a satisfactory plot, at least if any pretence of historicity is to be maintained. And Lucan was historically serious. His choice of Livy and Caesar rather than some of the more convenient summaries is significant in itself, especially since Livy was himself an author with a nostalgic regard for the lost Republic, a Pompeian, as Augustus had called him. But the events of the years 49–48 B.C. lent themselves to no surprises, no reversals of fortune, no great climaxes. Pompey handled the campaign in an uncharacteristically negative way. And in telling it Lucan concentrates more on melodramatic incidents than on any developing story. The first book in particular is disappointingly static, with its speeches of encouragement by Caesar and long lists of omens, prodigies and visions. Lucan does not lay the threads for a story that will build up to a climax.

Secondly there is no genuine characterization. In the *Aeneid* certain figures – Aeneas, Turnus, Dido, Evander – are given an individuality of their own and grow in stature as the poem evolves, but Caesar, Pompey and Cato all talk and behave in the same way, just as all the characters in Seneca's tragedies talk like Seneca. It is the technique of the student of oratory writing suitable speeches for set characters. And the characters are not even consistent. They are drawn on each occasion as the situation requires, without any regard for overall plausibility. Pompey alternates between statesmanlike dignity and abject pusillanimity.

But the most damning criticism is the overall lack of balance in the *Pharsalia*. Lucan was too self-indulgent a writer. He allowed himself to be carried away by the macabre and the supernatural. Sextus Pompeius, for instance, employs the witch Erichtho to summon up the ghost of Cato (the episode occupies the whole of 6.405–830). She selects a corpse and after making several cuts in it and washing out the contents of its veins

poured in warm menstrual blood mixed with every kind of unnatural poison – the froth of dogs suffering from rabies, a lynx's guts, the hump of a corpse-eating hyaena, the marrow of a snake-fattened stag, one of those remora fish that can keep a ship motionless on the high seas, though the east wind howls through her rigging; also dragon's eyes, eagle-stones which when warmed by the she-eagle explode with a loud noise, an Arabian seraph of the sort that pounces on travellers, a few of those Red Sea vipers that guard the pearl-oyster beds, the sloughed skin of a Libyan horned snake, and the ashes of the Phoenix stolen from the altar of Heliopolis. To these commoner [*sic*!] ingredients she added the bewitched leaves of plant that she had spat upon when they first appeared, thereby steeping them in the venom of her own body.   (tr. Robert Graves)

This is no isolated example. Given an opportunity for expansion and improvisation Lucan will produce catalogues of stunningly rhetorical virtuosity which completely defeat their own purpose. A hint, as in Virgil, would have been far more effective.

Similar is his overplaying of the role of fortune and fate (they are virtually synonymous in Lucan). In eliminating the gods as causative agents he had replaced them by the much more Stoic concept of Fate, which exercises a comparable control over events. Its endless repetition becomes boring in itself but also undermines the validity of human endeavour. This was the paradox. 'The virtuous man will obey his destiny [the fates] without fear' (2.286-7). But if all is predetermined by the Divine Providence, then why stand out for liberty against tyranny? Lucan never resolves this paradox and indeed the most subtle Stoics only resolved it by saying that, since we are ourselves a part of creative providence, we can create to some extent the destiny that is already created for us.

But if Lucan has many of the vices of his rhetorical education, he also has many of its greatest virtues. Perhaps even more than his uncle he was capable of writing epigrammatical lines which virtually defy translation, such as *victrix causa deis placuit, sed victa Catoni* ('the gods favoured the winning side, Cato the losing') or *magni stat nominis umbra* ('there stands the shadow of a great name').

Lucan is the supreme example of the poetry of protest, and his true place in the history of European literature can be gauged by comparison with another contemporary, Silius Italicus (or, to give him his full name, Tiberius Catius Asconius Silius Italicus). Silius was at least thirteen years older than Lucan. His background is unknown, but he must have come from a prominent and cultivated family because he had a successful political career under Nero, so successful in fact that he was consul in A.D. 68, the last year of Nero's reign. There is no doubt that he earned his promotion by collaborating with the regime to the full, for he is known to have been one of the more odious informers during the latter part of Nero's reign. On Nero's death he intrigued first with Vitellius and then established himself in the favour of Vespasian and gained a reputation as governor of Asia. He was (by Roman standards) too old for an active career under Domitian but, instead, he took up the pen and began to compose a long epic on the Carthaginian Wars. That he was *persona grata* to Domitian (an emperor whose reign resembled Nero's in many ways except for his lack of interest in culture) is clear both from the complimentary references paid to him by Martial in A.D. 88 and 92 and from his own respectful praise of Domitian's military exploits in A.D. 92–3. He lived on in secure and comfortable retirement until his death in A.D. 101 when the Younger Pliny records his obituary. Whatever inward anxiety and conscience he may have felt, outwardly Silius enjoyed a life of uninterrupted success and lived to see his younger son follow in his footsteps as consul. He was a rich man and a connoisseur, interested in his country's national heritage: he bought up one of Cicero's country houses and took pains to see to the conservation of Virgil's tomb; he even made a show of cultivating philosophy and is referred to by the Stoic ex-slave Epictetus (*Diss.* 3.8.7). He died an ostentatiously Stoical death by voluntary starvation.

But at no point throughout all the long seventeen books so laboriously written (Pliny says he wrote with more pains than flair) is there any suggestion that literature is anything more than a dilettante recreation suitable for retirement. Even though in style, language and technique his debt to Virgil and Lucan is obvious, he is merely going through the motions of writing an epic. All the elements are there – the gods, the catalogues, the digressions, the similes, the detailed combats, the speeches and so on. The narrative is not even illuminated by a sense of history, as if the events were to be understood as part of a Stoic vision of a divine plan, nor is it relieved by that brilliance of writing which can sometimes sustain Seneca's most vacuous passages. Only one quality shows it to be the work of a man who had witnessed and, no doubt, ordered countless deaths, and that is its fascination with the gruesome. Like Lucan, Silius is obsessed with blood.

The lifeless nature of the *Punica* can be matched by the equally lifeless *Argonautica* of Valerius Flaccus (*c.* A.D. 40–A.D. 90), an epic of eight books. Valerius, who is virtually unknown as a person, was clearly a less distinguished public figure, but he must also have been involved in the politics of his day, for he is known to have held the office of *XV vir sacris faciundis*, a religious office which like the pontificate and the augurate always went to magistrates.

The *Punica* and the *Argonautica* are nostalgic works of escapism. To a classical scholar they are of interest for their technique and language, but they have nothing to say. They are the fruits yet again of an educational system that encouraged facility in composition.

Must I *always* be stuck in the audience at these poetry-readings, never
Up on the platform myself, taking it out on Cordus
For the times he's bored me to death with ranting speeches
From that *Theseid*?   (Juvenal, *Sat.* 1.1 ff.; tr. Peter Green)

10

THE NEW DAWN

It is always dangerous to attempt to divide history into cut-and-dried periods. Such divisions are artificial, the work of academic hindsight. Nevertheless no one can deny that the reign of Domitian (A.D. 81–96) had a special impact on a small number of writers which singles them out, for all their individual differences, as being in a very real sense the children of their times. The facts are clear. No amount of white-washing can obscure the truth that Domitian equalled the excesses of his predecessors. It may well be that the very strain of being emperor, answerable to nobody and responsible for everything, told on his sanity and stamina, as it did on others. A.D. 93 alone saw the murder of his relations Clemens and Sabinus, and of the ex-consuls Acilius Glabrio, Helvidius Priscus, Arulenus Rusticus, Cornelius Salvidienus, L. Salvius Otho, Mettius Pompusianus, and L. Aelius Lamia, as well as the exile of Artemidorus, Plutarch, Epictetus, Junius Mauricus and others, including perhaps Juvenal.

The effect of such a succession of tyrannies was marked upon society. The first victims were the old aristocracy, not only from the time of the Republic but from the early years of the Empire. By the time of Nerva (A.D. 96–8) and Trajan (A.D. 98–117) virtually none of the old families survived, and those that did were the objects of respectful curiosity rather than the wielders of power. A second casualty was the old Italian families of equestrian standing, families like those of Propertius and Persius. They had been hit less by persecution than by economic factors. Traditionally accustomed to live off the rents of their estates and businesses rather than engage directly in trades and professions themselves, they had seen fortunes being made by a much more brash class of entrepreneurs, often tradesmen and Greeks of the type caricatured in Trimalchio. There is a certain shabby gentility about such families, portrayed in Pliny's letters and represented to some extent by Juvenal and even Martial. Martial wrote a cynical poem on the disadvantages of a liberal education which ends: 'Does your son wish to learn money-making arts? make him learn to be harper or flautist for the chorus; if the boy seems to be of dull intellect, make him an auctioneer or architect' (5.56).

On the other hand life went on. There was the same basic education, the same career structure in politics, the same need for lawyers, speakers and administrators. Only men now were content to find their satisfaction within their particular sphere rather than see political activity as a means to improving their position in the state as a whole. Cicero treated his province as a tiresome necessity which at best might improve his finances and secure him a triumph back in Rome; Agricola spent many years in Britain simply because his ambition was to be a good governor of Britain. As a result public men became much more professionally minded, taking their responsibilities seriously and discharging them unassumingly. Under Trajan and Hadrian we know the names of hundreds of senators who had worthwhile careers in public service. And the same professionalism began to affect other aspects of life, as the second century went on. History, for instance, and law and literary studies tended to be written not by versatile public figures such as Cicero and Seneca but by specialists such as Suetonius. An early but good example of this is Sextus Julius Frontinus (c. A.D. 34–c. A.D. 103), who had a distinguished public career, being consul three times (in 74, 98 and 100) and serving as a very competent governor of Britain before Agricola. He devoted his life to the practical business of government and wrote technical treatises on surveying, military science, stratagems and aqueducts, the last two of which have survived. Very many people suppressed whatever feelings they might have on wider issues and quietly got on with their own particular job. As Tacitus wrote, 'there can be good men even under a bad emperor'. Bitter experience had shown that there was nothing to be gained by dramatic protest: it had brought even the best like Lucan to a premature death. So if people did write, they settled for much smaller and more innocuous subjects – published in prose or verse on topics of everyday interest. These were the successes of Martial, Statius and even the Younger Pliny.

If you felt deeply, you were silent. The unexpected change came with the death of Domitian. Although none of the succeeding emperors from Nerva to Marcus Aurelius was an easy man, they were all conscientious and cultured, and they were sufficiently sure both of their own position and of public good-will to allow free expression to recover. Hadrian in particular, as countless inscriptions from all parts of the empire from Britain to the East display, gave great and genuine encouragement to the arts.

Nevertheless for people born in the mid-century the price of silence was heavy. Juvenal (D. Junius Juvenalis; *c.* A.D. 55–*c.* A.D. 128) did not publish his first satires until about A.D. 110, although the drafts of some of them must have been written earlier. Tacitus (P. Cornelius Tacitus; *c.* A.D. 56–*c.* A.D. 116) wrote his first work, the life of Agricola, in A.D. 96 and in it speaks of his fifteen years' silence – 'a long span in the life of a man'. Pliny the Younger (C. Plinius Caecilius Secundus, nephew of the polymath; A.D. 61–*c.* A.D. 114) wrote his letters intended for publication from A.D. 97 onwards. He wrote in his *Panegyric* of A.D. 100: 'Away then with expressions formerly prompted by fear: I will have none of them. The sufferings of the past are over: let us then have done with the words which belong to them.' Yet all three had had careers under Domitian. Pliny was praetor in the notorious year of A.D. 93 (he subsequently became consul in A.D. 100). Tacitus also was praetor under Domitian, in A.D. 88 (consul in A.D. 97). Juvenal, although from a humble background, had probably held a commission in the army (perhaps in Britain) and a priesthood of the deified Vespasian, although it is conjectured that he fell foul of Domitian in A.D. 93 and was exiled to Egypt.

Pliny, Juvenal and Tacitus were all past middle age when they did feel free to write openly. So it was inevitable that their thoughts were concerned not so much with the challenges of the present as with the experiences of the past. There is a perpetual looking backwards about them, a marked fascination with the horrors of their youth. Even Pliny contemplated writing a history of the Flavian period. 'I may probably give offence to many and please but few. For in an age so overrun with vice you will find infinitely more to condemn than approve; and your praise, though ever so lavish, will be thought too reserved and your censure, though ever so cautious, too profuse'. This factor, which has an important bearing upon the character of their writings, should be borne in mind as the increasing fashion for archaism, the re-creation of the past, gathers momentum throughout the century. Furthermore, although they were as familiar with Greek as their predecessors and took the same delight in imitating Greek authors, they did not derive their inspiration in the same way directly from them. Tacitus looked more to Sallust and Livy than to Thucydides, Martial to Catullus rather than Archilochus or Meleager. Pliny was very consciously treading in the footsteps of Cicero, as Juvenal was indebted to Horace and Persius. The epics of Statius owe much to Virgil, Ovid and Lucan but little to Homer or Callimachus. Latin literature had come of age and Romans now had classics of their own.

Finally these writers did not work in isolation. Pliny and Tacitus were closely associated. Martial was a friend of Silius Italicus and Juvenal and much in Pliny's debt. Both Statius and Martial were acquainted with Lucan's widow, Polla, and wrote about Domitian's page, Eiarinus. All of them were acquainted with Quintilian (p. 196). Although there is no suggestion of a literary coterie, nevertheless the educated world at Rome, the world that went to recitations and commissioned works of literature, was a small one, and a steady interchange of ideas was inevitable.

If all five of the major literary figures – Martial, Statius, Tacitus, Pliny and Juvenal – came to terms sufficiently with Domitian's regime to be able to survive and even prosper under it, it is important to distinguish the two, Martial and Statius, who were also able to *write* under it. An examination of their work helps us to understand at least one direction that literature was to take.

MARTIAL

Martial (M. Valerius Martialis; c. A.D. 40–A.D. 104) was born and educated in Spain. It was not until about A.D. 64 that he went to Rome to find his fortune under the patronage of his fellow-Spaniards Seneca and Lucan. Their disgrace the following year left Martial with the necessity of making his own way by whatever means he could. As he put it in a poem, 'What reason or what confidence draws you to Rome, Sextus . . .? "I will compose poems: hear them, you will call them Virgil's work." You are crazy. "I will haunt the halls of great men." Barely three or four has that procedure supported: all the rest of the crowd are pale with hunger. "What shall

I do? Advise me, I am bent on living in Rome." If you are a good man, Sextus, you may live by accident'. And by accident, by turning up every day at the doors of rich patrons and by writing occasional poetry, Martial does in fact seem to have lived until the publication in A.D. 80 of his first volume, which consisted of thirty-three short poems on different events to be staged by the emperor Titus at the inaugural games in the Colosseum. Over the next fifteen years Martial never missed the opportunity to seek imperial largesse by a well-timed poem, and he did indeed receive some minor privileges and some modest financial reward as well. 'If, Caesar, you have regard for the longing of your people and your Senate, if you care for the true joys of the citizens of Italy, we pray, return to us, our Lord and our God. Though the news of victory often comes, Rome envies her enemies because they see the Master of the World at close quarters, and in your face the barbarians find their terror and their joy' (7.5). Equally he would write to order short poems for other patrons (two of his volumes consist of verse-mottoes to accompany presents, an instructive catalogue of contemporary gifts to suit all purses).

The bulk of his poetry comprises twelve books of epigrams, brief poems principally in elegiacs but also in hendecasyllables and 'limping' iambics, issued annually from A.D. 86 onwards, with the exception of Book 12, which was finished in Spain about A.D. 100. His model was Catullus, and each poem is taken up with some little incident of everyday life. Martial is one of the sharpest observers of the ancient world. Nothing seems to escape his notice. And his range is enormous, from the most unspeakable sexual perversions to the most tender pictures of his friend's home (4.64: 'The few fields of Julius Martialis, more favoured than the garden of the Hesperides, rest on the long ridge of the Janiculum: wide sheltered reaches look down on the hills, and the flat summit, gently swelling, enjoys to the full a clearer sky and, when mist shrouds the winding valleys, alone shines with its own brightness: the dainty roof of the tall villa gently rises up to the unclouded stars'). In his pages you meet every type of person – the young boys who raked the sand at the Circus (2.75: 'A lion that used to put up with the blows of its master and meekly allow a hand to be put in its mouth forgot its peaceful ways and showed a savagery wilder than it might have shown in his Libyan hills. For with its ferocious fangs it suddenly killed two boys who were smoothing the blood-stained sand: the Field of Mars never saw a crueller crime...'), the stall-holders in the streets (7.61: 'The hucksters had robbed us of the whole city; one didn't know where houses began or ended. But you, Caesar, have ordered our narrow streets to expand and what was recently a track has become a road. Columns are no longer festooned with flagons chained to them; the praetor is not forced to walk in the middle of the mud; razors are not rashly drawn in a dense crowd; and the filthy tavern does not monopolize the whole street. Barber, café-owner, cook, butcher keep to their own premises. Now Rome exists: of late it was a huge shop'), the charioteers who fix the races (6.46), the affected reciters (6.41: 'He recites with his throat and neck wrapped up, declaring that he can neither speak nor keep silence'), the sordid auctioneers (6.66: 'Gellianus was selling a dubious prostitute the other day. The bidding was slow. So to prove to all that she was clean, he pulled the unwilling girl to him and kissed her three or four times. What happened? The highest bidder withdrew his bid'), the drunkards, bores, fortune-hunters, booksellers (1.117) and all the other flotsam and jetsam of the big city.

But Martial has no point of view. The poem may end with a caustic jibe, but it is the neatness of the jibe not the moral point of view behind it that one remembers. He may claim that his pages were dirty but his life was clean (Catullus was only one in a long succession who had said the same thing), but one doubts it. He was a brilliant scribbler, perpetually embittered that his talent never earned him the income that he felt he deserved. 'This morning I addressed you accidentally by your own name and didn't add "my lord", Caecilianus. How much did it cost me? £5 [the usual hand-out to a client]' (6.88). 'I asked for a small loan, from an old and well-to-do friend who has plenty in his coffers. His answer was "Be a barrister and you'll be rich." Give me what I ask, Gaius: I didn't ask for advice' (2.30).

In the end Rome, for all its bizarre fascination, seems to have sickened him. He had toyed earlier with the idea of withdrawing to Gaul or Venice, but in A.D. 98 he accepted financial help from Pliny and went home to Spain.

STATIUS

Statius (P. Papinius Statius; c. A.D. 45–96), despite his great reputation in antiquity and the Middle Ages, cannot be said to have offered such an insight into the life of Rome as Martial. The son of a schoolmaster, who had brought him up to read widely in Greek and Latin literature, Statius went to Rome and at an early age attracted the attention of literary circles, but it was not until the succession of Domitian in A.D. 81 that he seems to have received steady patronage. He wrote a libretto for Domitian's favourite artiste, Paris (before A.D. 83), and won the principal literary prize at the competition held in A.D. 90. He was flattered to be invited to dinner with Domitian even after the terrible pogroms of A.D. 93 (*Silvae* 4.2.1 ff.: 'The poet that brought great Aeneas to the Laurentian fields extolled the royal banquet of Phoenician Dido [= Virgil, *Aen.* 1.696], and the poet who ended Ulysses' story after long sea-faring portrays in lasting verse the supper of Alcinous [= Homer, *Od.* 8.57]: but I, on whom now for the first time Caesar has bestowed the unwonted rapture of a feast divine and granted me to ascend to the table of my prince, what skill have I to say my blessings, what power to express my thankfulness?'). He cheerfully turned his pen to composing an epic on Domitian's German Wars. He was rewarded with a country house near Alba and an adequate competence.

Yet Statius was, as all the evidence suggests, a warm-hearted and simple man. His affection for his family and friends shines through all his poetry, as in his poems of congratulation or consolation to his friends or in his grief over the death of his adopted son (*Silvae* 5.5.86–7: 'my name was your first speech, my play your infant happiness, my countenance the source of all your joy'). But first and foremost he was a professional poet with a living to make.

The fashion of the time, as quotations from Juvenal given earlier show, was for long and learned epics, not on dangerous subjects of recent history but on safe mythological themes. Statius began his twelve-book *Thebaid*, amounting to some 10,000 lines, in A.D. 80 and finally completed it in 91. The subject-matter was the story of the quarrel between Polynices and Eteocles, the two sons of Oedipus, and the subsequent campaign of the Seven against Thebes; but Statius introduces a great deal of other related material, often by way of digression, and creates some substantial secondary characters, like Hopleus and Dymas. In all this (even in the number of volumes) the influence of Virgil is very strong. There have to be funeral games to match *Aeneid* 5; there has to be an underworld scene, like *Aeneid* 6; there has to be a final duel in which Polynices and Eteocles re-enact the fight of Turnus and Aeneas. And Statius also borrows heavily from Virgil's language, often to great effect.

The *Thebaid* contains passages of great beauty, none finer or more celebrated than the description of the altar of Mercy at Athens (*Thebaid* 12.480 ff.):

> There stood an altar at the city's heart
> Reared to no God of Power: Mercy mild
> Made it her shrine, and human misery
> Has hallowed it. It never lacked for prayers
> Renewed, nor e'er repelled a suppliant.
> There whoso asks is heard, and day and night
> The way is open, and the offering
> The Holy One requireth is a cry.
>
> (tr. J. D. Duff)

This, like Persius's satire, reveals the noblest side of Roman religion. There is no doubt that Statius achieved great popularity by public readings of the work. Juvenal alluded to this in *Satire* 7.82 ff.:

> The city is all agog when Statius agrees
> To fix a recital-date. He's a sell-out, no one
> Can resist that mellifluous voice, that ever-popular
> Theban epic of his: the audience sits there spellbound
> By such fabulous charm.   (tr. Peter Green)

But the poem suffers from three major weaknesses. It lacks an overall structure, with a plot leading forcefully to a climax. There are too many episodic books (such as Book 6, the cremation of Archemorus) and too many irrelevant digressions (such as the 500 lines in Book 5 on the history of Hypsipyle). It reads as if it was designed in self-contained sections suitable for performance on their own. Secondly it is too studied, both in the enormous demands which it makes of a reader in mythological expertise (e.g. what does 'Echionian' signify?) and in its obsession with what can only be called the literary macabre (e.g. Tydeus gnawing Melanippus's head, Apollo as Amphiaraus's charioteer spreading havoc (7.776–7:

233

the reins are wet with gore, blood clogs the wheels and trampled entrails hinder the horses' hooves), Menoeceus plunging to his death from the top of a tower). Both of these faults, which recur in so many early imperial (or 'Silver') writers such as Seneca, are a direct product of Statius's education. Thirdly, the *Thebaid* cannot be said to be *about* anything. The poem is not in any sense the author's testament about the world, any more than, it seems, his second epic, on Achilles, which he left unfinished at his death, would have been.

Between A.D. 92 and his death Statius did, however, also write five volumes of short poems, mainly in hexameters, entitled *Silvae* (literally 'woods', but meaning 'new material'). Quintilian (10.3.17) defined *silva* as 'a rapid first draft of a subject made with the utmost speed of which the pen is capable and written in the heat and impulse of the moment'. Statius's *Silvae* are not as immediate as that, but they are occasional poems, inspired by some particular event or thing. In form and subject-matter they resemble both Martial's epigrams, although longer and less pointed, and some of Pliny's letters. Martial, for instance, had written about a friend's villa (p. 229). So Pliny, in a famous letter (2.27), gives a detailed description of his own villa. So too Statius (*Silvae* 2.2) paints the villa of his patron, Pollius Felix: '. . . the time I spent delighted me. The crescent waters of a tranquil bay break through the circling line of cliff on either hand. The spot is of Nature's giving: one single beach lies between sea and hill, ending towards the land in over-hanging rocks . . .' Pliny wrote many affectionate letters commemorating the death of friends, such as Fundania, who died at the age of thirteen (*Epist.* 5.16). Martial, in the same vein, wrote a touching memorial for his slave-boy Demetrius, who was his amanuensis and who died at the age of sixteen. On his death-bed Martial gave him his freedom. 'Though his strength was failing he felt the reward and called me "patron" as he passed, a freeman, to the waters below' (1.101). One of Statius's finest poems is a consolation to Flavius Ursus on the death of a favourite slave (*Silvae* 2.6: '... Peerless of soul was he and deserving to be mourned: but you have paid that debt and he is entering the company of the blessed and enjoys Elysian peace ...'), and he wrote several other similar pieces, including a lament for his father (5.3). Birthdays required to be noticed: like consolations, wedding songs, congratulations on recovery from illness and so on, birthday-odes had a long history in Greek literature and followed precise conventions. Martial and Statius both afford examples of such odes, Statius a notable one to Lucan's widow on the occasion of the anniversary of his birthday (2.7). They also both wrote poems on statues or other works of art (e.g. *Silvae* 4.6¹ on the statuette of Hercules belonging to a collector, Norvius Vindex), and it is a subject which also interested Pliny (*Epist.* 8.18.11 on the garden-statuary of Domitius Tullus; or 3.5.6 on Corinthian bronzes).

In these poems Statius shows his true gifts – charming fancy and (except in the fulsome allusions to Domitian) elegant language. But they are slight pieces, the work of a professional writer anxious to please everybody and offend nobody.

> What crime, O Sleep, thou God of calm confessed,
>   Brings my young heart alone to lack thy boon?
>   Wild things of earth or air in slumber swoon:
> The tree-tops droop the head in mimic rest:
> Loud streams are hushed: the rough sea smoothes his breast.
>   Fierce waves find peace upon the strand full soon.
>   But stars of eve and seventh returning moon
> Behold me ever in pale woe depressed.
> Dawn passing leaves me in her earth bedewed:
>   Even now some lover, clasping hand in hand
>   His love by night, repels thee, Sleep, with zeal.

Leave him – not on my eyes full-winged to brood,
  As joy might crave. Nay, touch me with thy wand:
  Enough if o'er me poised, thou lightly steal.

                    (*Silvae* 5.4.1–19; tr. J. D. Duff)

PLINY THE YOUNGER

There may be something disingenuous about Pliny's protestations that he was afraid to write until after the death of
Domitian. Although connected with the Stoic circles of
Helvidius Priscus and Herennius Senecio, he had in fact
pursued an active career as a lawyer and taken pride in the
publication of some of his speeches which he carefully
polished and tried out before selected audiences of his friends.
His forte was representing aggrieved provincials who brought
actions against corrupt governors (e.g. Baebius Massa in
A.D. 93, Marius Priscus in 100 or Caecilius Classicus in 101)
or defending governors against such charges (e.g. Julius Bassus
in A.D. 103 and Varenus Rufus in 107). But he had made his
name in chancery business, in particular in cases involving
disputed inheritances. Nor are the contents of his letters in
any way inflammatory or incriminating. There are no discussions of contemporary politics, no theorizing about autocracy
or liberty. Instead we have a fascinating portrait of a busy man
of affairs with all his interests and connections. There is
nothing here that could not have been published under
Domitian. And indeed Pliny must have written letters before
A.D. 97.

Yet the fact is that the 247 letters, addressed to over 100
persons (excluding the final volume of correspondence
between Pliny and Trajan), date from the years A.D. 97 to
about 109. They were published in nine volumes, not strictly
according to a chronological principle but so as to achieve a
balance of subject-matter within each volume, mixing anec-

dotes, trials, descriptions, literary criticism, business affairs, greetings, consolations, congratulations and the like. In his careful arrangement they differ from Cicero's letters, which were collected either chronologically or according to correspondent. They differ too in that although they were genuinely written to recipients and deal with real matters (that is, it is not an imaginary correspondence) they are self-conscious compositions intended also for a wider public. Each letter is not a spontaneous communication written in response to some request or situation but a carefully planned 'essay' dealing with one particular topic. On the other hand, unlike Seneca's letters, they are not meant to add up to some total synthesis. In effect, they are the prose companion of Martial's and Statius's poems without the vulgarity of the former and with a far wider sweep than the latter.

Some of the letters can stand on their own. Among these are the descriptions of the eruption of Vesuvius (6.18) or of Pliny's villa (2.7) or the ghost story of Athenodorus (7.27). But they deserve to be read, as Pliny intended them to be read, as a whole, so that you form an impression of the daily complexities of social life, down to the trivial details of wills and tutors. What emerges is a picture of Pliny and his friends as conscientious, hard-working, affectionate and moral people. His world is not just the world of Roman high society. He maintained his contacts with the associates of his youth in Como, like the town councillor Calvisius Rufus, and his school friends, Atilius Crescens and Renatius Firmus. We read of his endowment of an independent school (4.13) at Como, offering to match whatever contributions parents could raise for the purchase of buildings and hire of teachers with a contribution of his own ('the teachers must be appointed by the parents, who will choose wisely if they have to bear the cost'). He revisited his estates in the neighbourhood frequently and took great pride in his native land. His correspondence is a delightful change after the seediness of Martial. And that this is a true picture is confirmed by the final book of letters, probably published posthumously.

The Roman province of Bithynia was mainly self-administered. It contained a number of large and ambitious Greek cities (Nicaea, Nicomedia, Prusa, Apamaea) which were responsible for most of their own jurisdiction, administration and fiscal arrangements. The Roman governor, with his small staff, was concerned only with the bigger issues. This loose system had allowed the cities over a number of years to become uncontrolled. Civic pride led them to compete with one another in extravagant building programmes (fountains, colonnades, basilicas, shrines etc.) which had to be paid for by citizens who could ill afford it and tended bitterly to resent it. Hence the cities were at each other's throats, and the citizens in each city were at loggerheads with the municipal authorities. Serious matters had come to light in the trials of Bassus and Varenus, two corrupt predecessors of Pliny's as governor of Bithynia, and in *c.* A.D. 110 Trajan sent Pliny, already an elder statesman, out there as his special representative to reorganize the province and set it on a better footing. Pliny's main task was to cut back wasteful public expenditure, but his letters reveal many other thorny problems which he referred back to Trajan for guidance, none more notorious than that of the Christians (*Letters* 10.96 and 97). After speaking of his treatment of intransigent Christians, who refused to renounce Christ and do honour to the Statue of Trajan, he wrote that others, who had repented of Christianity, 'declared that the sum total of their error amounted to no more than this: they had met regularly before dawn on a fixed day to chant verses in honour of Christ as if to a god, and to bind themselves by an oath, not for any criminal purpose, but to abstain from robbery and adultery, to commit no breach of trust and not to deny a deposit when called upon to restore it. After this ceremony it had been their custom to disperse and reassemble later to take food of an ordinary, harmless kind'. Pliny was worried how to proceed in the matter and whether 'the mere name of Christian' was a punishable offence in itself. He also sensed that there was a religious revival in the air which might be turned to good account if he did not take too severe steps against the Christians. Trajan, concerned primarily with the social rather than the theological implication of the cult, replied:

You have followed the right course of procedure, my dear Pliny, in your examination of the cases of persons charged with being Christian, for it is impossible to lay down a general rule to a fixed formula. These people must not be hunted out; if they are brought before you and the charge against them is proved, they must be punished, but in the case of anyone who denies that he is a Christian, and makes it clear that he is not by offering prayers to our gods, he is to be pardoned as a result of his repentance, however suspect his past conduct may be. But pamphlets circulated anonymously must play no part in any accusation. They create the worst sort of precedent and are quite out of keeping with the spirit of our age.

(10.97; tr. Betty Radice)

Perhaps after all, then, it was the spirit of the age that induced Pliny to undertake the creative labour of his correspondence, not just the desire of a man of affairs for a cultivated occupation in his leisure.

JUVENAL

What matters about Juvenal is not his life but what he wrote. Even if Pliny and Tacitus had never penned a line, their public careers would have earned them a small place in history. Juvenal did not achieve such heights and his biography poses too many insoluble problems, although there are a number of ancient 'lives' of the poet, mainly building hypotheses out of the satires themselves. What can be said is that he was probably born about A.D. 55 at Aquinum near Mount Cassilo into a 'lower-middle-class' family which may have originated in Spain; that he served in the army (very conjecturally in A.D. 78–80 under Agricola in Britain, about which he shows surprising knowledge); that he was banished (presumably in A.D. 93 to Egypt); and that he published five books of *Satires*, which on internal evidence can be dated from about A.D. 110 to about A.D. 130. There is no suggestion that he held a higher magistracy or priesthood. But his poetry is among the most powerful, even vitriolic, ever written.

To understand it, therefore, it is best to look at the *Satires* themselves, leaving aside for the moment *Satire* 1 which, like most introductory poems in ancient literature, is programmatic and so written later than some of the satires it is designed to introduce. At the outset it must be said that although Juvenal castigates in appalling detail and with impressive eloquence a wide sweep of vices, he does not make any fundamental analysis of the society of his day. He criticizes people who abuse and mistreat their slaves but not the system of slavery itself; he attacks vicious emperors but does not question whether the very institution of the principate was bound to lead to such excess; he laments the decline of the solid, Italian middle class in favour of *parvenu* Greeks and orientals but does not ask why, or even suggest how it could be reversed; he accepts the inevitability of gladiatorial shows and expresses concern only at extraordinary outrages; he laments the poverty of himself and his kind but does not look for any constructive alternatives. He is not in any sense a reformer. But there are other enigmas about him.

Satires 2 and 9, two of the most unpleasant pieces ever written, even when compared with some of Martial's products, are concerned with the degradation of male homosexuality – the aristocratic perverts who wear drag, use cosmetics and even go through 'marriages' and the discarded sodomite, Naevolus. Homosexuality was not uncommon in the time of Trajan and Hadrian. Hadrian's favourite, Antinous, was responsible for a new and widely diffused ideal of male beauty. Hadrian's contemporary Herodes Atticus, one of the most generous patrons the arts have known, had several boy-friends, one of whom, Polydeucion, can be seen in a hauntingly beautiful relief at Brauron. And male prostitution continued officially in Rome and elsewhere. But, as we can see from Plutarch and later writers, there was a widespread revulsion in the second century from the blatant homosexual practices which had been current, both in court circles and in the world of Trimalchio, under the reigns of Tiberius, Nero and Domitian.

Satire 6, the longest of Juvenal's poems, is a denunciation of marriage, warning a friend, Postumus, not to marry and in no circumstances to marry a rich and noble wife. The theme was an old satiric one, treated by Lucilius and also by popular philosophers. In the first section Juvenal claims that there is no such thing as a chaste woman, and every wife will be as unfaithful as Messalina, Claudius's wife:

> The minute she heard him snoring
> His wife – that whore-empress – who dared to prefer the mattress
> Of a stews to her couch in the Palace . . .
> would make straight for her brothel
> With its odour of stale, warm bedclothes, its empty reserved cell . . .
>   (tr. Peter Green)

Secondly even if Postumus were to think that he was one of the lucky ones marrying for love, he will find himself dominated and deceived by his wife. Juvenal goes on to assert that Roman women have been debased by luxury, using a contrast, by now familiar from historians and moralists, between the 'good old days' of Republican simplicity and the decadance brought on by imperial wealth. Finally he illustrates his point by a dozen examples of wives' intolerable behaviour, ranging from hen-pecking to abortion and murder.

> There's nothing a woman
> Baulks at, no action that gives her a twinge of conscience
> Once she's put on her emerald choker.   (tr. Peter Green)

It is impossible to produce comparative statistics about permissiveness that are sociologically valid for any society, still less for an ancient one. But once again the hundreds of inscriptions testifying to happy marriages in the second century, the charming pictures of married life in Plutarch and Pliny or the devotion of men like Tacitus or Statius to their families indicate that at the very least Juvenal's strictures are grossly exaggerated. One reason for this is that the *political* importance of marriage (and divorce) had declined together with the *political* importance of individual families. There was now no place for the competition of power and influence by the great, aristocratic houses.

This point emerges clearly from *Satire* 8, a noble poem addressed to a young aristocrat named Ponticus. It warns him that blue blood is not enough ('What good are family trees? . . . You may line your whole hall with waxen busts, but virtue,/And virtue alone, remains the one true nobility') and gives him serious advice as to how he should conduct himself when he becomes a provincial governor:

> Set some curb on your anger and greed, pity the destitute
> Local inhabitants . . . observe what the law prescribes,
> Respect the Senate's decrees.   (tr. Peter Green)

Juvenal follows it up with examples of aristocrats who have disgraced their lineage, such as Lateranus, who drove high-speed gigs, Gracchus, who fought in the arena, and Rubellius

Blandus, who claimed descent from the Julii and despised everyone else as 'the rabble, the very dregs'. In the course of the poem the names of all the great families of Rome, e.g. the Aemilii, the Valerii, the Cornelii, the Antonii, the Fabii, are brought in for effect. We do not know who Ponticus was (he may have died young before he even achieved his province), but the advice is wise and humane. Yet were there any decadent aristocrats in Juvenal's day? The last Aemilius was executed in A.D. 39; the last Valerii and Cornelii to hold the consulship were in Nero's reign; the last Antonius was banished by Augustus to the University of Marseilles; the last Fabius was a friend of Claudius. Assassination and sterility had taken its toll. As for the specific examples, Plautius Lateranus is best known for his adultery with Messalina in A.D. 48; Gracchus is uncertain, because the last Gracchus of the noble line died as a humble merchant in Africa under Tiberius; and Rubellius Blandus was probably the brother of the Stoic great-grandson of Augustus executed by Nero in A.D. 62. In other words Juvenal is talking about a situation over fifty years old, and, although of course there were still, and always would be, corrupt governors, the new pattern was much more that of Agricola and Pliny – professional and conscientious.

Satires 5 and 11 form a pair. 5 is concerned with a dinner-party given by Virro. Its point is the contrast between the fine fare served to Virro and his special guests while the rest, humble clients and others, are treated to filthy wine and

> A grey-mottled river-pike, born and bred in the Tiber,
> Bloated with sewage, a regular visitor to
> The cesspools underlying the slums of the Subura.
>
> (tr. Peter Green)

Satire 11 is an invitation to Juvenal's friend Persius to have a quiet cultured meal with him: it is race-day, so everyone will be in the Circus. The invitation-poem is a familiar medium (developed by Catullus, Horace and Martial, to name only three) and Juvenal uses it to expatiate on the folly of extravagance and the pleasures of literature. 'We'll hear the Tale of Troy from Homer, and from his rival/For the lofty epic palm, great Virgil.'

We do not know if Virro was a real person. The name is rare, and one of the few holders of it was Vibidius Virro, expelled from the Senate by Tiberius in A.D. 17 for wanton extravagance. The dependant to whom the poem is addressed has the name Trebius, which is common in Juvenal's hometown of Aquinum. He may even be the Trebius Sergianus who eventually became consul in A.D. 132. However, the point is that such descriptions of banquets had for long been a stock weapon in the satirical armoury, as Nasidienus's and Trimalchio's dinner-parties testify. Probably the worst offender in this respect was the short-lived emperor Vitellius, who once created a dish in which he mixed 'the livers of pike, the brains of peacocks and pheasants, the tongues of flamingoes and the milt of lampreys, brought back by his captains and ships from the whole Empire, from Parthia to the Spanish Strait' (Suetonius, *Vitellius* 13). Martial, too, writes nauseating accounts of gluttony and singles out discrimination between guests as specially repellent.

Since I am asked to dinner, why is not the same meal served to me as to you? You have oysters fattened in the Lucrine lake, I cut my lips sucking a mussel from its shell ... You gorge on a bloated turtle-dove, golden with fat: I got a magpie that died in the cage. (3.60)

But it seems clear that the practice had virtually died by the time Juvenal was writing. Hadrian had always disapproved (*Hist. Aug.* 17.4), and Pliny tells a story to a young friend in about A.D. 97 which is so obviously *ben trovato* that discrimination cannot really have been common in his day. 'The best dishes were set in front of himself and a select few, and cheap scraps of food before the rest of the company. He had even put the wine into tiny flasks, divided into three categories . . . one lot was intended for himself and for us, another for his lesser friends, and the third for his and our freedmen.' Pliny, in true Senecan spirit, naturally disapproved. He gave the same fare to everybody. 'That must cost you a lot?' 'On the contrary . . . my freedmen do not drink the sort of wine I do, but I drink theirs.'

One's doubts are intensified by poems like *Satire* 4, which describes a cabinet-meeting called by Domitian for the special purpose of deciding what to do with a big turbot, or *Satire* 12, which begins with Juvenal's performance of a vow for the safe return of his friend Catullus, despite having been shipwrecked with the loss of all his valuable cargo, and ends with a bitter attack on people who preyed on the childless rich in the hope of being remembered in their wills. The latter theme is, once again, a conventional one. Horace and Persius treat it, and Petronius tells of the ironic twist to a will which laid down that the legatees would inherit only if they ate the dead man (*Sat.* 141: 'Just close your eyes and pretend you are eating a million'). No doubt there were scandalous legacy-hunters and no doubt Juvenal, as an impoverished, middle-class man, resented it; but was it really a vice relevant to the state of contemporary society? Again *Satire* 7 deals with the miseries of intellectuals – poets, historians, lawyers and school-masters who slave away but make no money out of it. Culture and education came lowest in a rich man's list of priorities. '"Be a perfect teacher", you're told, and when the school year's ended,/You'll get as much as a jockey makes from a single race.' Now *Satire* 7 opens with an address to Caesar (who can only be Hadrian) – 'All hopes for the arts today, all inducement to study, depend/Upon Caesar alone' – and Hadrian had not only refounded the Athenaeum as a centre for literary study but also established not ungenerous salaries

and pensions for schoolmasters in the principal towns of the
empire. So too Pliny, fifteen years earlier, had endowed the
teaching profession at Como and done much to stimulate its
library (p. 237). Indeed under Trajan and Hadrian poets and
writers, provided that they were not charlatans, seem to have
earned a very respectable living.

Juvenal's most famous satires are 3 (on Rome) and 10 (on
the vanity of human wishes), both of which were to be
powerfully imitated by Johnson. In 3, Umbricius, a simple
friend of Juvenal, has decided to give up the struggle and
retire to the seaside at Cumae. As his belongings are packed
on to a cart beside the Capuan Gate, he and Juvenal walk off
to the little grove of Egeria, which has now been modernized
and turned into a marble park, where Umbricius pours out
his troubles. No honest man can make a living in Rome
nowadays.

> What can I do in Rome? I never learnt how
> To lie. If a book is bad, I cannot puff it, or bother
> To ask around for a copy; astrological clap-trap
> Is not in my stars.

All the jobs have been taken over by Jews, Greeks, Syrians,
oiling their way into positions of power and influence:

> schoolmaster, rhetorician,
> Surveyor, artist, masseur, diviner, tightrope-walker,
> Magician or quack, your versatile hungry Greekling
> Is all by turns.

In any case Rome is so uncomfortable and dangerous. You
live in a garret that can be swept by fire; you are mugged
and burgled; you are kept awake all night by the rumbling
traffic; you are jostled in the street.

> We're blocked by the crowds ahead, while those behind us
> Tread on our heels. Sharp elbows buffet my ribs,

Poles poke into me; one lout swings a crossbeam
Down on my skull, another scores with a barrel.
My legs are mud-encrusted, big feet kick me, a hobnailed
Soldier's boot lands squarely on my toes.   (tr. Peter Green)

The Rome is a perennial one, London in the eighteenth century, Chicago in the twentieth, and because it is a perennial one it rings true. Besides, we can reconstruct, from archaeological and literary sources, proof that Umbricius's description is no exaggeration. Rome was just such a big city: it was Martial's city too.

Satire 10, one of the most clearly structured satires, also deals with a perennial problem. Is there anything in life worth praying for? Persius had dealt with the theme (p. 215), which was a popular one, but Juvenal views it in his own terms. All the things that men pray for bring them unhappiness. Wealth? 'But you'll never find yourself drinking/Belladonna from pottery cups'. Power? Look at Sejanus. 'The ropes are heaved, down come the statues'. Long life?

But old men all look alike, all share the same bald pate,
Their noses all drip like an infant's, their voices tremble
As much as their limbs, they mumble their bread with toothless
Gums.

Good looks? 'So you're proud of your handsome son? Fair enough – but don't ever forget/The extra hazards that face him'.

Still, if you must have something to pray for . . . then ask
For a sound mind in a sound body.   (tr. Peter Green)

Juvenal's treatment of the tragedy of human ambitions is marked both by an uncanny accuracy of detail and by a wealth of unforgettable epigrams.

A brief survey cannot possibly do justice to the richness of

247

Juvenal's satires, but one fact should already have emerged. In his first, programmatic satire, he claimed:

> Though talent be wanting, yet
> Indignation will drive me to verse, such as I – or any scribbler –
> May still command. All human endeavours, men's prayers,
> Fears, angers, pleasures, joys and pursuits, these make
> The mixed mash of my verse. Since the days of the Flood ...
> has there ever
> Been so rich a crop of vices?　　　　　　　　(tr. Peter Green)

Yet the vices that he attacks are not the vices of his times. They are either those eternal weaknesses of human nature which inspired Horace as they had inspired Aristophanes, or they are the vices of a bygone age, the grim nightmare of Juvenal's childhood.

It is here that another side of Juvenal's writing has to be considered. Juvenal had had a rhetorical education; he was certainly acquainted with Quintilian, if only at a distance (he is the lawyer any wife turns to if her husband finds her in bed with a slave: *Sat.* 6.280), and he knows all about the teaching and practice of declamation.

> Of course, it's the teacher's fault
> If some bumpkin pupil isn't thrilled to the marrow
> Week after week, while dinning his awful Hannibal speech
> Into my wretched head, whatever the set theme
> Up for discussion – should Hannibal march on Rome
> From Cannae?　　　　　　　　(7.158 ff.; tr. Peter Green)

Juvenal's work is the product of rhetoric, not just in the paradoxes, dramatic apostrophes, hyperboles, but in its very substance. For instance, to ram home the point in *Satire* 8 that blue blood does not guarantee virtue and that mere upstarts have often proved saviours of the state, he brings in a series of examples: but they are not examples from living times, they are the examples of the rhetorical handbooks.

The wicked aristocrats are Catiline, Cethegus and the sons
of the first consul of the Republic, Brutus, who were spoiled
and arrogant enough to plot the restoration of the Tarquins.
The fine patriots are Cicero, Marius, the Decii, King Servius
Tullius and the three heroes of the Republic – Horatius guard-
ing the bridge, Mucius, and Cloelia. Such a list confirms the
suspicion mentioned above when in the same satire Juvenal
listed all the grand names of Roman families (no less than
eleven in all) despite the fact that not one single one of them
existed any longer. Every satire depends for its copious store
of illustrations upon the rhetorician's stock-in-trade (as, for
instance, the tricks of fortune-tellers in *Satire* 6), and almost
every argument is planned in the long run with an eye to a
neat conclusion or an epigram (e.g. 14.139: 'the appetite for
riches will expand in direct proportion/To your actual
wealth'), which may be too clever and, in fact, leave the
argument vulnerable or incomplete.

   Yet it would be quite wrong to infer from this that Juvenal
was simply an ingenious writer giving a new twist to old,
hackneyed themes and to argue that his claim to be driven by
indignation to write is just a hollow piece of pretence. The
proof, if any proof is needed beyond the vitality of every page,
is that Juvenal is himself well aware that he is very rhetorical
and undercuts this idle verbosity by making fun of it. In
Satire 2.24–8 he gives a string of examples to match the
insincerity of a man who self-righteously attacks homosexual
behaviour and then proceeds to lend himself to it:

Who would endure the Gracchi complaining about revolution?
Who would not bring down heaven and earth
If Venus found fault with a thief or Milo with a murderer,
If Clodius were to reproach adulterers or Catiline Cethegus?

These examples are stock (notice Catiline and Cethegus
above), but also grotesque in the context. They are not

rhetoric but a parody of rhetoric. To be a satirist Juvenal had to use the literary tools of his day, but to be a true satirist he had to be able to satirize them as well.

> Put Hannibal in the scales: how many pounds will that peerless
> General mark up today? This is the man for whom Africa
> Was too small a continent, though it stretched from the surf-beaten
> Ocean shores of Morocco east to the steamy Nile ...
> > On, on, you madman, drive
> Over your savage Alps, to thrill young schoolboys
> And supply a theme for speech-day recitations.
>
> > > (10.148 ff.; tr. Peter Green)

TACITUS

Juvenal never recovered from the experiences of his long years of silence under Domitian. If his satires cannot be called a social commentary on his own day, they are a bitter commentary on how a man's mind can become warped by suffering. It was this same urge to break silence that drove Tacitus – or so he says – to compose his historical volumes. As he himself freely admitted, he had owed the start of his career to Vespasian, its continuance to Titus and its success to Domitian. His family seems to have come from the same area north of the Po as Pliny's and there was an association between them, but we know nothing of his father unless he is connected with a financial procurator called Cornelius Tacitus who served in Gallia Belgica, perhaps under Claudius. Tacitus made his mark at Rome by his speaking ability and strengthened it by marriage to the daughter of Agricola in A.D. 77. From then on office and preferment came his way – the praetorship, the command of a legion followed, perhaps, by a small provincial governorship (A.D. 90–93), and the consulship in the second half of A.D. 97, although it is possible that he had been nominated for the position by Domitian. All through this period Tacitus had witnessed and taken part in crimes which haunted him for the rest of his life. 'Ours were the hands that dragged Helvidius to prison' (*Agr.* 45.2). To purge himself of this he wrote first of all a biography of his father-in-law (A.D. 98), then the *Histories* (dealing with the period A.D. 69–96), of which only the first four and a half books survive out of a probable twelve (*c.* A.D. 100–109), and finally the *Annals*, eighteen books dealing with the period from the accession of Tiberius to the death of Nero, of which Books 1–6 (partly fragmentary) and 11–16 survive (*c.* A.D. 110, or later – *c.* 120). There are also surviving an ethnological account of Germany (A.D. 98) and a *Dialogue on Oratory* (*c.* A.D. 106), already discussed (p. 197).

Tacitus makes his purpose quite clear. In the *Agricola* (3.3) he writes 'I shall not regret the task of recording our former slavery and testifying to our present blessings, although with unpractised and stammering tongue.' Again, 'Whatever we have found in Agricola, whatever we have admired, abides and will abide in the hearts of men through the endless course of ages by the fame of his achievements ... Agricola will outlive death as his story is told and handed down to posterity.' He makes just the same point in the *Annals*, 3.65.1: 'My conception of the first duty of history is to ensure that merit shall not lack its record [literally: "that virtues should not be kept in silence"] and to hold before the vicious word and deed the terrors of posterity and infamy.' Unlike Livy, his aim is not primarily moral, to use history as a means of improving the standard of contemporary life. He is simply concerned that the memories of good men should not go by default and that the evil deeds of wicked men should not be passed over in silence. He had had to keep silence himself for too long.

Because his aim was to bring the truth out into the light he had a special obligation to discover that truth in a way neither Sallust nor Livy did. Both in the *Catiline* and in the

Jugurtha Sallust was using a historical episode as an illustration of a historical point of view; Livy was not unduly particular about his material, provided that it could be moulded to his requirements. Tacitus was well placed to get at the facts both by his contacts (he wrote to Pliny, for instance, for a first-hand account of Vesuvius, and he refers to several conversations which he had with his father-in-law about the British campaigns) and by his position, which gave him access to many archives, including the proceedings of the Senate, the 'Daily Gazette' (a news-sheet posted every day in Rome) and other official records. His thoroughness in this respect is proved by a passage in the *Annals* (11.24) where he gives a speech by Claudius to the Senate on the admission of Gallic senators to that body. By chance large fragments of the actual speech survive from a copy in bronze that was set up in Lyons. It is clear also that Tacitus made extensive use of earlier historians who had written on the period, in particular Pliny the Elder and Fabius Rusticus. One can be sure that Pliny's work was thorough and well researched. Historians did not, of course, normally parade their sources (except for self-advertisement), and their aim was to create a work of art, not a work of reference. The *Agricola* affords a good example of this. At first its content seems rhetorical and its knowledge minimal. It was after all designed to be recited to a sophisticated Roman audience with little interest in the minutiae of provincial administration and a taste for epigram and paradox. Yet the more profound our archaeological knowledge of Agricola's campaign becomes, the more fully it supports the clues which Tacitus gives – the division of the army into three parts, the early advance to the Tay, the supporting role of the fleet, the concave face and numerous tops of Mons Graupius, and so on.

The order of composition of his works shows that, as he worked over the years, his historical awareness grew and deepened. The *Agricola* remains for many readers, not just because of its British associations, the most moving and readable of all Latin prose works. Agricola's life was bound up with Britain, where he had served before being appointed governor in A.D. 78. When he left, seven years later, he had extended the Roman province to the Forth–Clyde line and beyond, had 'Romanized' the greater part of England and was within sight of the complete annexation of the island. A remarkable achievement, sustained by rare humanity and justice, all the more remarkable in that it was done against the background of increasing tyranny at Rome. 'There can be good men even under bad emperors'. But Agricola was too close to Tacitus for him to be able to write the record of his life as other than a personal one: there is no view of Britain as one of many provinces within the Roman empire, each with its own problems, no view of the role of the central government at Rome (was it simply jealousy that made Domitian recall Agricola?) and no view of the affairs of these years as part of the much wider canvas of Roman history as a whole. But hints as to the direction in which Tacitus's thought was to go are here. For all Agricola's greatness, Roman success is not an attractive phenomenon. 'They make a desert and they call it peace', Calgacus says. The primitive virtues of the Britons are enervated by the vices of Roman civilization.

The *Histories* is a much more ambitious work and, although it is an incalculable loss that the books which dealt with the times that Tacitus was most personally involved in, namely the reign of Domitian, do not survive, nevertheless one can form a clear impression of its scope and penetration. Right from the start Tacitus's interest is focused upon the characters of the men who held the stage during a period which was 'rich in disasters, appalling in battles, and rent asunder by mutinies'. Galba, with his out-of-date strictness and severity, a 'man capable of governing, had he never been emperor'; Mucianus, a blend of 'dissipation and energy, courtesy and arrogance': Vitellius, a glutton, terrified by the silence of his empty palace; Otho, effeminate and pusillanimous; Vespasian, bluff, rugged, unassuming, one of the few men whose character, in Tacitus's opinion, improved during the course of his life.

Tacitus is often criticized for over-emphasizing the role of individual character in history. It was, of course, part of the literary inheritance that he took over, that the course of events was determined by the psychology of the various participants and that psychology was a datum, implanted at birth. This attitude undoubtedly coloured the whole of his approach to the reign of Tiberius, a period of which he did not have first-hand knowledge. He had read the sources and pondered on them; a picture of Tiberius grew in his mind; he then used that picture to interpret and make sense of the material he had accumulated. His obituary of Tiberius sums up his approach:

His character, too, had its different stages. While he was a private citizen or holding commands under Augustus, his life was blameless; and so was his reputation. While Germanicus and Drusus still lived, he concealed his real self, cunningly affecting virtuous qualities. However, until his mother died there was good in Tiberius as well as evil. Again, as long as he favoured (or feared) Sejanus, the cruelty of Tiberius was detested, but his perversions unrevealed. Then fear vanished, and with it shame. Thereafter he expressed only his own personality – by unrestrained crime and infamy.

(*Annals* 6.51; tr. Michael Grant)

Tiberius's personality (*ingenium*) was fixed. When he acted out of character, he did so from ulterior motives. Everything that happened in his reign can, therefore, be explained in the light of his proven cruelty, vindictiveness and deceit. Such an approach is, certainly, restrictive. Tiberius's motives cannot be so simplicistically analysed, nor can everything that happened be explained so easily. There were grave social and economic forces, such as the influx of immigrants to Rome, the rise of the municipal families in provincial government, the role of freedmen, administrative bureaucracy, the inflationary consequences of an artificially restricted metal currency, reliance on imports, and so on, of which Tacitus displays, for some, regrettable ignorance. Yet, although such things were undoubtedly factors that had to be taken into account, the ancient world was smaller, less complex and, above all, more personal than the modern. The power of an emperor or his ministers had direct and immediate repercussions throughout society, and that power was not conditioned by such external, sociological pressures. Caligula may have been mad but it was Caligula, not some clinical psychosis, that murdered M. Silanus.

Tacitus's gifts do not lie simply in the synthesis of material and the delineation of character. No ancient writer, except Thucydides, is so much a master of the atmosphere and organization of narrative. Almost always there is some sinister undertone, as in the account of the murder of Agrippina (*Annals* 14.1–13) or the 'marriage' of Messalina and C. Silius (*Annals* 11.30 ff.: 'the frightful storm over Ostia'). None is more horrific than the visit paid by Germanicus and his troops to the site of Varus's disaster (*Annals* 1.60):

Now they were near the Teutoburgian Wood, in which the remains of Varus and his three divisions were said to be lying unburied. Germanicus conceived a desire to pay his last respects to these men and their general. Every soldier with him was overcome with pity when he thought of his relations and friends and reflected on the hazards of war and of human life. Caecina was sent ahead to reconnoitre the dark woods and build bridges and causeways on the treacherous surface of the sodden marshland. Then the army made its way over the tragic sites. The scene lived up to its horrible associations. Varus's extensive first camp, with its broad extent and headquarters marked out, testified to the whole army's labours. Then a half-ruined breastwork and shallow ditch showed where the last pathetic remnant had gathered. On the open ground were whitening bones, scattered where men had fled, heaped up where they had stood and fought back. Fragments of spears and of horses' limbs lay there – also human heads, fastened to tree-trunks. In groves nearby were the outlandish altars at which the Germans had massacred the Roman colonels and senior company-commanders.

Survivors of the catastrophe, who had escaped from the battle or from captivity, pointed out where the generals had fallen, and where the Eagles were captured. They showed where Varus received his first wound, and where he died by his own unhappy hand. And they told of the platform from which Arminius had spoken, and of his arrogant insults to the Eagles and standards – and of all the gibbets and pits for the prisoners. (tr. Michael Grant)

The composition of the *Histories* showed the dark side of human nature, but it also revealed the fact that the process of corruption in Roman society went very much further back than the death of Nero. It was the task of the *Annals* to trace this inevitable tendency back to the very inception of the Principate. It is, therefore, no accident that the times of Domitian seem to be mirrored in the times of Tiberius – informers, corrupt ministers, conspiracies, treason trials, scheming women and the like. Tacitus had known Domitian's world, and when he turned to the history of a world which he had not personally known he could not but see it through the same spectacles, even at the cost of distortion. But it would be wrong to see him as a reformer or someone who wished to put back the clock. The old Republic could never be restored (*Hist.* 2.37); it was inevitable that the anarchy of the first century B.C. should give way to some form of absolutism (*Hist.* 1.1). There is a stark realism about his thinking.

The *Histories* and the *Annals* reveal a formidable command of the evidence and a devastating sense of history. They are permeated by an ineradicable pessimism, which shows itself not only in general comments (e.g. his complaint at *Annals* 4.33, which foreshadows Gibbon's immortal words, that he has to deal with 'barbarous edicts, perpetual prosecutions, treacherous friendships') or reflections (e.g. *Annals* 2.41: 'brief and ill-starred are the favourites of the Roman people') but by his incessant habit – it is almost a mannerism – of qualifying one explanation by another, more sinister one (e.g. *Annals* 1.3, Gaius and Lucius Caesar cut off by destiny – or by their stepmother Livia's treachery; *Agr.* 40, was it true or was it an Imperial fiction that the messenger sent to offer the province of Syria to Agricola returned without even speaking to him?) and introducing morbid innuendoes into every story. Tacitus has much in common with Juvenal in his outlook on life.

What ensured, however, more than anything else that such virtues as did exist should not be buried in silence is Tacitus's command of Latin. His vocabulary is chosen with exquisite care; he perpetually surprises by giving an unexpected twist to the shape of a sentence (*Agr.* 35.2: Agricola stationed his Roman legionaries behind the battle-line 'to secure the great glory of a victory that involved a battle without shedding Roman blood or as reinforcements if the others were routed'); and his prose is laced with phrases which once read can never be forgotten even if they can never be satisfactorily translated: for example, *deorum iniurias dis curae* ('the gods can look after the wrongs done to them'); *et in luctu bellum inter remedia erat* ('war is one of the cures for grief'); *omne ignotum pro magnifico* ('what is unknown is always exaggerated'). What is strange is that his work had such a precarious survival. Rarely quoted except at the end of the fourth century, the *Agricola*, the *Annals* and the *Histories* all survived into modern times through the accidental preservation of a single manuscript each.

II

FULL CIRCLE

FEW gestures have been as significant in the history of taste as Hadrian's decision to grow a beard. For centuries it had been the practice for Romans of good family to shave; beards were the symbol either of grief or of decadent adolescence (Cicero refers contemptuously to 'young ne'er-do-wells with their little beards' and Nero prided himself on his fringe). An unreliable story says that Hadrian grew his to conceal a disfigurement on his face, but it was taken to symbolize a reversion to the manners of old times, and to the ways of the Greek philosophers. In 386 B.C. barbarian Gauls could pull senators by the beard. Socrates, Plato and Aristotle were all full-bearded, and this was one respect in which their successors managed to imitate them.

Hadrian's beard is symptomatic of other transitions. Much of his reign he spent in travel, visiting almost every part of the empire. A more conservative imperialist than Trajan, as his construction of Hadrian's Wall and his withdrawal from the most easterly provinces indicate, he was much taken up with the problem of good administration. And it was only on the spot that the needs and the difficulties could be properly appreciated. As a result the centre of gravity of the empire began to shift from the West to the East because it was the eastern, Greek-speaking, half which was the real economic heart. It is probable that more than half of the Senate by now consisted of Easterners. It was no longer necessary for an emperor to spend all his time in Rome, and Rome, as a result, no longer exercised quite the same pull on artists and writers from elsewhere. The second century witnessed the great flowering of the Hellenistic cities of the East – Ephesus, Smyrna, Antioch, Nicaea and so on – under imperial patronage and that of rich men like Herodes Atticus. From the speeches of Aelius Aristides and Dio of Prusa one can form a vivid picture of the cultivated and thriving life of these great cities, which outshone any of the cities of the West except Rome – the dramatic performances, the recitations and orations, the philosophical discussions. Admiration for Hellenic culture had, as we have seen, always possessed the Romans, but it had been a fertilizing influence which enabled them to create their own original means of expression. Horace read Alcaeus and Sappho not so much as an admirer of the classics but as a writer seeking to mould his own style. Now, however, the mood had changed. The great writers of the early part of the century had looked to Roman not Greek predecessors for models to emulate and surpass. Pliny, Tacitus and Juvenal owe very little directly to Greece.

This change had certain important consequences, the chief of which is that the Greek and Roman worlds can be seen to be beginning to drift apart. The process was, of course, a long and slow one, only completed by political and theological differences which came over the next three centuries. Romans, at least down to the anarchic times of the third century, continued to be bilingual and to study Greek literature with the same thoroughness, and Latin remained the language of government in the East. At the same time, they were not much in touch with the upsurge of Greek literature which was going on. The most spectacular phenomenon was the popularity of the 'Sophists' in the East. These were educated and talented men, drawn from far and wide, who made a profession out of public speaking. The names and careers of dozens of them are known, and the works of Aelius Aristides for one have survived. Such a climate was favourable for other literary enterprises. Lucian (c. A.D. 120–c. A.D. 185) began life as a Sophist but turned to the successful composition of semi-satirical essays and dialogues. Two considerable historians, Appian, an Alexandrian, who wrote chiefly on Roman history, and Arrian, a Bithynian, who was a successful provincial governor under Hadrian and composed a fine history of Alexander the Great, both reflect the renewed pride in Greek letters. In the scientific fields Galen (c. A.D. 129–A.D. 199) re-established the great Aristotelian tradition of empirical investigation. It is, therefore, perhaps not surprising that Hadrian preferred to write in Greek rather than Latin and that Marcus Aurelius chose Greek as the medium for his *Meditations*.

This remarkable renascence had very little effect on Rome, where the fashion was rather to look back on the Roman past. Ever since the first century B.C. there had been archaizers but, like Sallust (p. 94), they were, in the main, people who were seeking to create a new language at a time when styles were still very fluid. Their aim was to devise a vocabulary that was appropriate for subjects which had never been treated in Latin before. Purely antiquarian archaism does not really emerge until the Empire. Seneca criticizes people whose language recalls that of the Twelve Tables (*Letter* 114); Persius parodies those 'who could pore over the shrivalled tome of Dionysian Accius, or Pacuvius and his warty Antiopa whose dolorific heart resteth on tribulation' (1.76–8); the speakers in Tacitus's *Dialogue* deplore the taste that prefers Lucilius to Virgil ('the old is praised, the modern despised'); even Martial (5.10) adds his testimony – 'Rome reads Ennius and leaves Virgil untouched'. But as authors, like Pliny and Martial, Juvenal and Tacitus, sought their own models in the works of their predecessors rather than in classical (or even contemporary) Greeks, the archaizing vogue ceased to be a mere eccentric craze and became established principle. Hadrian himself led the way, explicitly favouring the old kind of writing and preferring Cato (the Elder) to Cicero, Ennius to Virgil, and Caelius (Antipater) to Sallust. Obviously such a fashion could go to ridiculous lengths. Aulius Gellius tells the story of Favorinus, the philosopher friend of Hadrian, rebuking a youth for his preciosity.

Curius and Fabricius and Coruncanius, men of the olden days, and, from still earlier times, the three Horatii talked clearly and intelligibly with their fellows, using the language of their own day, not that of the Aurunci, Sicani or Pelasgi who are said to have been the earliest inhabitants of Italy. You, on the contrary, just as if you were talking with Evander's mother, use words that have already been obsolete for many years, because you want no one to know and comprehend what you are saying. Why not accomplish your purpose more fully, goodish fellow, and say nothing at all?   (tr. J. C. Rolfe)

Yet Aulius Gellius (c. A.D. 130–c. A.D. 180) was himself one of the main proponents of the new movement. His background is unknown, although the Gellii came from Samnium and members of the family had risen to considerable eminence in the Roman Republic. We first know of him as a student in Athens about A.D. 148. He studied Plato and Aristotle under Calvenus Taurus and was on intimate terms with Herodes Atticus. It was during his stay in Athens that he conceived the idea of making a commonplace book of interesting and various information, which he named *Attic Nights* because he had devoted his evenings to it as he stayed at a country-house near Athens. He continued it on his return to Rome, where for a short time he was a professional lawyer and where he enjoyed the society of leading intellectuals such as the philosopher Favorinus, the poets Julius Paulus and Annianus, the rhetorician Antonius Julianus, and above all Fronto (see p. 267).

The *Attic Nights* is a store-house of oddities. Gellius had read widely and gleaned many curiosities from the works of

Varro and others, but he also recorded personal speech, such as an argument with Julianus, after listening to a public reading of the seventh book of the *Annals* of Ennius, as to whether the poet had written *equus* (horse) or *eques* (rider) in a certain line. The scholar Sulpicius Apollinaris closed the argument by saying that 'he had procured at great trouble and expense, for the sake of examining one line, a copy of heavy and venerable antiquity which had almost certainly been edited by the hand of Lampadio: and in that copy *eques* not *equus* was written in that line'. Passages such as this give us a charming insight into the world of ancient book-sellers in Shoemakers' Street, into the discussions that went on about the meanings of words and the origins of ceremonies, and into the tastes of men of letters. Aulus Gellius was interested in old books for their own sake. He talks of old copies of Cato, Fabius Pictor, Claudius Quadrigarius, Sallust and Catullus which dealers had let him consult. He is fascinated by obscure points of etymology, grammar and syntax! 'When I say "he is in the field or in the *comitium*", I refer to the present time; also when I say "he will be in the field or in the *comitium*", I indicate future time; but when I say *factum est* ['it has been done'], although the verb *est* ['is'] is in the present tense, it is nevertheless united with the past and ceases to be present'; 'The Elder Cato in his speech "Against the Exile Tiberius" certainly wrote *stitisses* not *stetisses*'. He loves antiquarian lore, such as the deference formerly shown to the old (2.15) or the proper etiquette at dinner-parties (13.11). And, in addition to a hundred anecdotes from Greek and Roman history, he knows how hellebore can cure madness and why heat affects the urine (19.4).

Gellius makes no pretension to a literary style himself. His work was meant to be a work of reference. However, it was natural that his own writing should be affected by archaism and he cannot conceal his liking for older and more pretentious words. But the great value of the *Attic Nights*, apart from its significance as a symbol of the age, is the immense amount of facts and quotations which it preserves. Without it our knowledge of early Latin literature would be incomparably the less. It is, for example, Gellius who preserves the annalistic narratives of the duels of Corvinus and Torquatus against the Gauls (9.11, 9.13) which were utilized and adapted by Livy, enabling us to see very clearly what Livy's technique was.

Gellius accumulated his material out of a curiosity about the earlier history of his own language and literature – a very different attitude from that of Varro, who searched earlier writers for knowledge.

SUETONIUS

The same antiquarianism fired the biographer Suetonius (C. Suetonius Tranquillus; c. A.D. 69–c. A.D. 135). He was the son of a soldier who had fought as a tribune in the Battle of Bedriacum (A.D. 69). After a few years as a lawyer, he devoted himself to a literary career and made the acquaintance of Pliny the Younger, who gave him valuable assistance. A recently discovered inscription shows that, after minor religious and judicial appointments under Trajan, he served Hadrian as Secretary of Studies, of Libraries and of Correspondence – that is, he was Hadrian's private secretary and general adviser on literary matters, in charge of the imperial library. A late, and not necessarily reliable, source says that he was dismissed in A.D. 121/2 for some offence with regard to the Empress. This may be borne out by the fact that there is a marked difference in documentation between the first two *Lives of the Caesars* and the others, as if Suetonius had been cut off then from official files. But otherwise his life does not seem to have suffered or his literary career been curtailed.

Suetonius was a voluminous writer, but the greater part of his output – on textual criticism, eminent courtesans, Greek and Roman games, Greek terms of abuse, the proper names of different articles of apparel etc. – has perished. One work, *On Famous Men*, probably an early work written under Trajan, consisted of biographies of Roman literary figures, arranged in different categories (poets, orators, historians, grammarians, and so on). Some of these, including the lives of Terence, Horace and Lucan, and brief notices of grammarians and rhetoricians have come down to us. They show, as one would expect, the same sort of interest that Gellius showed in collecting interesting tit-bits of information.

It is, however, for his *Lives of the Caesars* that Suetonius is read and remembered. Strangely enough, although he had moved in the same circles as Tacitus and often used the same sources, he shows no certain knowledge of him. But then his purpose was a very different one. Tacitus was writing history in order to say something affirmative about his times; Suetonius is compiling a series of portraits based upon anecdote, scandal and fact, which are meant to divert, amuse and, on occasion, shock. It is, once again, the attitude of Aulus Gellius, compiling details because of their intrinsic fascination but drawing no profound lessons and passing no judgement. The *Lives* are also different in kind from Tacitus's *Agricola*. Agricola's personality emerges gradually from the texture of the whole narrative, whereas Suetonius adopts a mechanical system for arranging his material. First come the details of family background and birth, then education and the years before accession to the Principate. At that point Suetonius usually gives a description of the emperor's appearance and dress.

Physical characteristics of Nero:

> Height: average.
> Body: pustular and malodorous.
> Hair: light blond.

Features: pretty, rather than handsome.
Eyes: dullish blue.
Neck: squat.
Belly: protuberant.
Legs: spindling.

His health was amazingly good: for all his extravagant indulgence he had only three illnesses in fourteen years, and none of them serious enough to stop him from drinking wine or breaking any other regular habit. He did not take the least trouble to dress as an emperor should, but always had his hair set in rows of curls and, when he visited Greece, let it grow long and hang down his back. He often gave audiences in an unbelted silk dressing-gown, slippers and a scarf.   (*Nero* 51; tr. Robert Graves)

Suetonius then proceeds to illustrate the emperor's moral character with a profusion of anecdotes, mainly scandalous. At this distance of time it is not always easy to decide whether the emperors were really as depraved and immoral as Suetonius alleges or whether the historian had a basically prurient mind. But even apart from their sexual depravities, Suetonius would list their characteristics – Claudius's gluttony, bloodthirstiness, scatter-brainedness and short-sightedness ('After executing Messalina, he went in to dinner, and presently asked: "Why is her ladyship not here?" '), Caligula's deranged cruelty ('At one particularly extravagant banquet he burst into sudden peals of laughter. The Consuls, who were reclining next to him, politely asked whether they might share the joke. "What do you think?" he answered. "It occurred to me that I have only to give one nod and both your throats will be cut on the spot" ') or Vespasian's irrepressible talent for joking (as on his deathbed, 'Alas, I think I am becoming a God'). The virtues and vices of each emperor are carefully balanced up. The events of each reign are formally divided into civil and military. Again, however, Suetonius merely piles up incident and anecdote. Reading the *Lives* of Otho, Galba and Vitellius, you can form no idea of the real fight for power in that troubled and confused year or what the issues and the pressures were. From the *Agricola* you gain a distinct view of the stages and policies by which the province of Britain grew and was consolidated; but from the *Life of Claudius* you would never suspect that that emperor, for all his eccentricities, did have a coherent and practical programme for the Empire.

Finally Suetonius turns with evident relish to the various portents which presaged the emperor's death.

> Many omens of Caligula's approaching death were reported. While the statue of Olympian Jupiter was being dismantled before removal to Rome, at his command, it burst into such a roar of laughter that the scaffolding collapsed and the workmen took to their heels ... On the night before his assassination he dreamed that he was standing beside Jupiter's heavenly throne, when the God kicked him with the great toe of his right foot and sent him tumbling down to earth ...
> (*Gaius* 57; tr. Robert Graves)

The reporting of such omens was a traditional feature of Roman historiography, to be found in Livy and Tacitus, both of whom, although accepting the validity of religious actions as a means of maintaining the equilibrium of the universe, were by inclination sceptical about such phenomena. Livy includes them because they were part of the basic raw material of history – the ancient archives of the priests; Tacitus, because they added a note of sombre foreboding to the narrative. Suetonius, however, is genuinely fascinated by them. Such a fascination with the occult is worth stressing not only because of its prominence in the *Lives* but because it reflects the increasing superstition of Suetonius's age in a matter of some note.

For the *Lives* of *Julius* and *Augustus* Suetonius was evidently able to ransack the imperial files. He unearthed, for instance, Augustus's correspondence and made good use of it; he had scrutinized the wills of Augustus and Tiberius; he seems to have read the Edicts of M. Bibulus, Caesar's rival consul in 59 B.C., the addresses of Tiberius and Claudius to the Senate, the proceedings of the Senate, the 'Daily Gazette', as well as a mass of secondary sources. For the late *Lives* there is little documentary evidence and much reliance on generalized gossip and rumour. This change may well reflect Suetonius's dismissal in A.D. 121/2, but, however he succeeded in continuing his task, he did not lack for material, and his simple delight consisted in recording it all, without any particular concern for style or literary artifice. It is only when he comes to relate the deaths of his heroes that a change comes over his plain and matter-of-fact manner of writing. His account of the death of Nero is a finely constructed and dramatic story, and there is something strangely impressive about Otho's last hours:

While making final preparations for suicide Otho heard a disturbance outside, and was told that the men who had begun the drift away from camp were being arrested as deserters. He forbade his officers to award them any punishment and, saying 'Let us add one extra night to life', went to bed, but left his door open for several hours, in case anyone wished to speak with him. After drinking a glass of cold water and testing the points of two daggers, he put one of them under his pillow, closed the door and slept soundly. He awoke at dawn and promptly stabbed himself in the left side.

(*Otho* 11; tr. Robert Graves)

FRONTO

If Suetonius mirrored one side of Aulus Gellius's tastes, his antiquarian interests, M. Cornelius Fronto was the greatest exponent of the literary fashion to which Gellius subscribed. Fronto was born about A.D. 100 at Cirta in Africa, which was more and more to take over from Spain the role of breeding-ground for Latin writers. He followed a public career at Rome, being quaestor under Hadrian and achieving the consulship in A.D. 143. At some unknown date, perhaps about A.D. 135, he became Latin tutor to the future emperor M. Aurelius (M. Annius Verus) and later also to L. Ceionius Commodus, better known as L. Verus, who together with M. Aurelius was adopted by Antoninus Pius in A.D. 138 in order to secure the long-term succession to the Principate. Fronto remained on the closest terms with both men from then on. He probably outlived Verus (who died in A.D. 169) and may have survived as late as A.D. 176.

Although he had travelled in Greece and Egypt, it was at Rome that Fronto made his residence and, in addition to his imperial pupils, attracted a circle of like-minded scholars and writers. Even if longer fragments of his correspondence had not been discovered in the early nineteenth century in Milan and the Vatican, he would have been known from Aulus Gellius. 'I remember that I once went with Julius Celsinus to Numidia to visit Fronto, who was then seriously ill with the gout. When we arrived and were admitted, we found him lying on a Greek couch and sitting around him a large number of men famous for learning, birth or fortune' (19.10). The party proceed to discuss the meaning of *praeter-propter* ('more or less'). One can reconstruct some of the members of that circle: the consular Festus Postumius, 'the finest orator of his day in Greek or Latin', Sulpicius Apollinaris, a grammarian who wrote commentaries on Terence and Virgil, and Favorinus, the philosopher. Their discussions tended to revolve round linguistics – the proper use of the phrase *multi mortales* or the meaning of *pumiliones*. As Gellius said, 'Whenever I saw him and heard him speak, I almost never failed to come away improved and better informed.'

His correspondence, however, gives us a distinct idea of what Fronto's approach to literature was. Essentially an orator – he distrusted philosophy, despite Marcus Aurelius's devotion to it, and regarded history as a branch of panegyric, as a fragment of his *Principia Historiae* betrays – he attempted to define a new style (*elocutio novella*, he called it). In a letter to Marcus dated possibly about A.D. 162 he wrote 'most things in your late speech, as far as the thoughts go, I consider excellent; very few required alteration to the extent of a single word; some parts here and there were not sufficiently marked with *elocutione novella*.' What he meant by this becomes clear from other letters:

I commend you greatly for the care and diligence you show in digging deep for your word and fitting it to your meaning. But, as I said, there lies a great danger in the enterprise lest the word be applied unsuitably or with a want of clearness or a lack of refinement, as by a man of half-knowledge, for it is much better to use common and everyday words than unusual and far-fetched ones, if there is little difference in real meaning.

In other words, what Fronto sought to create was an original style without verbiage or bombast, where each word was carefully chosen for its special duty. Mere empty periods and sounding phrases were to be banished. But at the same time archaic words were not to be chosen simply because they were archaic. The Latin of Cicero and Caesar had, surprisingly, greatly reduced the size of the vocabulary that was regarded as suitable for serious literature. New words had, it is true, been introduced or invented, but many that had figured, for instance, in Plautus, and had sometimes even remained in common speech, had been dropped. It was these which Fronto sought to recall in order to give greater precision and greater piquancy to expression. It was an eclectic and artificial vocabulary which depended for its success on academic scholarship rather than spontaneity.

His letters are, by and large, couched in this style, but

perhaps because their contents are so natural and unaffected the style is never allowed to obtrude. Fronto reveals himself as very much of an invalid, but a tender-hearted, gentle and deeply good person – a fit tutor to the philosopher-emperor. He writes to his son-in-law:

Your little Fronto prattles no word more readily and more constantly than his 'Sire'. I on my part do my best to supply him with scraps of paper and little tablets, things which I think him to want. Some signs, however, even of his grandfather's characteristics he does show. He is very fond of grapes: it was the very first food he sucked down, and for whole days almost he did not cease licking a grape with his tongue or kissing it with his lips and mumbling it with his gums and amusing himself with it. He is also devoted to little birds.

But pretty and charming as such vignettes are, they do not constitute important literature and there is no evidence that Fronto ever did write any work of consequence. It could be argued that his over-riding concern for style suggested that he was more interested in how he said a thing than what he said. And the fact of the matter is that during this period very few important works were written in Latin at all. It is not just that they do not happen to have come down to us. We are relatively well-informed about who was writing what, and literary activity seems slight. Many reasons have been given for this, not least the resurgence of Greek. It may be, too, that because it was politically and socially a relatively stable time there were not the same provocations to write as there had been under the Republic and early Empire.

Yet the veneer of civilization is a thin and brittle thing. Behind the façade of the fine buildings and temples that Hadrian and Herodes Atticus had built, underneath the cultural brilliance of the Sophists and the philological enthusiasms of Fronto, a force was at work which Pliny had sensed in Bithynia and Suetonius echoed in his *Lives*. The Romans had always been superstitious and turned at times of stress to magic, witchcraft, mystery-cults like the Bacchanalia, astrologers, diviners and the rest, but for most of the time such superstition was held down and did not surface openly. From the first century A.D. onwards, however, men turned more and more to the occult. Whatever the reasons – and it may have something to do with the sheer size of the Roman empire, making ordinary people feel that the old cults which had held together the Peace of the Gods (*pax deorum*) were remote and too impersonal; or it may have been the increasing influence of Egypt and the Orient – the facts are indisputable. Demons were everywhere. Unless you accept this, you cannot understand St Paul or the impact that Christianity initially made. Minucius Felix, one of the earliest and most persuasive Christian apologists in Latin, wrote:

There exist unclean and wandering spirits whose heavenly vigour has been overlaid by earthly sins and lusts . . . These unclean spirits as revealed to Magi and philosophers find a lurking place under statues and consecrated images and by their breath exercise influence as of a present God; at one while they inspire prophets, at another haunt temples, at another animate the fibres of entrails, govern the flight of birds, determine lots, and are the authors of oracles mostly wrapped in falsehood.   (*Octavius* 26)

One feature of this was the revival of oracles. Not Delphi, which was too rational and tranquil and had been in decline for centuries, but shrines like that of Clarian Apollo which issued a stream of oracles on personal, political and theological subjects during the second century A.D. Or the strange poems in Greek hexameters, known as the Sibylline Oracles but more properly the work of Jewish-Christians foretelling the overthrow of Rome, which were much used by the Apologists. The passion for communication with the supernatural could easily be abused. Alexander of Abonuteichus, a contemporary of Lucian's (c. A.D. 160) and a strikingly handsome man, claimed to possess a snake that was a new manifestation of the God Asclepius. He built up a substantial following – even Marcus Aurelius consulted him – and his oracles were so successful that the cult lasted after his death. As Lucian saw, he was a total impostor. 'He would receive enquiries in elaborately sealed scrolls, melt the wax with a hot needle, read the question, reseal the scroll, and then emerge to astonish the questioner by handing back the scroll, apparently unopened and give him an appropriate answer'. He was adept at planting treasures which he would then 'reveal' by prophecy and sending oracle-mongers to spread his successes all over the Empire. Yet his popularity and prestige were immense.

A rather different, but no less significant, figure was Apollonius of Tyana, who died at an advanced age at the end of the first century and became a kind of pagan saint in subsequent years. His life was written by a Sophist, Philostratus of Tyre, as a counter to the life of Christ. He was a true shaman with miraculous powers of healing and prophecy. He could disappear at will, free himself from chains (as he did when imprisoned by Domitian), and tame wild animals. Adopting a vigorously ascetic life of abstinence and vegetarianism, he travelled the Empire bare-foot, preaching a mystical doctrine of a supreme and spiritual God.

Apollonius and Alexander are only two examples that testify to the universal credulity and superstition of the times, which spread even to Christianity. Montanus, a Phrygian Christian, about the year A.D. 172 saw a vision in a trance and began to speak in ecstatic utterances. He attracted a group who practised spontaneous prophecy and trances. The Montanists, as the sect was known, continued a vigorous if heterodox branch of the church until the end of antiquity.

Magical charms, amulets, stones, spells were in constant

demand. At Pergamum, for instance, a magician's work-case of the second or third century has been found, including a bronze triangular table engraved with magical letters, a round dish displaying the letters of the Greek alphabet and other magical signs and two rings. The whole served as a ouija-board, the rings moving automatically to different letters to spell out words. Egypt has produced hundreds of papyri with magical formulae and incantations. Theurgy was practised even in Italy.

These then were the fears and hopes that occupied the minds of men and women. Writers were not interested in personal ambition or Roman civilization, but they were interested in the supernatural because it was their most pressing reality. Many of the greatest Latin literary talents became Christians – men like Tertullian, Minucius Felix, Origen, Cyprian and Lactantius – and often in so doing gave up promising careers in politics, law or education. But their writings, although grounded in the old classical tradition, belong to a different world and cannot be discussed here. There was, however, one non-Christian author who did respond to the spirit of the age to such effect that his novel is at once a remarkable social commentary and a profound manifesto. It is the last Latin masterpiece before the first Renascence at the end of the fourth century.

APULEIUS

Apuleius (his full name is not preserved) was born about A.D. 123 at Madaura in Africa. His family was well-to-do, so that he received the best education available in his day, studying at Carthage, Athens and Rome. About A.D. 155 he married the wealthy widowed mother of a friend of his, Pudentilla, a marriage that so scandalized other members of the family that he was prosecuted in A.D. 158/9 before the governor at

Sabrata on a charge of having used black arts to procure her not inconsiderable fortune. He defended himself successfully in a speech, the *Apology*, which is one of the liveliest forensic defences to survive. In it he showed himself a serious philosopher, committed to Platonism, and an honourable man. But the work also contains passages of brilliant farce, in which he brings out for ridicule the sort of superstitions which every educated Roman in Africa evidently believed. It was, for instance, alleged that he used a fish as a magical tool to win over Pudentilla. 'A fish indeed! What could be less conducive to kindling the fires of love than a dumb, cold fish, something caught from the ocean.'

Apuleius's acquittal established him as the leading thinker and speaker in Africa, and fragments of his declamations made at Carthage in the years after A.D. 160 are preserved in the *Florida*. He became chief priest of the province, and a statue was erected in his honour. But he was not content with the empty duties of a Sophist. The prevalence of magic (and it is to be presumed that he regarded Christianity, which was by then widespread in N. Africa, as a comparable superstition, since Christian 'magic' was an early phenomena in the Church) was to him a subject both of abhorrence and amusement. It was to expose it and to advance the faith that in the years after A.D. 160 he composed the *Metamorphoses* or *Golden Ass*.

The plot is an old Milesian tale. A young man called Lucius makes some imprudent experiments in sex and displays an unhealthy curiosity in magic. In consequence, he is transformed into an ass, while retaining his human senses. He undergoes a series of adventures as he passes from owner to owner (a sadistic boy, robbers, farmers, eunuch-priests, baker, market gardener, cook), until he ends up in the hands of a Corinthian, Thiasus, who is anxious to make the star attraction of his gladiatorial show the public copulation of an ass with a woman. So much for Books 1-10. We are fortunate in possessing among the works attributed to Lucian a Greek version of the same story, which although much briefer and certainly not the direct model of the *Golden Ass*, enables us to see very clearly the changes which Apuleius had made. The various adventures common to both stories are of a traditional kind – the comic anecdotes of a Greek romance such as can be found in existing novels (e.g. that by Achilles Tatius) or in Petronius, which usually involve some sexual ingenuity or deception. But Apuleius has greatly extended the story. His major addition is the beautiful folk-tale of Cupid and Psyche which occupies much of Books 4-6, but his other additions seem designed to emphasize the magical rather than the sexual side of the story. Such is the anecdote told by Thelyphron in Book 2. He was hired to make sure that nobody mutilated a corpse during the night before its burial, on condition that if any parts were mutilated he would supply equivalent parts from himself to patch the corpse up. In the course of the night, a witch-mouse hypnotized him, but to his relief nothing was missing when he awoke. Just before the actual burial, the dead man's uncle produced an Egyptian medium, who resuscitated him so that he could accuse his widow of having poisoned him to pursue an adulterous love. The corpse proved his credentials by telling of all that had happened in the night. In alarm Thelyphron put his hand to his face, and his waxen nose and ears fell off. There are at least five other magical anecdotes of the same kind which are not to be found in 'Lucian'.

It might be thought that they are intended merely to add spice to the story. At the very beginning Apuleius appears to disclaim any serious purpose.

Soon after (as a stranger) I arrived at Rome where by great industry and without instruction of any schoolmaster, I arrived at the full perfection of the Latin tongue; behold, I first crave and beg your pardon, lest I should happen to displease or offend any of you by the rude and rustic utterance of this strange and foreign language. And verily this change of speech doth correspond to the enterprise and matter whereof I purpose to treat, like a reader leaping from horse to horse; I set forth unto you a Grecian story: whereto, gentle reader, if thou attend and give ear, thou shalt be well contented withal.

It is a Grecian story, a Milesian tale. And it is told in the most affected Latin style possible, a truly *diamanté* prose, which can be only faintly recaptured by Adlington's sixteenth-century translation. Apuleius carried to the furthest possible limits Fronto's taste for the choice of archaic words. His sentences are a riot of obscure words jostling with vulgar words; diminutives vie with intensives, neologisms with Graecisms; parallel clauses end in lilting rhymes. The total effect can only be compared with the style of *Euphues*. Yet it is achieved with such gusto and vivacity that the reader is swept breathlessly along from one anecdote to the next. The pose that the author is a Greek who has only just mastered Latin is, of course, bogus. Latin was Apuleius's native tongue, and it is noteworthy that the hero, Lucius, who begins the story as a Greek ends it very firmly as a citizen of Madaura. And despite all the conventional fairy-tale elements, one begins uncomfortably to feel that a good deal is derived from the travels and experiences of Apuleius himself as a young man.

Book 11, however, which is entirely original, finally disproves the frivolous purpose of the work. In 'Lucian', Lucius was saved from a fate worse than death by eating some rosepetals from the basket of a passing flower-seller and so being transformed back into a man. In Apuleius he runs away from the games down to the sea-shore, where the great goddess Isis appears to him in a dream.

Behold, Lucius, I am come; thy weeping and prayer hath moved me to succour thee. I am she that is the natural mother of all things, mistress and governess of all the elements, the initial progeny of worlds, chief of the powers divine, queen of all that are in hell, the principal of them that dwell in heaven, manifested alone and under one form of all the gods and goddesses.

She bids him attend her great ship-procession that is to be held that night. Lucius describes it with loving detail until he comes to the chief priest who carries a timbal in one hand and a garland of roses in the other. Lucius eats and, in thanksgiving for his transformation, becomes an initiate of the cult of Isis. With great solemnity he tells of the initiation service and of the mystical vision that he was vouchsafed.

> Then were all the laity and profane people commanded to depart and when they had put on my back a new linen robe the priest took my hand and brought me to the most secret and sacred place of the temple ... Thou shalt understand that I approached near unto hell, even to the Gates of Proserpine, and after that I was ravished throughout all the elements. I returned to my proper place: about midnight I saw the sun brightly shine. I saw likewise the gods celestial and the gods infernal before whom I presented myself and worshipped them.
> (tr. W. Adlington)

Book 11 has such a different tone from the earlier books that one is forced to conclude that Apuleius's aim was to expose the hollow frauds and immoral tendencies of the popular superstition of his day, by which he had himself nearly been victimized at his trial, and to put in their place the true faith of Isis. For the worship of Isis was one that deserved to command respect. The myths had many variants but the central thread was that Osiris, Isis' brother-husband, was killed by the evil power Seth. Isis travelled far and wide looking for the body and when she found it conceived from it miraculously a son, Horus. Then Seth dismembered the body and scattered the parts all over the earth, but Isis patiently recovered all the pieces, except the genitals, and raised Horus from the dead, conferring on him eternal life. He grew up to wage ceaseless war against Seth. In all this there are many deep strains, the principles of male and female, good and evil, dying and resurrection, the sun, vegetation and water. When the Greek world first came into contact with the worship of Isis, they identified her with their own deities, with Artemis, or Demeter, so that, for all the exotic symbols and chants, Iseism was readily naturalized in the Hellenistic world too. Greeks and Egyptians brought her to Rome, and her shrines are familiar from Pompeii, Ostia, Beneventum and many other Latin towns. The resistance to her was half-hearted and ineffectual. Despite destruction of her altars in the Capitol in 58 B.C., the triumvirs, Octavian, Antony and Lepidus, ordered the construction of a new temple only fifteen years later. It was sometimes felt that Isis was foreign to the innermost heart of the city of Rome, but nothing could keep her out, and Roman religion was by its nature accommodating to the gods of other countries. Caligula gave the cult official recognition; Otho openly took part in the rites; Domitian built a temple to her in the Campus Martius and thought of himself as reincarnation of Isis' later consort, Serapis. Under Trajan and his successors Isis took her place in the official and conventional Roman pantheon. But unlike the other Roman deities, she met certain special needs. The growing feeling for monotheism found an answer in her. She was invoked as 'the one whose names cannot be numbered', who subsumed in herself all other deities. As she says in the *Golden Ass* (11.5): 'my name, my divinity is adored through all the world, in diverse manners, in variable customs, and by many names'. Mother of the gods, Minerva, Venus, Diana, Proserpine, Ceres, Bellona, Juno, Hecate, all are but approximations to the true name – Isis. Secondly her cult placed quite extraordinary emphasis upon morality. Her priests preached chastity, asceticism, contemplation and goodness. Apuleius, after his past life, doubted whether he could live up to such standards.

'But I, although I was endued with a desirous good-will, yet the revered fear of the same held me back, considering that as I had heard by diligent enquiry her obeisance was hard, the chastity of the priests difficult to keep, and the whole life of them, because it is set about with many chances, to be watched and guarded very carefully.' Thirdly it offered spectacle and excitement – the great ship-procession, the mysteries and the bizarre representations of Isis' attendants that can be seen in mosaics, paintings and sculptures. But above all it offered companionship in this life and the hope of salvation after death. It contained nothing Satanic.

CONCLUSION

Apuleius ends a continuous tradition of Latin literature which began with Ennius, Cato and their immediate predecessors. And it is perhaps appropriate that he should do so. Roman society had come full circle. In the first period religion was uppermost in men's minds. The climax of the Second Punic War was the transportation of Cybele, the great mother-goddess of Anatolia, to Rome in 205 B.C. Cato had believed that a farmer's first duty was to respect the gods. In the intervening period the Romans had become much more humanist, interested in man's emotions, aspirations, dreams, sorrows and doings, and their religion much more spiritual-ized. In the last period the old gods, and some new ones, had reasserted their power.

But Latin literature did not die. It found new fields – in the propagation of Christianity and in the opposition to Christian-ity. For the brilliant revival of classical Latin in the fourth century, the writings of Ammianus, Claudian, Macrobius, Servius, Ausonius, Symmachus and others, can only be under-stood in the context of a Christian empire. And that was another world and another society. Tertullian pregnantly summed it up when he wrote:

What has Athens to do with Jerusalem?

APPENDIX I

A Selective Bibliography about Roman Writers

APULEIUS   Apuleius (full name not known; *c.* A.D. 123–*c.* A.D. 170), from Madaura in Africa. Orator and philosopher. Surviving works include an *Apology*, the *De Deo Socratis* and the *Metamorphoses* or *Golden Ass.*

TRANSLATIONS: Robert Graves, *The Golden Ass* (Penguin, 1950)
W. Adlington (1566), rev. S. Gaselee (Loeb, 1915)

STUDY: P. G. Walsh, *The Roman Novel* (Cambridge, 1970)

CAESAR   C. Julius Caesar (102–44 B.C.), consul 59 B.C., governor of Gaul 59–49 B.C. Defeated Pompey at Pharsalus in 48 B.C. Composed seven books of *Commentaries* on his Gallic campaigns and three books on the Civil Wars which survive.

TRANSLATIONS: Jane F. Mitchell (Gardner), *The Civil War* (Penguin, 1967)
S. A. Handford, *The Conquest of Gaul* (Penguin, 1951)

STUDIES: M. Gelzer, *Caesar, Politician and Statesman* (Blackwell, 1968)
J. P. V. D. Balsdon, *Julius Caesar and Rome* (E.U.P., 1967)
Stefan Weinstock, *Divus Julius* (Oxford, 1971)

CATO THE ELDER   M. Porcius Cato (234–149 B.C.), consul 195 B.C., censor 184 B.C. A famous orator and statesman, who also wrote a history in seven books (*Origines*) and a treatise on agriculture. Only fragments of his speeches and of the *Origines* survive, but the *De Re Rustica* is preserved.

TRANSLATION: W. D. Hooper and H. B. Ash, *Cato on Agriculture* (Loeb, 1935)

STUDIES: G. Kennedy, *The Art of Rhetoric in the Roman World* (Princeton, 1972)
K. D. White, *Roman Farming* (Thames and Hudson, 1970)

CATULLUS C. Valerius Catullus (*c.* 87–54 B.C.), from Verona. Versatile poet, celebrated for his poems about Lesbia.

TRANSLATIONS: James Michie, *The Poems of Catullus* (Hart-Davis, 1969)
P. Whigham, *The Poems of Catullus* (Penguin, 1966)

STUDIES: E. A. Havelock, *The Lyric Genius of Catullus* (Blackwell, 1939)
K. Quinn, *Catullus* (Batsford, 1972)

CICERO M. Tullius Cicero (106–43 B.C.), consul 63 B.C., from Arpinum. Orator, writer and politician. Among his surviving works are fifty-eight political and legal speeches; sixteen books of letters to his friends, sixteen to Atticus, three to his brother and two to Brutus; twelve philosophical treatises; and six works on oratory.

TRANSLATIONS: Michael Grant, *Selected Works* (Penguin, 1960)
Michael Grant, *Murder Trials* (Penguin, 1975)
Michael Grant, *Selected Political Speeches* (Penguin, 1969)
Michael Grant, *Letters to Atticus* (Penguin, 1978)
H. C. P. McGregor, *The Nature of the Gods* (Penguin, 1972)

282

D. R. Shackleton Bailey, *Cicero's Letters to his Friends* (2 vols., Penguin, 1978)

L. P. Wilkinson, *Select Letters* (Arrow Books, 1959)

Complete works in the Loeb Classical Library

STUDIES: D. L. Stockton, *Cicero: a political biography* (Routledge, 1971)

D. R. Shackleton Bailey, *Cicero* (Duckworth, 1971)

T. A. Dorey (ed.), *Cicero* (Routledge, 1964)

ENNIUS Q. Ennius (239–169 B.C.), from Rudiae in Calabria. Wrote tragedies and comedies on Greek models, an epic history of Rome (*Annales*) and other poems. Regarded as the father of Latin poetry. Only fragments survive.

TRANSLATION: E. H. Warmington, *Remains of Old Latin* I (Loeb, 1936)

STUDY: A. S. Gratwick in *Cambridge History of Classical Literature*

FRONTO M. Cornelius Fronto (c. A.D. 100–c. A.D. 176), from Cirta in Africa. Scholar and professor, friend of the emperor M. Aurelius.

TRANSLATION: C. R. Haines (Loeb, 1919)

STUDY: M. D. Brock, *Studies in Fronto and his Age* (Cambridge, 1911)

AULUS GELLIUS A. Gellius (c. A.D. 130–c. A.D. 180). Author of *Attic Nights*.

TRANSLATION: J. C. Rolfe (Loeb, 1927)

HORACE Q. Horatius Flaccus (65–8 B.C.), from Venusia in Apulia. Patronized by Maecenas and Augustus. Author of four books of *Odes*, two books of *Satires*, two books of *Epistles* and seventeen *Epodes*. Celebrated as a writer of satire and lyric poetry.

TRANSLATIONS: James Michie, *The Odes of Horace* (1964; Penguin, 1967)

Niall Rudd, *The Satires of Horace and Persius* (Penguin, 1973)

Gordon Williams, *The Third Book of Horace's Odes* (Oxford, 1969), with useful introduction and commentary

H. R. Fairclough, *The Epistles of Horace* (Loeb, 1908)

STUDIES: E. Fraenkel, *Horace* (Oxford, 1957)

Niall Rudd, *The Satires of Horace* (Cambridge, 1966)

David A. West, *Reading Horace* (Edinburgh U.P., 1967)

L. P. Wilkinson, *Horace and his lyric poetry* (Cambridge, 1951)

JUVENAL D. Junius Juvenalis (*c.* A.D. 55–*c.* A.D. 128), from Aquinum. Author of sixteen *Satires*.

TRANSLATION: Peter Green, *The Sixteen Satires* (Penguin, 1967)

STUDY: G. Highet, *Juvenal the Satirist* (Oxford, 1954)

LIVY T. Livius (59 B.C.–A.D. 17), from Padua. Historian, author of 142 books (thirty-five survive) on the history of Rome from its foundation to his own times.

TRANSLATIONS: Aubrey de Sélincourt, *The Early History of Rome* (Penguin, 1960)

Aubrey de Sélincourt, *The War with Hannibal* (Penguin, 1965)

Henry Bettenson, *Rome and the Mediterranean* (Penguin, 1976)

The surviving books are translated in the Loeb Classical Library

STUDIES: P. G. Walsh, *Livy: His Historical Aims and Methods* (Cambridge, 1961)

T. J. Luce, *Livy: The Composition of his History* (Princeton, 1977)

T. A. Dorey (ed.), *Livy* (Routledge, 1971)

LUCAN M. Annaeus Lucanus (A.D. 39–65), nephew of Seneca (q.v.). Writer of unfinished epic *Pharsalia* (ten books).

TRANSLATION: Robert Graves, *Pharsalia* (Penguin, 1956)

STUDIES: M. D. O. Morford, *The Poet Lucan* (Oxford, 1967)

F. W. Ahl, *Lucan: an Introduction* (Cornell, 1976)

LUCRETIUS T. Lucretius Carus (*c.* 94–55 B.C.). Epicurean poet, author of *On the Nature of the Universe* in six books.

TRANSLATIONS: R. E. Latham, *On the Nature of the Universe* (Penguin, 1951)

M. F. Smith, *Lucretius* (Loeb, 1977), with good introduction

C. Bailey, *Lucretius, De Rerum Natura* (3 vols., Oxford, 1947), with invaluable commentary

STUDIES: David A. West, *The Imagery and Poetry of Lucretius* (Edinburgh U.P., 1969)

D. R. Dudley (ed.), *Lucretius* (Routledge, 1965)

MARTIAL M. Valerius Martialis (*c.* A.D. 40–*c.* A.D. 104), from Spain. Author of twelve books of *Epigrams*.

TRANSLATIONS: W. C. A. Kerr (Loeb, 1968)

James Michie (Hart-Davis, MacGibbon, 1973; Penguin, 1978)

OVID P. Ovidius Naso (43 B.C.–A.D. 18), from Sulmo in the Paeligni. Poet, banished to Tomi in A.D. 8. Author of three books of *Amores*, three books on the *Art of Love*, fifteen books of *Metamorphoses*, six books of *Fasti*, five books of *Tristia*, four books of *Letters from Pontus*, and other shorter pieces.

TRANSLATIONS: Mary M. Innes, *The Metamorphoses* (Penguin, 1955)

Horace Gregory, *Love Poems of Ovid* (Mentor, 1962)

STUDIES: Brooks Otis, *Ovid as an Epic Poet* (Cambridge, 1966)

L. P. Wilkinson, *Ovid Recalled* (Cambridge, 1955)

J. W. Binns (ed.), *Ovid* (Routledge, 1973)

G. V. Galinsky, *Ovid's Metamorphoses* (Blackwell, 1975)

Sir Ronald Syme, *History in Ovid* (Oxford, 1978)

PERSIUS   A. Persius Flaccus (A.D. 34–62), from Etruria. Writer of six *Satires*.

TRANSLATIONS: G. G. Ramsay (Loeb, 1918)

Niall Rudd, *The Satires of Horace and Persius* (Penguin, 1973)

STUDY: R. G. M. Nisbet in J. P. Sullivan (ed.), *Critical Essays in Roman Literature: Satire* (Routledge, 1963)

PETRONIUS   T. Petronius Niger, probably consul in A.D. 61, Nero's Arbiter Elegantiarum (Master of Elegance). Author of the *Satyricon*, a novel.

TRANSLATIONS: J. P. Sullivan, *Petronius, the Satyricon, and Seneca, the Apocolocyntosis* (Penguin, 1965, 1977)

W. Arrowsmith, *Petronius, the Satyricon* (Michigan, 1960)

STUDIES: B. E. Perry, *The Ancient Romances* (Berkeley, 1967)

J. P. Sullivan, *The Satyricon of Petronius* (London, 1968)

P. G. Walsh, *The Roman Novel* (Cambridge, 1970)

PHAEDRUS   C. Julius Phaedrus (*c.* 15 B.C.–*c.* A.D. 50), from Thrace, freedman of Augustus. Author of five books of *Fables of Aesop*.

TRANSLATION: B. E. Perry, *Babrius and Phaedrus* (Loeb, 1965)
S. A. Handford, *Fables of Aesop* (Penguin, 1954)

PLAUTUS T. Maccius Plautus (*c.* 254–184 B.C.), from Sarsina in Umbria. Adapted Greek New Comedy for the Roman stage. Twenty-one plays have come down to us.

TRANSLATIONS: E. F. Watling, *The Rope and other plays* (Penguin, 1963)
E. F. Watling, *The Pot of Gold and other plays* (Penguin, 1965)

STUDIES: G. E. Duckworth, *The Nature of Roman Comedy* (Princeton, 1952)
E. Segal, *Roman Laughter* (Harvard, 1968)
A. S. Gratwick in *Cambridge History of Classical Literature*

PLINY THE ELDER C. Plinius Secundus (*c.* A.D. 23–A.D. 79), from Comum. Scholar and scientist, killed at the eruption of Vesuvius. Author of the *Natural History* in thirty-seven books and other works which do not survive.

TRANSLATION: Loeb Classical Library (1938–62).

PLINY THE YOUNGER C. Plinius Caecilius Secundus (A.D. 61–*c.* A.D. 114), nephew of Pliny the Elder (q.v.); consul in A.D. 100. Politician and writer, author of ten books of *Letters*.

TRANSLATION: Betty Radice, *The Letters of the Younger Pliny* (Penguin, 1963)

STUDY: A. N. Sherwin-White, *The Letters of Pliny* (Oxford, 1966), with useful introduction

PROPERTIUS Sextus Propertius (*c.* 50 B.C.–*c.* A.D. 1), from Assisi. Author of four books of elegies, predominantly about love.

TRANSLATIONS: S. G. Tremenheere, *The Elegies of Propertius* (London, 1923)

A. E. Watts, *The Poems of Propertius* (Penguin, 1966)

STUDY: Margaret Hubbard, *Propertius* (Duckworth, 1974)

SALLUST C. Sallustius Crispus (86–*c.* 34 B.C.), from Amiternum; praetor in 46 B.C. Politician and historian. Author of the *Catiline*, *Jugurtha* and (fragmentary) *Histories*.

TRANSLATION: S. A. Handford, *The Jugurthine War* and *The Conspiracy of Catiline* (Penguin, 1963)

STUDIES: D. C. Earl, *The Political Thought of Sallust* (Cambridge, 1961)

Sir Ronald Syme, *Sallust* (Cambridge, 1964)

SENECA THE YOUNGER L. Annaeus Seneca (*c.* 4 B.C.–A.D. 65), from Cordoba in Spain. Statesman and Stoic philosopher, counsellor of the emperor Nero. His surviving works are 124 *Letters to Lucilius*, twelve essays (*Dialogues*), seven books of *Natural Questions*, nine tragedies, and a satirical work on the deification of Claudius (*Apocolocyntosis*).

TRANSLATIONS: Robin Campbell, *Letters from a Stoic* (Penguin, 1969)

E. F. Watling, *Four Tragedies and Octavia* (Penguin, 1966)

J. P. Sullivan, *Petronius, the Satyricon, and Seneca, the Apocolocyntosis* (Penguin, 1977)

STUDY: M. T. Griffin, *Seneca, A Philosopher in Politics* (Oxford, 1976)

SILIUS T. Catius Asconius Silius Italicus (*c.* A.D. 26–A.D. 101), perhaps from Padua; consul in A.D. 68. Author of an epic poem, *Punica*, in seventeen books.

TRANSLATION: J. D. Duff (Loeb, 1934)

STATIUS P. Papinius Statius (*c.* A.D. 45–A.D. 96), from Naples. Author of an epic, *Thebaid*, in twelve books, an unfinished *Achilleid*, and five books of occasional poems, *Silvae*.

TRANSLATION: J. H. Mozley (Loeb, 1928)

SUETONIUS C. Suetonius Tranquillus (*c.* A.D. 69–*c.* A.D. 135), private secretary to the Emperor Hadrian. Author of *Lives of the Caesars* and (largely lost) *On Famous Men*.

TRANSLATION: Robert Graves, *The Twelve Caesars* (Penguin, 1957)

STUDY: D. R. Stuart, *Epochs of Greek and Roman Biography* (Berkeley, 1928)

TACITUS P. (?) Cornelius Tacitus (*c.* A.D. 56–*c.* A.D. 116), perhaps from Southern Gaul; consul in A.D. 97. Politician, orator and historian. Author of a biography of his father-in-law Agricola, the *Germania*, a *Dialogue on Oratory*, *Histories* (from A.D. 69 to 96; some five books survive), and *Annals* (from A.D. 14 to 69 in at least eighteen books).

TRANSLATIONS: H. Mattingly, *Tacitus on Britain and Germany* (Penguin, 1948)
Kenneth Wellesley, *The Histories* (Penguin, 1964)
Michael Grant, *The Annals of Imperial Rome* (Penguin, 1956)

STUDIES: Sir Ronald Syme, *Tacitus* (2 vols., Oxford, 1958)
B. Walker, *The Annals of Tacitus* (Manchester, 1952)
H. Benario, *An Introduction to Tacitus* (Georgia, 1975)

TERENCE P. Terentius Afer (185–159 B.C.), from Carthage. Befriended by the Younger Scipio. Adapted Greek New Comedy for the Roman stage. Wrote six plays.

TRANSLATION: B. Radice, *The Comedies* (Penguins, 1976²)

STUDIES: G. Norwood, *The Art of Terence* (Cambridge, 1923)

G. E. Duckworth, *The Nature of Roman Comedy* (Princeton, 1952)

TIBULLUS Albius Tibullus (c. 55–c. 19 B.C.). Author of sixteen elegies.

TRANSLATION: Philip Dunlop, *The Poems of Tibullus* (Penguin, 1972)

STUDY: F. Cairns, *Tibullus* (Cambridge, forthcoming)

VALERIUS Valerius Flaccus (c. A.D. 40–A.D. 90), author of an epic poem, *Argonautica*, in eight books.

TRANSLATION: J. H. Mozley (Loeb, 1934)

VARRO M. Terentius Varro (116–27 B.C.), from Reate. Scholar.

TRANSLATIONS: R. G. Kent, *De Lingua Latina* (Loeb, 1938)
W. D. Hooper and H. B. Ash, *De Re Rustica* (Loeb, 1934)

VELLEIUS C. Velleius Paterculus (c. 19 B.C.–c. A.D. 31), from S. Italy; praetor in A.D. 15. Historian.

TRANSLATION: F. W. Shipley (Loeb, 1924)

STUDY: A. J. Woodman, *Velleius Paterculus: the Tiberian Narrative* (Cambridge, 1977)

VIRGIL P. Vergilius Maro (70–19 B.C.), from Mantua. Poet, patronized by Pollio, Maecenas and Augustus. Author of ten *Eclogues*, four books of *Georgics* and twelve books of the epic, the *Aeneid*.

APPENDIX I

TRANSLATIONS: E. V. Rieu, *The Pastoral Poems* (Penguin, 1949)

C. Day-Lewis, *The Georgics of Virgil* (Cape, 1940)

C. Day-Lewis, *The Aeneid of Virgil* (Hogarth Press, 1952)

W. F. Jackson Knight, *Virgil, The Aeneid* (Penguin, 1956)

STUDIES: Brooks Otis, *Virgil: A Study in Civilized Poetry* (Oxford, 1963)

W. A. Camps, *An Introduction to Virgil's Aeneid* (Oxford, 1969)

V. Poschl, *The Art of Vergil* (Michigan, 1962)

K. Quinn, *Virgil's Aeneid* (Routledge, 1968)

L. P. Wilkinson, *The Georgics – A Critical Survey* (Cambridge, 1969)

VITRUVIUS Vitruvius Pollio (full name not known; *c.* 80–20 B.C.). Architect and author of a treatise *On Architecture* in ten books.

TRANSLATION: F. A. Granger (Loeb, 1931)

APPENDIX 2

A Selective Bibliography on Roman Literature and Civilization

The following list contains a selection of recent books of a more general kind in English on Latin literature and society.

J. P. V. D. Balsdon (ed.), *Roman Civilization* (Penguin, 1969)

M. Coffey, *Roman Satire* (Methuen, 1976)

T. A. Dorey (ed.), *Latin Historians* (Routledge, 1966)

D. R. Dudley, *The Romans* (Hutchinson, 1970)

J. W. Duff, *A Literary History of Rome* (Unwin, 1909)

J. W. Duff, *A Literary History of Rome in the Silver Age* (Unwin, 1964³)

G. Kennedy, *The Art of Rhetoric in the Roman World* (Princeton, 1972)

M. L. W. Laistner, *The Greater Roman Historians* (Berkeley, 1947)

G. Luck, *The Latin Love Elegy* (Methuen, 1955)

H. I. Marrou, *A History of Education in Antiquity* (Mentor, 1964)

K. Quinn, *Latin Explorations* (Routledge, 1963)

H. J. Rose, *A Handful of Latin Literature* (Methuen, 1936)

J. P. Sullivan (ed.), *Critical Essays: Elegy and Lyric* (Routledge, 1962)

J. P. Sullivan (ed.), *Critical Essays: Satire* (Routledge, 1963)

Sir Ronald Syme, *The Roman Revolution* (Oxford, 1939)

L. P. Wilkinson, *The Roman Experience* (Elek, 1975)

G. W. Williams, *Tradition and Originality in Roman Poetry* (Oxford, 1968)

G. W. Williams, *The Nature of Roman Poetry* (Oxford, 1970)

ACKNOWLEDGEMENTS

Grateful acknowledgement is made to the publishers and translators who have kindly granted permission to reproduce passages from the following:

Caesar, *The Conquest of Gaul*, tr. S. A. Handford (Penguin Classics, 1951). © S. A. Handford, 1951. Reprinted by permission of Penguin Books Ltd.

Catullus, *The Poems*, from *The Works of Catullus in Modern English Verse*, tr. James Michie (Hart-Davis Ltd, 1969). © James Michie, 1969. Reprinted by permission of Granada Publishing Ltd.

Cicero, *The Second Philippic against Antony*, from *Selected Works*, tr. Michael Grant (Penguin Classics, second revised edition 1975). © Michael Grant, 1960. Reprinted by permission of Penguin Books Ltd.

Cicero's Letters to his Friends, tr. L. P. Wilkinson (Arrow Books, 1959). © L. P. Wilkinson, 1959. Reprinted by permission of Hutchinson Publishing Group Ltd.

Juvenal, *The Sixteen Satires*, tr. Peter Green (Penguin Classics, revised edition 1974). © Peter Green, 1967, 1974. Reprinted by permission of Penguin Books Ltd.

Lucretius, *On the Nature of the Universe*, tr. R. E. Latham (Penguin Classics, 1951). © R. E. Latham, 1951. Reprinted by permission of Penguin Books Ltd.

Plautus, *The Swaggering Soldier* and *Pseudolus*, from *The Pot of Gold and other plays*, tr. E. F. Watling (Penguin Classics, 1965). © E. F. Watling, 1965. Reprinted by permission of Penguin Books Ltd.

Sallust, *The Jugurthine War* and *The Conspiracy of Catiline*, tr. S. A.

INDEX

Most Romans had at least three names. This index has been deliberately compiled so that people are listed under the names by which they are commonly known today. This may be unsystematic and unscholarly but should make it easier to use.

INDEX